AN INTRODUCTION TO CHRISTIAN ENVIRONMENTALISM
Ecology, Virtue, and Ethics

Kathryn D. Blanchard

and

Kevin J. O'Brien

BAYLOR UNIVERSITY PRESS

Cover Design by Emily Weigel, Faceout Studio

Library of Congress Cataloging-in-Publication Data

Blanchard, Kathryn D'Arcy, 1970–
 An introduction to Christian environmentalism : ecology, virtue, and ethics / Kathryn D. Blanchard and Kevin J. O'Brien.
 230 pages cm
 Includes bibliographical references and index.
 ISBN 978-1-4813-0173-2 (pbk. : alk. paper)
 1. Human ecology—Religious aspects—Christianity. 2. Ecotheology. 3. Christian ethics. I. Title.
 BT695.5.B555 2014
 261.8'8—dc23
                              2014010729

Printed in the United States of America on acid-free paper.

"This is an excellent book, written with brio and precision, about the most vital ecological and economic issues facing Christian theology today. An excellent choice for college classrooms, reading circles, or church groups."
—**Mark I. Wallace**, *Professor of Religion and Interpretation Theory, Swarthmore College*

"This well-written and insightful book demonstrates how the four moral virtues and the three theological virtues that have guided the church for millennia can help Christians address the complex environmental problems we face today."
—**James Martin-Schramm**, *Professor of Religion, Luther College*

"Scholarly without being stodgy, in understandable and often winsome prose, *An Introduction to Christian Environmentalism* is a creative contribution to the fledgling field of Christian environmental virtue ethics."
—**Steve Bouma-Prediger**, *Hope College, author of* For the Beauty of the Earth: A Christian Vision for Creation Care

To our students

CONTENTS

ACKNOWLEDGMENTS

Much of the work for this book was completed during our concurrent research leaves in 2012–2013. We offer sincere thanks to the Louisville Institute, which offered us a generous year-long Sabbatical Grant for Researchers, and to Alma College and Pacific Lutheran University for allowing us time away from our teaching and service duties. We are also grateful to the Property and Environment Research Center (PERC), which hosted us for an inspiring one-week fellowship in beautiful Bozeman, Montana, in 2012.

Our heartfelt gratitude goes also to the many scholars and friends who offered us their time and their thoughts on this project, as well as moral support, at various stages from beginning to end. In alphabetical order, they are Terry Anderson, Jennifer Ayres, Spencer Banzhaf, Whitney Baumann, Trevor Bechtel, LeeAnne Beres, Rick Bohannan, Letitia Campbell, Kristen Chase, Forrest Clingerman, Jessie Dye, Laura Hartman, P. J. Hill, Laura Huggins, Rusty Pritchard, Ashton Ritchie, and Bart Scott. In addition, we extend thanks to members of the Society of Christian Ethics who attended our panel at the 2013 annual meeting in Chicago and asked stimulating questions, and to the anonymous referees of both the *Journal of the Society of Christian Ethics* and Baylor University Press who gave us important feedback on earlier drafts of this work. Special thanks go to our editor, Carey Newman, who somehow managed to make us feel that ours was the most interesting and exciting book he had ever encountered. We are also indebted to Emily Brower, Jordan Rowan Fannin, Karla Garrett, Jenny Hunt, Savanah Landerholm, Diane Smith, and others at Baylor University Press who were charged with herding us toward the finish line. We sincerely apologize to others who have undoubtedly offered us support that we have neglected to name here.

Above all, we express our gratitude to Mary O'Brien and to Chris and Gus Moody, who tolerated us while we worked from home for an entire school year, who put up with our many work-related travels, and who made that year—and make our lives—better, more fun, and more meaningful.

Finally, we thank our students at Alma College and Pacific Lutheran University, to whom we dedicate this book. We are grateful for their questions, for the ways they challenge us, for their willingness to work and to learn, and for their commitment to think and act in ways that will make the world better. They give us hope.

INTRODUCTION
Seven Virtues, Seven Problems, One World

Talking about the environment is hard.

First of all, there are so many different environmental problems that it is hard to know where to begin. Even simple actions in daily life connect to multiple environmental issues. Say, for example, you walk into a convenience store to buy a banana. The land where it was grown, now essentially a banana factory, was once a habitat for birds and other native species. Unless it is organic, that banana was produced with synthetic pesticides, herbicides, and fertilizers that are harmful to nearby soil, water, and creatures. The people who picked that banana from the plant were also likely exposed to those chemicals, and they were probably paid well below what most of us in the developed world think of as a living wage. Even if the fruit is organic, it was grown far away—unless you live in the tropics—so fossil fuels were consumed and pollution was released in order to get it to you. Plastic and cardboard were used to pack and label it, and those materials will eventually be put into a landfill, or else energy will be consumed in the process of recycling them.

All this for one banana. It can be frustrating to think about such things while trying to enjoy a quick snack, but these considerations are inevitable in a time of global environmental challenges. The information age means that none of us can plead total ignorance anymore, but the complexity of our world means that none of us can completely understand even a simple banana—much less broader issues like climate change, loss of biodiversity, or toxic pollution.

Environmental issues are also deeply personal. Every problem facing ecosystems has implications for how individuals live their lives—whether it is acceptable to drive or fly, where we should live, what we should wear, and what kind of work we should do. We can no longer wonder only whether bananas are part of a nutritious breakfast, but now we must also ask whether our breakfast is sustainable, and wonder what exactly that means. Such questions can become so overwhelming that it is tempting just to shut down and forget all about environmental problems, especially because to talk about the environment is to talk about ethics.

Talking about ethics is also hard.

Like questions about the environment, questions about ethics (from the Greek word *ethos*, meaning "custom" or "habit") are fraught with hot buttons and land mines. For someone to criticize our everyday habits and customs is to hit us right where we live, where we are most vulnerable: eating, working, parenting, loving, voting, relaxing, and spending. Throw Christianity into the mix, and things get even messier, with everyone fighting over whose side God is on. The deceptively simple question of "What would Jesus do?" often rubs people the wrong way because it tends to imply that there is only one answer (and only one group who knows it). Christians through the centuries have chosen Bible verses that supported their own views while minimizing those verses and stories that might be interpreted to question the wisdom they hold dear. As a result, debates about ethics—Christian or otherwise—are often marked by the kind of shouting and vitriol that most of us have come to expect from talk radio hosts, political representatives, and Internet trolls. People of faith may end up feeling victimized by ideological opponents and may, with Martin Luther, bemoan the poor quality of ethical discourse: "I am not worthy in the sight of God that a godly and honorable person should discuss these matters with me in a Christian way."[1] In worst-case scenarios, people may just decide that difficult conversations are not worth the effort.

It is easier to shut down than to talk about the environment, or to scream across ideological divides rather than discuss ethics civilly, but it is better to resist these temptations. This book is intended to help Christians do the hard work of talking about environmental ethics by drawing upon the ancient (yet still occasionally trending) tradition of virtue ethics. Virtue ethics is a way of thinking about moral problems that goes beyond lists of fundamentals, of "thou shalts" and "thou shalt nots." It pays attention instead to human *character*—habits of mind and habitual behaviors. Instead of thinking only about what humans should *do* in any given situation, virtue ethics asks first about who we *are*, followed up by what kinds of people we want to be. The pertinent question for Christian virtue ethics, then, is not "What would Jesus do?"

but instead, "Who does Jesus call us to be?" This shift in ethical talk—away from rules and toward character—has the potential to move ethical debate beyond dueling fundamentalisms—left and right, orthodox and liberal, tree hugger and job creator—and instead enable thoughtful conversations about how to obtain and preserve commonly held goods.

This book is for Christians who already believe that human beings are called to take care of God's creation, but who struggle with the specifics of how to do this in private and public life. It brings together diverse voices from various traditions to engage the challenges of talking about the environment and virtue. In a world of increasing pollution, endangered species, and extreme weather events triggered by a changing climate, Christians cannot afford to bury our heads in the sand and ignore the challenges that face humankind and the rest of creation.

There are no easy solutions to these highly complex struggles with environmental issues or Christian ethics, but addressing them can become easier through compassionate listening and genuine dialogue. Open-hearted conversations stretch the imagination in new ways, introduce new and different ideas, and reassure participants that no one faces these challenges alone. Perhaps most importantly, conversations offer the chance for all of us to think a bit differently. This is particularly vital when facing environmental problems that are, at their core, problems of thought.[2] No one will sacrifice for, invent, or invest in new paths out of toxic waste or species extinction, soil depletion, or climate change unless they first learn to understand these problems in new ways. Environmentalism is a challenge to think better and more creatively, to move beyond strident positions or absolutes, and to create a new sense of human purpose and meaning. What the earth needs is a new generation of human beings who neither ignore the environment nor give up on it, but whose minds have been shaped through constructive conversations about ecological problems as they intersect with human character, including classical and Christian virtues. In other words, the plight of creation calls for humans trained in a renewed sense of virtue.

Operating Assumptions

Environmental questions are inevitably personal, with implications for individual choices about what each person will consume and how each person will live. Environmental questions are also inherently political, affecting the ways people live together in public and organize social institutions. Disagreements in both the personal and the political realms invite the temptation to focus on differences rather than common ground. This book seeks to nurture Christian environmentalism beyond fundamentalism in order to make personal and political conversations less divisive and more fruitful. The path forward responding to today's environmental problems will require diverse people working together in a multitude of social systems, avoiding unnecessary fundamentalisms that prematurely cut off conversation. When it comes to the earth, sensible solutions and accomplishable goals are more important than ideological purity or narrow extremism.

But lest this approach of eschewing fundamentalisms in favor of dialogue begin to sound totally relativistic, it is important to add that fruitful conversation does indeed depend upon at least a few common boundaries and starting points.[3] What follows are four operating assumptions that underlie the rest of this book's discussion of Christian environmentalist virtue.

Assumption 1: Christians Are Called to Love God and Our Neighbors

Any book for "Christians" needs to be clear about whom it addresses, because Christians are a tremendously diverse group—over two billion human beings on every continent, divided into some forty thousand (and counting) denominations and traditions—with many disagreements among us about authority, ritual, and theology. Reflecting the context of its authors, *An Introduction to Christian Environmentalism* primarily addresses Christian readers in the United States—one of the wealthiest nations on earth—and focuses on those who have enough resources to exercise at least some degree of choice in response to environmental problems. This book is for those who have the luxury of worrying about whether their banana is organic rather than those who are barely scraping by. Beyond that, the arguments in this book are for interested Christians of every stripe (Catholic, Orthodox, Protestant, liberal, conservative, evangelical, spiritual but not religious, and those who are "Christians in name only") and across the political spectrum (Republican, Democrat, Libertarian, Independent, Socialist, Green, and those who seek to separate themselves entirely from secular government). Readers are invited to see the ways in which Christians and all people of goodwill can act together for creation's benefit, despite critical theological differences.

While the diversities of Christianity are important, the heart of the tradition assumes a common heritage, well expressed in Jesus' concise summary of his teachings into two commandments: first, "You shall love the Lord your God with all your heart, and with all your soul, and with all your mind," and second, "You shall love your neighbor as yourself."[4] The first commandment is about making the God of creation, incarnate in Jesus Christ, central to one's identity—what one might call "the ground of our being" or "the habitual center of our personal energy."[5] To love God, in other words, is not just about attending church or saying the occasional prayer when one needs a parking space. It is an orientation of character, an awareness that the whole self exists by God's grace and for God's purposes—that in God "we live and move and have our being" (Acts 17:28).

If the love of God defines *who we are*, the love of neighbor defines *what we do*. Loving our neighbors as we love ourselves means practicing a deep and abiding care for people that includes a refusal to distinguish our own good from others', focusing on what connects us rather than what separates us. When asked to clarify who he meant by "neighbor," Jesus told the parable of the Good Samaritan, a traveler who reached out to help a foreign stranger he noticed beaten and bloodied on the side of the road. The message is clear: the neighbor is "the one who showed him mercy," who responds to someone in need; Christians are called to "go and do likewise" (Luke 10:29-37).

No human being is perfect, yet Christians do believe that grace makes it possible to love God and our neighbors. Vice is a reality, and cultivating virtue is a lifelong task for everyone. As Paul put it, "with my mind I am a slave to the law of God, but with my flesh I am a slave to the law of sin" (Romans 7:25). But despite our imperfections, selfishness and greed are not the sum total of human destiny; we are also capable of great faithfulness, kindness, and compassion. The theological notion of humans as *simul justus et peccator* ("simultaneously justified and sinners") means that Christians are called, through grace, to live into the lofty goals of loving God and our neighbor as ourselves—assignments worth attempting and failing at again and again. This is true no less in our environmental behavior than it is with regard to money, sex, or violence.

Assumption 2: Christian Love Includes Care for the Environment

Because so many Christians have already made the case that creation is valuable in and of itself, and not merely as material for humans to use, this book assumes as a starting point that loving God includes caring for God's creation.[6] The God of Christianity took on a human body in Jesus Christ; the "word became flesh" in order to participate fully in the created world. This radical act of self-emptying occurred because, according to the Gospel of John, God "so loved *the world*" (John 3:16), and not just "people."[7] In other words, this famous biblical verse is a claim about God's regard for the whole of creation, a reminder that the same divine power that made the world also declares every aspect of it to be "good" (Genesis 1). Loving God surely includes a regard for the world God made and loves, including the arctic tundra and the polar bears that live upon it, the grasslands of Africa and the blue cranes that fly over them, and even our own backyards and the worms that dig underneath.

Environmental concern also naturally and logically grows out of love for the neighbor, because our neighbors require healthy ecosystems in order to flourish. If Jesus is to be found among "the least of these," then surely our neighbors include those who suffer as environmental refugees—whether driven from their homes by floods in Bangladesh, droughts in China's Sichuan province, wildfires in California, or hurricanes in New Jersey. Such extreme weather events are becoming ever more common as the climate changes, meaning that more and more neighbors will find themselves in need of help. Our neighbors also include victims of pollution: urban children with skyrocketing asthma rates, rural families struggling to support themselves as soil erodes, and citizens whose water quality has been destroyed for someone else's short-term financial gain. Environmental problems threaten the health and well-being of some people more immediately and severely than others, but one way or another, they eventually affect everyone. Once we understand that our neighbors' fates are tied up with our own, Christians cannot help but respond in love. In more than just a symbolic way, we see that our neighbors *are* ourselves.

Assumption 3: Environmental Problems Are Real

Humankind faces serious environmental challenges. The signs are clear for those with eyes to see and ears to hear: climate change is already inflicting significant suffering; pollution is a desperate threat to human health and particularly to the health of the poor; biodiversity is on the decline; the earth and its resources are finite; and the fate of the human species is inextricably bound to the fates of other creatures and ecosystems with whom we share this planet.

There is overwhelming agreement in the scientific community that the earth really is in danger, and that our neighbors are already threatened by environmental degradation in both the near and the long terms. This book is not designed to offer persuasive scientific evidence to those who remain skeptical about whether climate change is real or significant, or whether it is affected by human beings; there are many excellent books already available that offer arguments about the reality of environmental problems.[8] Of course, there is still a great deal that is unknown about the earth's systems, and there remains plenty of room for debate about the relative urgency of various issues (e.g., climate change vs. species extinction vs. poverty) and how to address them. But important debates can be productive only if all parties agree that, at the very least, we *are* living in a time of real and serious ecological challenges and that humans have at least *some* power and responsibility to address these challenges in meaningful ways.

Assumption 4: Environmental Problems Are Complex

In an inspiring book about social and environmental change called *Getting to Maybe*, the authors make a helpful distinction among three kinds of problems: simple, complicated, and complex. *Simple problems* are clear-cut and can be solved by following a few easy steps, like baking a cake: the goal is clear, and anyone who follows the recipe is likely to achieve it. *Complicated problems* are much more involved, requiring many steps and expert knowledge to solve. For example, sending a rocket to the moon is complicated, because it requires enormous attention to detail. But complicated problems deal with predictable factors: if we understand rocket propulsion and gravitational forces and orbital patterns and have the resources to build powerful enough rockets, human beings can land on the moon. Complicated problems, like simple problems, can also be solved. This is not true for the third type, *complex problems*, which are never clearly and finally solved because they continue to change throughout time, such that following a formula or achieving expertise is no guarantee of success. An example is the raising of a child—a task in which one is constantly adjusting; there is no reliable guidebook, there is no final conclusion in success or failure, and even a parent with a Ph.D. in child psychology and an M.D. in pediatric medicine can never know enough to be absolutely certain that every decision she makes is contributing to the formation of a perfect child.[9]

Based on this typology, environmental problems are complex problems: there are no simple formulae that will always provide guaranteed solutions, no single area of expertise that qualifies any individual to make all of our decisions for us. When faced with a changing climate, poisoned air, dying species, and dwindling resources, people must make the best decisions possible, both individually and together, drawing upon information and expertise from multiple sources, always prepared to adapt in the process. This is a daunting reality, but it is also a call to creative and collaborative thinking of the sort that depends on *character* rather than simple rules. Dealing with environmental problems may not be as clear-cut as baking a cake, nor as gratifying as landing a rocket on the moon, but perhaps it can be as rewarding and hope filled as raising a child, offering meaning and common ground in a world that often has too little of both.

Seven Virtues, Seven Problems

Talking about the environment and talking about ethics are hard because both are big, complex, personally and politically challenging topics. *An Introduction to Christian Environmentalism* seeks to make these conversations a little easier by bringing them together and emphasizing issues of character. The next chapter will introduce the traditional seven Christian virtues and outline the approach that animates this book. Each of the remaining chapters will then address a single environmental problem by pairing it with a single virtue. Chapter 2 explores how prudence can guide responses to species extinction, seeking a balance between caring selflessly for other creatures and owning them as private property. Chapter 3 discusses courage, which is desperately needed to make responsible energy choices and policy. Without courage, people will flee from the specter of economic or ecological apocalypse by panicking or pretending all is well. Chapter 4 applies temperance to the moral and environmental issue of food. Eating is the most intimate connection humans have to the environment, and it should be guided by informed intentions rather than unfiltered desires. The conversation centers most resolutely on human communities in chapter 5, on justice. The burdens of pollution and toxic waste must be justly distributed rather than inflicted upon the poor and oppressed masses by the wealthy and powerful few.

The final three chapters deal with the "theological" virtues as expounded by Christian tradition: faith, hope, and love. Chapter 6 discusses the relationship between faith and the need for concerted action on climate change.

Throughout Christian tradition, trusting God has always involved deep commitment to the complexities of contemporary life, and climate change requires a renewal of such commitment. Chapter 7 uses Christian hope to reflect on the challenges of human population growth. People of faith must welcome every person as the image of God but must also be aware of the natural limits of God's creation. Finally, chapter 8 explores the need to establish balance between individual action and political activism with the virtue of love. Some people are better equipped to readily make significant changes in their personal or family lives, while others are called to push political and social structures to change, but no Christian is exempt from doing works of love for God, neighbor, and creation.

Each chapter introduces a conversation, bringing thinkers and activists who disagree into a dialogue about how to respond virtuously to environmental problems. It is likely that every reader will encounter some perspectives that seem self-evidently true and others that seem utterly false. Readers are asked to try to take all positions seriously and to approach every voice in this book with compassionate listening and careful attention. The ideas in this book all come from neighbors who are worthy of respectful consideration. The goal is not to agree with everything—that would be impossible—but rather to practice the work of Christian virtue by fully participating in a conversation about how to live well in a world of environmental degradation.

This is not a book of straightforward answers to environmental problems, because complex problems do not have simple solutions, and because virtue ethics is about who we are before it is about what we do. Careful reflection on the virtues can help Christian environmentalists respond thoughtfully and well to these problems in our personal lives, in communities, in the voting booth, as members of the human race, and as creatures of God. Virtue is an alternative to fundamentalisms in that it draws insights from multiple sources, rather than resting on easy answers. This book is for people who want to love God and neighbors by cultivating virtuous characters through practical action and living well in the world. It is also for those who understand that such work will never be completed, who accept that these are complex, ongoing challenges humans can expect to face anew every day of our lives. Taking care of one another and the world upon which all life depends is a lifelong challenge—indeed, a never-ending series of challenges. Loving God and neighbor in ever-changing ecosystems, amid human-created global economies and societies, is the complex task of Christian virtue.

1

CHRISTIAN ECO-VIRTUE
In Search of the Golden Mean

Complex Ethics for Complex Problems

E thics and morality are sometimes treated like a quiz in class: you are pre-sented with hypothetical moral dilemmas, such as "who would you throw out of a lifeboat—the old sailor or the critically injured child?" Then you are supposed to use logic to figure out the right answer in order to get a good grade. Some moral systems do indeed work in the way of right and wrong answers. A law such as "thou shalt not commit adultery," for example, is fairly cut and dried (at least at first blush)— either you obey or you do not. When it comes to the environment, however, simple laws and slogans are just not up to the task. Complex problems require complex ethics.

Christian virtue ethics is well suited to moral complexity, because it focuses not on universal rules to be obeyed or applied to specific choices but on habits of human character nurtured over time through daily practice and multiple interactions. Virtue ethics is less like a math quiz than it is like a spin class: the only test is the day-to-day exercise of pedaling the bike; there is no one-time success and no one-time failure. The people who do well at spin class are those who show up again and again to develop their muscles and their discipline until the exercise becomes a natural part of who they are. Like physical fitness, character is about habits. It is about developing excellence by practicing virtues, over and over again, in everyday life. Aristotle argued that it was "no small matter" whether human beings develop good or bad habits from childhood: "On the contrary, it makes considerable difference, or, rather, all the difference" that people train themselves and their children to cultivate habits of goodness.[1]

As readers know all too well, fitness does not come from one workout but requires long-term discipline. Similarly, virtue traditions do not label someone "faithful" after hearing them say that they believe in God; instead, virtue is about the ongoing practice of faithfulness, passing not just one test but living an entire life shaped by fidelity to God and neighbor. Christian environmental virtue is likewise not about saying "I love trees," recycling a can, or signing a petition. It is about the habits and character that shape every perception, thought, and action over the course of an entire lifetime. For this reason, virtue is far more important and powerful than memorizing a few simple right answers. Complex environmental problems will persist from generation to generation, so they call for virtuous habits that will sustain people for the long term and help us continue adapting and learning from the world around us.

While environmentalists sometimes offer lists of commandments ("Thou shalt carpool!") or a vision of the future ("The promised land runs entirely on renewable energies!"), virtue ethics instead calls for a different way of *being human*. The focus here is on character formation—the process of shaping human beings into people who can respond well to complex problems specific to their times and places. Environmental virtue ethics, then, is about helping Christians to become people who understand that creation is God's, who care enough to notice when our neighbors around the globe are sick and dying from environmental degradation, who take responsibility for the ways our choices and social structures create waste and alter the global climate, and who are prepared to take constructive action.

Defining Virtue

Christian tradition has classically emphasized seven moral virtues. Four are shared with pre-Christian virtue traditions: prudence, temperance, courage, and justice. The last three are based in New Testament teachings: faith, hope, and love. It can be tempting to dismiss such old-fashioned virtues as irrelevant to our modern lives. Some sound stuffy and out of date: Who really wakes up in the morning hoping to be temperate and prudent? (Yawn!) Even for those who do aspire to virtue, these classical virtues can seem inaccessible: How often in your daily grind do you have the opportunity to demonstrate your courage, your justice, or your hope? Most days you are probably just trying to get your work done. Moreover, virtue can feel like a purely private matter: citizens of the United States, in particular, tend to resent others' scrutiny and think that it is no one else's business, beyond perhaps family and close friends, how we choose to express faith or love.

Nevertheless, Christian communities teach that character still matters, that the virtues are relevant to every human life, and that they need to be debated and reestablished in each new generation of congregations, families, and communities. Indeed, one purpose of Christian churches is to shape Christians into people whose characters make them distinct from other citizens and societies of the world. Virtue calls Christians to resist the self-serving materialism of our popular culture and to instead embrace wholehearted orientation toward God and neighbor.[2] It also, increasingly, calls Christians to respect the natural world that God created and of which humanity is a part.[3]

Christians are not the only ones turning to virtue ethics in response to environmental problems. Secular environmental philosophers have noted that environmental discourse is filled with virtue language. For example, the movement has shown courage in its responses to terrifying environmental truths.[4] Also on display are virtues that do not appear on the lists of classics—one philosopher argues that perhaps the most important virtue for our time is "simplicity."[5] In addition, there are entirely new virtues that have developed in response to environmental problems, such as "sustainability."[6]

Rather than inventing new virtues or prioritizing one particular virtue over another, *An Introduction to Christian Environmentalism* promotes the idea that the seven moral and theological virtues passed down through Christian tradition can be vital resources for responding to environmental problems and ordering our environmental lives; for millennia, these virtues have offered guidance about Christian character in the context of political, sexual, and economic life.[7] Believers who nurture these seven virtues are successfully living the lives for which humankind was created, in service to God and neighbors. Said another way, people are most fully human when they are prudent, temperate, just, courageous, faithful, hopeful, and loving. Humans were made precisely for such habits of character, which in turn foster the good life. Meanwhile, those who ignore the virtues do not experience their full humanity; they are ruled instead by lesser models of the good life provided by thoughtless appetites, profit-driven marketers, or corrupt cultural norms. This is not to claim that the virtues offer a clear solution or set of solutions to environmental problems; again, complex problems do not lend themselves to simple, universal answers. But virtuous habits, formed and practiced over time, can help people to respond with wisdom when facing new and ongoing problems.

One of the most famous thinkers in Christian tradition and a vital guide to the virtues is the medieval European theologian Thomas Aquinas (1225–1274), who borrowed heavily from Aristotle (384–322 B.C.E.). In his great work, *Summa Theologica*, Aquinas argues that the seven virtues are what enable people to "do good work well." He also articulates an important division between the first four and the last three virtues. The four "moral virtues" (also called "principal" or "cardinal"), borrowed from ancient Greeks, are open to all human beings, given our natural endowments. The first, prudence, is the foundation for the other three; it is, simply put, the practical application of human rationality—doing the right thing at the right time for the right reason. The next three virtues can be understood as prudence directed toward particular purposes. When human reason curbs unhealthy desires and passions, it is temperance; when it responds to threats and fears, it is courage; and when reason is directed toward enabling humans to live well together in community, it is justice.[8] Every human being is naturally capable of these habits of good character.

Aquinas argues that the latter three "theological" virtues surpass basic human nature and are "infused" by God's grace. These virtues relate not only to how to be good as natural persons and communities but more specifically to how to serve God in Christian communities. In the scriptures, these virtues are discerned specifically through the revelation of Christ: faith is defined in the Letter to the Hebrews as "the assurance of things hoped for, the conviction of things not seen" (11:1); this is the habit of fidelity toward God, of orienting one's whole life toward the unseen truth behind all of creation. Hope is the habit of working for the world God wants to create, even though it is not yet here: "Surely there is a future," writes the author of Proverbs, "and your hope will not be cut off" (23:18). Finally, love is the ultimate perfection of all the other virtues, "for love is from God, and everyone who loves is born of God and knows God" (1 John 4:7). Love is about spiritual union and friendship with God, developed over time through faithful and hopeful service to and friendship with the neighbor.

While each virtue is unique, the virtues are best understood together as aspects of a whole rather than as seven separate character traits. Just as flowers and bees and bears depend upon one another for survival, no single virtue can exist in isolation without the others. Virtue is about living well, which one cannot truly do without the complete set. The virtues are ultimately unified or else they become unbalanced. One might do the right thing for the wrong reason or at the wrong time or possibly a wrong thing for the right reason. Think of Charles Dickens' infamous Ebenezer Scrooge (or *The Simpsons'* Mr. Burns), who demonstrates an enormous amount of prudence: he invests his money wisely and refuses to spend it on frivolous things. But because he lacks the ability to give lovingly from his excess to those in need, or to recognize the justice of paying a fair wage or a fair share into the communal coffers, he cannot be called a virtuous man nor does he fully embody the virtue of prudence. Character and the good life are not about developing just one virtue; humans become whole persons by cultivating all of them together. In a world beset by complex environmental challenges with no precedents, nurturing all seven virtues may be the most crucial ecological work that humans can do.

The Golden Mean

Virtue is a journey rather than a destination. Human beings are not perfect, an,d according to traditional Christian teaching, no one, at least not on this side of the resurrection, can ever fully embody a character that perfectly integrates all of the virtues. Sometimes courage fails, sometimes love falters, sometimes justice feels impossible, and often communities and nations settle for much less than the ideal. However, virtue ethics is about a lifetime of habits rather than any single choice. Christians can learn from our failures but must continue to practice being more loving, more hopeful, more faithful, more just, more temperate, more courageous, and more prudent. Just like a sport or a musical instrument, those who put effort into practicing habits of virtue will excel. Even if one never perfects all of these virtues, it is worth a lifetime of attempts and failures to try to become fully human.

Christians have learned a great deal about virtue ethics from Greek philosophy, which teaches that the virtuous path arises as a balance between extremes, a happy medium between polar opposites. Consider, for example, the well-known story of Icarus, whose father Daedalus built him a set of wings out of feathers and wax to free him from the island maze where they were imprisoned. When Daedalus taught his son to fly, he instructed Icarus to stay on the middle course, safely above the ocean waves and below the sun's heat. Icarus, however, was tempted to excess by the joy of his flight. He flew too close to the sun, which melted his wings' wax and sent him plummeting down to a watery death. The moral of the story is clear: extremes are deadly. Better to keep to the middle way.

Virtue is therefore best understood as a middle way, or what Aristotle called a "mean," between two vices, "one of excess and the other of deficiency . . . some vices exceed and others fall short of what is required in emotion and action, whereas virtue finds and chooses the median."[9] Sometimes we miss virtue because we seek to fly too high toward the sun; sometimes because we dip too low and get soaked. For example, the virtue of courage can be seen as the sensible middle ground between the extremes of cowardice (too little courage) and recklessness (too much). Justice is, similarly, the middle ground between overly strict legalism and indiscriminate lawlessness. The theological virtues, too, can be understood as "golden means." While it is not possible to have "too much faith" in God, faith is nevertheless a middle course between what Aquinas called "contrary heresies"—potentially good ideas taken too far in a single direction.[10] When measured in human terms, it is possible to have too much hope (presumption or blind optimism) as well as too little (despair); love can likewise be too extreme when one is tempted to turn it away from God and toward something unworthy of ultimate devotion. Virtue is thus always about discerning the sweet spot between vicious excesses in one direction or the other.

This is no less true in a time of environmental problems. Virtue in the context of Christian environmentalism is about looking for sensible answers in a polarized political and cultural landscape, about seeking the middle path in response to environmental problems. This requires looking to many different sources to understand environmental challenges and consulting multiple experts for ideas on how to respond. The path of virtue assumes that the best way to approach complex challenges is likely to be found somewhere in the uncomfortable middle territory between dangerously clear extremes that tend to present themselves in our political debates. In Christian terms, seeking the middle path is part of the lifelong work of learning to love one's human neighbors and the rest of God's creation.

The Middle Path of Eco-virtue

Virtue is particularly useful in environmental conversations because environmentalism has too often been perceived as a polarizing force, an extreme to be avoided. For example, a group of conservative evangelicals called the

Cornwall Alliance asserts that "without a doubt one of the greatest threats to society and the church today is the multifaceted environmentalist movement."[11] They identify environmentalism as the "cult of the green dragon," a religion all its own that competes against Christianity with "deceptions" about the seriousness of environmental problems. According to this argument, traditional environmentalism gets its values from a heretical pantheistic belief system in which nature takes the place of the one transcendent God. For these critics, environmentalism is not only a theological threat but also a social one, because the green dragon de-emphasizes human importance, distracts people from concern for the poor, and encourages the expansion of impersonal and inhumane government regulations.

In stark contrast to the concern that the environmental movement is a vast and threatening conspiracy against Christianity, others worry that environmentalism is entirely too mild mannered. Philosopher Patrick Curry worries that the movement is no threat to the status quo at all and is in fact not nearly influential or radical enough to handle the seriousness of environmental degradation. Noting that the biggest environmental organizations collaborate with and take money from the same polluting industries they purport to fight, Curry argues that environmentalism has been "colonized by the anthropocentrism it was originally meant to counter." Corporately sponsored environmentalism is focused on human health and the sustainability of modern capitalist cultures rather than on protecting ecological integrity and the nonhuman world.[12] Curry advocates an even more expansive "ecological" ethics that goes further and deeper than traditional environmentalism in its argument against human domination of the rest of nature.

Thus is environmentalism attacked from two sides: theological conservatives worry that it radically de-emphasizes the importance of humans as the center and purpose of God's creation, which threatens our way of life. Leftist critics worry that it clings too closely to the status quo and fails to challenge human dominance and our current way of life. Such attacks are evidence of the preexisting commitments that each side brings to environmental problems. Patrick Curry is certain that anthropocentrism and capitalism are at the roots of environmental degradation. The Cornwall Alliance declares that environmental stewardship requires anthropocentrism, human dominion, and free markets. Because both sides have already made up their minds and neither leaves much room for conversation, it is difficult to imagine such opponents working together to try to solve, or even fully understand, a real environmental problem.

This book uses the Christian virtues to bolster an environmentalism beyond fundamentalism, advocating an approach of "eco-virtue" that discerns common ground between political and economic extremes. The virtuous person seeks broad participation in shared endeavors toward the earth's and humanity's flourishing, without knee-jerk reactions to political or theological buzz words. Twenty-first-century environmentalism need not be radically anthropocentric nor radically antihuman. In its most basic terms, environmentalism is simply about having a particular kind of orientation toward the earth—one concerned with taking good care of the planet that sustains us. Environmentalism does not lift people far above the rest of the world; rather it requires attention to how we are connected to ecosystems and nonhuman creatures. At the same time, environmentalism does not lift the world far above people; rather it requires care for human health and flourishing, especially "the least of these" among our human sisters and brothers. Eco-virtue resists false dichotomy; it includes the core concerns of both sides while refusing to accept any extreme on its own terms.

For those who feel that there is always a right answer, and that someone must therefore always be "wrong," eco-virtue may be unsatisfying. Finding a life-affirming golden mean between the extremes of anthropocentrism and ecocentrism will not work for anyone who wants to absolutely dismiss either the intrinsic value of the natural world or the uniqueness of humanity. But given the reality that all human ideologies exist together in the same ecosystem (whether they want to or not), it seems high time for a holistic conversation about commonly held goods in the middle ground. This does not mean refusing to pick a side, being wishy washy, or spectating passively while others fight it out in the ring of fire. Environmentalism beyond fundamentalism stands up decisively for positions that are flexible and broad enough to make cooperation possible. It is about finding a way to bring people together in action, based on shared goals, rather than pushing them apart with ideological arguments that demonize each other. Eco-virtue has many philosophical and theological implications, but it should not rest upon exclusive philosophical or theological doctrines; it has many political implications, but it should not rest upon party politics.[13]

Everyone shares one planet, so environmental stewardship can be a broad and wide-ranging movement that involves people from all over the world with all sorts of interests. Avid hunters can partner with endangered species proponents to preserve wilderness. Lawyers working for international NGOs can team up with local stay-at-home parents to ensure clean drinking water. Communities in the developing world can collaborate with university scientists to understand the intricacies of climate change. Vegans who seek to eat without causing suffering to any other being can research agricultural policy alongside activists who chomp fast food between meetings.

In other words, eco-virtue develops out of conversations among a broad and diverse range of environmentalists. The coming chapters will show that there are some earnest and concerned people who believe capitalism is destroying the planet and others who see capitalism as the only way to save it. There are some who see technological innovation as the key to humanity's future and others who advocate a return to simpler lives with fewer—or no—energy-hogging gadgets. What unites the diverse sources in this book is not any ideology or belief but rather a desire to be persons of character who live well in relationship, both with the natural world of which we are part and with one another. Eco-virtue is an environmentalist project and a Christian project, but it is also a human project. The strength of virtue-based environmentalism is that it does not have to embrace narrow political or religious boundaries but rather invites collaboration from all people of goodwill who seek to care for the habitats of human beings and other creatures. That is the power of the golden mean.

Learning Virtue

If virtue is about forming habits, then it is not enough simply to read and think about it; virtues must be learned and actually practiced in communities. Virtue is about habits, and the people with whom we associate undeniably shape our habits (for better or worse). So most of us probably wish to choose our conversation partners carefully: perhaps we want to discern eco-virtue in our churches through reading and interpreting the Bible. Perhaps we hope to achieve eco-virtue in secular contexts such as public schools, democratic exchanges, or the marketplace. Or perhaps we think the nuclear family is the one and only appropriate place to shape children into virtuous environmentalists, citizens, or Christians. Yet while our chosen communities are of deep importance, more often than not we will find ourselves thrown into communities that are not of our own choosing. These communities offer the opportunity to test and to expand our understanding and our practice of virtue.

One path to virtue is to try to relate, as broadly as possible, to all people. To a great extent most of us are already doing this through the global marketplace, which offers opportunities to learn virtuous (and vicious) habits from negotiations with diverse communities. Perhaps the most eloquent spokesperson for this market-centered perspective is the Episcopalian and economic philosopher Deirdre McCloskey, who argues in *The Bourgeois Virtues* and elsewhere that capitalism is a powerful force—indeed perhaps the most powerful source—for global virtue formation.[14] She argues that global capitalism—far from creating selfish, greedy monsters—is in fact a school of virtue in its own right, teaching people to live together justly, to steward their resources prudently, and even to have a fruitful hope for the future. In our attempts to feed, clothe, and house ourselves and our families, human beings naturally end up cooperating by building relationships of specialization and exchange. If these relationships are lawfully undertaken, with networks of free and voluntary trade rather than coercion or theft, they are known as "markets." As these markets develop and grow, we encounter different people, we engage one another as equals in mutual need, we see the results of our actions, and we concoct innovative solutions to problems.

More importantly, McCloskey argues, once our own needs are met, we can also begin to think creatively about ways to help others; this includes not only services for the sick or hungry but also the luxury of a cleaner environment.[15] Thus, she suggests, even the theological virtues—faith's steadiness, hope's eye to the future, and love's care for others—are nurtured better by the marketplace than by any other system. Against those who would accuse capitalism of degrading human virtue, McCloskey insists that "capitalism has not corrupted our souls. It has improved them." It was people trained in capitalist virtues, she says, who "ended slavery and emancipated women and founded universities and rebuilt churches, none of these for material profit and none by damaging the rest of the world. Bourgeois virtues led us from terrified hunter bands and violent agricultural villages to peaceful suburbs and lively cities."[16] McCloskey suggests that it is precisely people trained to be virtuous by the school of capitalism who will innovate and lead the way into a sustainable future.

Not all Christians are comfortable with McCloskey's analysis of capitalism's virtues or her belief in the character-building qualities of markets; capitalism has done great harm as well as much good to the world and to human character.[17] But it is not necessary to agree with all the details of McCloskey's argument in order to engage with her broader point about the virtue-shaping potential of markets.

Christian virtue, however, has traditionally been nurtured in relationships of mutual care rather than mutual profit, by charity rather than competition. Theologian and virtue ethicist Stanley Hauerwas argues that the church, when grounded in the biblical narrative and the promise of God's peaceable society, represents an ethos that is radically different from the logic and the practices of the capitalist marketplace. "By virtue of the distinctive narrative that forms their community," he writes, "Christians are distinct from the world."[18] Those who believe Jesus Christ to be God—incarnate, crucified, and resurrected—are shaped by a narrative unknown to those outside the church, and thus are able to cultivate virtues that are unavailable to those living apart from that narrative. Echoing Thomas Aquinas' insistence that certain virtues require grace and revelation beyond natural human faculties, Hauerwas believes that Christians are those who learn and practice in the context of a unique "community of virtues" known as the Christian church. Once one learns the gospel narrative from the church, "the nature and meaning of the virtues are essentially changed" from anything we could learn elsewhere, creating a distinctive understanding of faith, hope, love, justice, temperance, courage, and prudence.[19] Christian virtues, he believes, simply cannot be found in a world that does not know the gospel. The market system that serves the goals of progress, growth, and profit is therefore incompatible with the faith, hope, and love of Christianity.

Both Hauerwas and McCloskey make sophisticated arguments about how virtues are learned and nurtured, and neither should be lightly dismissed. Hauerwas emphasizes the tradition of Christian virtues as distinct from natural or worldly virtues, while McCloskey believes true virtue is possible for not just Christians but everyone through attentive participation in the world, especially in global capitalism. The middle path of eco-virtue tries to learn from both of these approaches, seeking the always-elusive golden mean. Environmental problems demand more breadth than either McCloskey or Hauerwas alone can offer. These problems are profoundly theological, determined and shaped by our commitment to love God, God's creatures, and our neighbors. But they are also practical problems, facing not just Christian communities but the whole human race and the entire planet. Eco-virtue means working from the particularities of Christian faith, but it also makes room for dialogue among multiple perspectives and prudently refuses to be ruled by any single ideological or philosophical foundation. Christians did not invent compassion or wisdom, so we have much to learn from interactions with others, whether businesspeople in the marketplace; activists in the political sphere; philosophers and scientists in universities; or Buddhists, Muslims, and other religious folks. Learning virtue in a broad global context introduces us to neighbors who may not share our faith, our habits, or our stories. This makes it possible to engage the whole wide world—the world that God calls Christians to love.

If environmental problems are truly complex, then no single person or community has all the answers. Environmentalists can, instead, unite around our uncertainties about how human beings should relate to the rest of the world, how to derive the energy that contemporary life requires, how to make moral choices about consumption, how to distribute the risks and burdens of pollution fairly, how to respond constructively to climate change, and how to build toward a sustainable future. Christian environmentalists on the left and right must avoid self-righteous fundamentalisms, moving beyond the false security of ideologies and "us versus them" mentalities into a more uncertain space where everyone has a voice in a broad conversation.

Virtues in Action

Of course, listening to others and hewing to the middle ground comes with its own dangers. Clinging too rigidly to the middle course—becoming fundamentalists about the golden mean—poses the risk of too much compromise and complacency, the paralysis that comes from constant second-guessing or the muddle that comes from trying to please everyone. Christians who strive for environmental virtue must beware the temptation to take quick and thoughtless actions, but we must also beware the temptation to sit and think or pray endlessly without ever actually acting upon our commitments. Eco-virtue finds another middle ground here: between the fundamentalism of callously rejecting enemies and the opposite fundamentalism of trying to accept every contradictory perspective. Christian environmentalists must be committed not only to listening and conversing broadly but also to *doing* something from those conversations, responding virtuously to the problems we face.

A helpful guide here is the work of Martin Luther King Jr., who identified his own activism as a middle course between extremes while also offering an uncompromising and scathing critique of the wrong kind of moderation. King's struggles against racism, segregation, and injustice were defined by the alternatives he resisted. He passionately railed against those who paid lip service to his cause, while also urging passivity, complacency, and patience in the face of systemic injustice; King insisted that the basic rights of all people demanded an immediate overthrow of segregationist policies and practices and sought concrete civil rights alongside social and economic justice for all people. At the same time, though, he also argued against the other extreme, those who claimed that racial injustice justified the use of violence and separation to overthrow the status quo.

The middle course King preached, between those who would wait patiently and those who would start a violent revolution, was nonviolent *resistance*: powerful and concrete enough to bring about change but deliberate and loving enough to maintain respect for human character and foster lasting community. Responding to a critic from the Black Power movement who had dismissed him as too moderate and too willing to compromise, King said, "I think moderation on the one hand can be a vice; I think on the other hand it can be a virtue. If by moderation we mean moving on through this tense period of transition with wide restraint, calm reasonableness, yet militant action, then moderation is a great virtue which all leaders should seek to achieve. But if moderation means slowing up in the move for justice and capitulating to the whims and caprices of the guardians of the deadening status quo, then moderation is a tragic vice which all men of good will must condemn."[20]

To cultivate virtue in our communities is to learn how to discern when our moderation or our passions have become vicious.

In seeking to become faithful environmentalists, Christians should strive to follow in the footsteps of King, who refused to respond to the extreme terror of white supremacy with violence but whose moderation was far from weak. Complex environmental challenges require the "wide restraint, calm reasonableness, yet militant action" that King advocated and demonstrated throughout his life. This reminder that being virtuous does not preclude bold action reflects another lesson taught by Thomas Aquinas, who argued that Christians are called to invest fully and without reservation in the virtuous life: "Virtue overcomes inordinate passion," he says, but "it produces ordinate passion."[21] Being reasonable and moderate in the spirit of Christian virtue does not mean we stop caring deeply and urgently about the problems facing our world and our neighbors. It does not mean we must be robotic or tame. On the contrary, eco-virtue is about being passionately aware of our surroundings and passionately loving toward our fellow creatures.

Responding to complex environmental problems with Christian virtue means seeking the golden mean, finding ways to end paralysis and gridlock, and enabling productive action with openness and resolve. This means recognizing that the earth cannot sustain the way we—especially we in the developed world—currently live. Our way of life is doing harm to many of our neighbors, and this calls for resolute and immediate action from all who have been blessed with the luxury of choices. The next seven chapters begin the work of discerning what that resolute and immediate action should be.

Questions for Discussion

1. This chapter introduces seven classical and theological virtues: prudence, courage, temperance, justice, faith, hope, and love. Which of these seems most important to you when it comes to environmental questions? If you could add another virtue to that list for the challenges of the twenty-first century, what would it be?

2. How might thinking in terms of "who should I be?" as opposed to "what should I do?" change conversations about environmental ethics?

3. Virtues are traditionally thought of as habits that involve finding the golden mean between extremes, identifying the well-ordered passion that drives one to do good work well. About what social or environmental problem are you most passionate? Can you discern a golden mean between extremes in response to that problem?

4. Which makes more sense to you: that virtue is learned from the trading and commerce of the global free market (as Deirdre McCloskey asserts) or that Christian virtue can only be learned in the church as it distinguishes itself from the world (as Stanley Hauerwas argues)? Can both be right? If so, how? If not, why not?

5. Which do you think is a bigger risk for the environmental movement: de-emphasizing the central place of human beings in creation (as the Cornwall Alliance worries) or making human beings too central (as Patrick Curry worries)? Why? What is the danger you foresee?

2

PRUDENCE
Between Selfless Conservation and Self-Interested Stewardship of Other Species

A Tame Virtue for a Wild Problem

Prudence may be the dullest and stuffiest sounding of the classical and Christian virtues. Prudence is a laughable wallflower, sitting on the sidelines and frowning while everyone else is out being creative. Prudence is a legalistic Puritan, ruining everyone else's fun with her caution, anxiety, and disapproval. Prudence sounds old-fashioned and backward; she pinned a scarlet letter on Hester Prynne and tried to keep everyone in *Footloose* from dancing. In short, dear prudence is a killjoy, never coming out to play.[1]

Having fallen out of general favor in the personal lives of contemporary U.S. citizens, prudence shows up most often these days in economic conversations, motivating discussions of "rational choice," "marginal utility," and "maximized efficiency." But this economic picture is hardly any better than the old-fashioned prude, because prudence is now reduced to cold and humorless calculation. Prudence is the boss who begins by instituting shorter breaks and higher quotas for workers and ends by outsourcing jobs overseas where laborers are cheaper, less demanding, and have fewer rights. Prudence is still ruining everyone else's fun, but now she is counting her money and plotting how to get more of it, with as little cost to herself as possible.

Both these visions of prudence contain important truths, but it is time for a revival of this most basic virtue; without prudence, none of the other virtues could accomplish anything. It takes prudence to tell the difference between courage and foolhardiness, between hope and wishful thinking, between real love and self-centered infatuation. The root is the Latin word *prudentia*, meaning "foresight"; at its core, prudence is not about being a judgmental prig or a miserly bore, but about intelligence, sagacity, and discretion—traits that enjoy almost universal approval (celebrity gossip magazines notwith-standing). All of this becomes more obvious when our prudish heroine takes off her bonnet and goes by her other, more palatable name: "reason." Among all of the other virtues, it is precisely prudence—intelligent, forward-looking, practical reason—that allows the virtuous person to discern the golden mean between vicious extremes.

In the context of environmentalism, prudence has a very important role to play—namely, to bring balance in the midst of competing interests. A much-beloved prayer asks God for "the wisdom to know the difference" between the things one can change and the things one cannot, something that environ-mental problems require in abundance. Prudence implores us neither to turn a blind eye to climate change, nor to run around in a panic screaming, "The sky is falling!" Prudence understands that human beings need meaningful work in order to flourish but does not rush to encourage wanton consump-tion to stimulate markets ("Go shopping!"). Prudence appreciates the cultural importance of certain kinds of food and habits of eating but is open to con-sidering dietary changes that would be more beneficial for human, animal, and plant life. Prudence, in sum, avoids law-bound fundamentalisms of all kinds and instead pays careful, reasoned attention to the complexities and particularities of context.

To understand how useful prudence is, consider the rampant and grow-ing crisis of species extinction. At this very moment, human beings are liv-ing through an unprecedented process of biodiversity loss. Never before in human history—indeed, not since the demise of the dinosaurs sixty-five mil-lion years ago—have so many species been driven extinct so quickly. The history of humanity is a history of expansion: spreading across the globe, expanding population, and increasing levels of consumption, with new tech-nologies allowing us to live in and take resources from ever more remote and inhospitable places. As the footprint of humanity expands, the space and food available for the rest of God's creatures shrinks. The result is extinc-tion, and the most threatened species are those who do not thrive alongside human populations: spotted owls, Sumatran rhinos, coral reefs, tree frogs, polar bears, and many more.

Perhaps the key challenge facing those who care about mass extinction is that no one fully understands it. While scientists have identified many endan-gered species, there are countless others out there not yet identified. There are species in the shrinking rainforest and the melting arctic that have never been seen by human eyes, some of which may never be seen before they are gone. We do not know exactly how many species have been driven extinct or how many are now endangered, because we do not even know how many species there are in the world. As of one recent study, scientists had catalogued a total of 1.2 million species and were adding over fifteen thousand to that list each year.[2] However, all estimates suggest that there are still millions of species yet to be found and identified. This is a problem that cries out for prudence: given limited knowledge, practical reason becomes all the more important. Prudence offers guidance in balancing the interests of other species—including the ones who remain unknown to us—with the needs and wants of the expanding human species.

At the moment though, human beings are wantonly and often unconsciously consuming the earth's resources to the detriment of other species. Extinctions deplete the knowledge, the wonder, and the safety that comes from a biologically diverse world. Prudence looks beyond short-term gain and calls attention to the long term. Prudence helps people wrestle with species extinctions and the moral problems they raise for future generations, preparing virtuous communities to face difficult choices about which species to save when resources are limited, to deal humanely with invasive species in delicate ecosystems, and to preserve wild habitats without unduly derailing human civilization. Prudence is central to the human work of preserving God's creation while continuing to benefit from the wild variety of life.

Learning to Care a Whole Awful Lot

The most common environmentalist appeal to prudence asks people to overthrow the selfishness and consumption that have previously defined our relationships to other species. While it is easy to think of other species as existing purely for human benefit—as resources, food, labor, company, materials, or even sights to be seen—environmentalists frequently ask people to stop thinking of other species in terms of what they can do for human beings and instead to conserve and care for them prudently.

A powerful example of this kind of thinking comes from one of the most popular but unlikely environmental ethicists of the past forty years: Dr. Seuss. He beautifully crystallizes the ongoing debate over the environment and the economy in his classic children's book *The Lorax*. The story chronicles a showdown between a businessman, the "Once-ler," and the Lorax, who famously "speaks for the trees." The story begins "at the far end of town where the Grickle-grass grows," a dark, desolate landscape of weeds and dilapidated buildings that signal trouble.[3] A scared-looking child pays fifteen cents and a nail to hear the Once-ler tell his tale.

The book then flashes back to a brightly colored world, "way back in the days when the grass was still green and the pond was still wet and the clouds were still clean." The most prominent features of the landscape are the Truffula Trees, which look like multicolored puffs of cotton candy. Into this picture drives the Once-ler Wagon, reminiscent of the prairie schooners of the Old West seeking out their manifest destinies. The Once-ler is immediately taken with the trees: "The touch of their tufts was much softer than silk. And they had the sweet smell of fresh butterfly milk."[4]

Like any good entrepreneur, the crafty Once-ler figures out how to profit from this beauty. He quickly chops down a Truffula Tree and knits its tuft into a "Thneed," which looks like a musical instrument made of thermal underwear. At this point, his titular antagonist enters the tale; a "shortish, brownish, and mossy-looking" mustachioed creature pops out of the tree stump and begins to throw his tiny weight around:

> "Mister!" he said with a sawdusty sneeze,
> "I am the Lorax. I speak for the trees.
> I speak for the trees, for the trees have no tongues.
> And I'm asking you, sir, at the top of my lungs"—
> he was very upset as he shouted and puffed—
> *"What's that THING you've made out of my Truffula tuft?"*

The Once-ler protests that he's making himself useful by creating the Thneed, "a Fine-Something-That-All-People-Need!" He promptly sells his creation to a customer—also faceless but significantly wearing a business suit—and the Thneed trade starts to boom. Soon the Once-ler's family members join him in a full-on industrial revolution, building a huge factory, chopping down trees in multiples with a custom-made machine, knitting, and then selling the inexplicably appealing products at a startling rate.[5]

The Lorax spends the rest of the story helplessly crying out against the destruction of Truffulas and the creatures who rely on them. He demonstrates that the ecosystem is interdependent, such that the destruction of one species hurts others: the Brown Bar-ba-loots have to leave town because of the scarcity of Truffula Fruit, the Swomee-Swans have to fly away to avoid the smog, and the Humming-Fish are driven away by polluted waters. The story reaches its terrible, ironic climax when the Once-ler, finally tired of the Lorax's parental nagging, angrily asserts his right to go on "biggering" his Thneed business at the exact moment that the very last Truffula Tree is cut down. With this last whack, the Once-ler's factory closes, his employees leave town, and the Lorax picks himself up by the seat of his pants and flies away, never to be seen again. All that remains of him is "a small pile of rocks, with the one word . . . 'UNLESS.' "[6]

When he finishes recounting this sad story to the bewildered boy, the now ruined Once-ler hands over the last remaining Truffula seed with this poignant exhortation: "Unless someone like you cares a whole awful lot, nothing is going to get better. It's not."[7] The moral is simple: the next generation must care more about the earth than the Once-ler did. The entrepreneur appreciated the monetary value of the trees but nothing else; he made no allowance for other creatures, for the beauty of his environment, or for the renewal of his stock. He was, in short, imprudent.[8]

In contrast, our hero the Lorax cares deeply for others, as is evident in the way he advocates for the innocent and vulnerable trees, bears, birds, and fish. He understands that prudence requires respecting and valuing other species and, that, if they are used purely for human economic benefit, they will soon be gone forever. He calls on the audience to care for other species "a whole awful lot," and this requires modifying, perhaps even banishing, business as usual. When it comes to endangered species, the teaching of *The Lorax* is that prudence comes from those who care rather than those who seek to make a profit.

Dr. Seuss reflects a popular position in the environmental movement. For example, the Sierra Club leads wilderness excursions to inspire members to care a whole awful lot about national parks, World Heritage sites, and other precious ecosystems that support endangered species.[9] The idea is that non-human species are best preserved by teaching people to love them and to see the reason behind treating them as inherently valuable creatures rather than mere commodities. The natural world should not be bought and sold in the marketplace, because markets teach people that other creatures exist as products for human enjoyment. For this school of conservationists, endangered species should be protected from trade and commerce at all costs.[10]

Christians might hear this call to stop our economic consumption of the environment as a contemporary expression of Jesus' command to the rich young man to "sell all that you have and distribute to the poor" (Luke 18:22), with the understanding that in this case the poor are threatened frogs, reefs, and trees, impoverished by the ways people get rich off buying and selling nature's goods. The Baptist farmer and essayist Wendell Berry writes that Christians can steward God's creation only if we utterly reject "the industrial economy—which is an economy firmly founded on the seven deadly sins and the breaking of all ten of the Ten Commandments." He continues that "Christ's life, from the manger to the cross, was an affront to the established powers of his time," and so urges Christians to reject established economic structures in favor of less exploitative and destructive practices.[11]

To his credit, Berry works to practice what he preaches. In 1964 he left a prestigious job as a professor in New York City to return to his native Kentucky, and shortly thereafter he moved to a farm that he plows with a mule rather than a tractor. He refuses to use a computer and speaks out against nuclear and coal power, consistently opposing business and industry in order to stand up for God's creation. Berry has not sold all that he owns, but he has worked to separate himself as much as possible from mainstream economics, which he sees as sinful, in order to have a more caring relationship to the land he farms and the other creatures that share it with him. Prudence for Berry, a real live Lorax, consists of rejecting the prevailing economic logic in order to care for the creatures of God's earth for their own sake. Of course, Berry is part of the system he tries to critique: he privately owns his farm, and he spreads his ideas through the capitalist world of publishing, but he seeks to use both to encourage others to resist manipulative ownership and destructive capitalism. He asks his audience to learn to care a whole awful lot.

Caring by Owning

There is much to be learned from such strident rejection of economics in relating to other species and the created world. But there is also something to be learned from those who believe that the best way to learn prudence is in fact through an *embrace* of economic logic and practices. Instead of the rich young man whom Jesus asked to sell all that he owned, perhaps Christianity's guide in relating to endangered species should be the wise servants in the parable of the talents, who use and invest the wealth with which they are entrusted to increase the wealth of their master (Matthew 25:14-30). Perhaps, in other words, humans are most likely to learn prudence from treating other species with the respect due the master's property.

Free market environmentalism (FME) is a school of thought that has emerged at the intersection of environmentalism and libertarian economics. It explicitly opposes the business-versus-nature perspective favored by traditional green thinkers and argues that private property and market systems, much beloved by conservative economic thinkers, have enormous potential for natural conservation. For free market environmentalists, good business *is* good environmentalism, and the best way to take care of the earth and its diversity of species is to ensure that their thriving is in at least one human's economic interest. Private ownership is precisely the key to environmental conservation.

Economist Terry Anderson, one of the most prolific proponents of FME, argues that "all environmental issues ultimately boil down to property rights issues."[12] The core claim of FME is that well-defined, stable, and consistently enforced property rights are the most effective tool for conserving natural resources. In general, people care responsibly for what they own and are all too likely to neglect, abuse, or deplete resources that belong to everyone (or no one) and seem to be free for the taking. This is the so-called tragedy of the commons, a famous principle in environmental ethics, which teaches that it is simply human nature to care more for one's own property than for property owned in common. Good policy, FME suggests, should accept this reality of human nature and do its best to "harness self-interest," defining private property and protecting people's rights to control their own property through the rule of law.[13]

Take, for example, fish. Free market environmentalists argue that it is disastrous for fish when governments control oceans, lakes, and rivers, setting limits on how many fish can be caught, thereby making the waters a "commons" that belong equally to all. Although the government's intention is to protect fish, it brings about unintended consequences: fishers have perverse, short-term incentives to overfish, catching as many as they can before their competitors get all the fish or before the government lowers the quota. By contrast, if the waters or the rights to fish them are privately owned, then the owners have a self-interested incentive that actually serves fish populations. When they are owners as well as anglers, fishers have incentives to make sure that fish populations stay healthy so that they can be harvested for many years to come.[14] In other words, the fish populations benefit from being owned by human beings.

A more colorful example comes from our old friend the Lorax. The story as it stands presents a prime example of the destruction of an unowned ecosystem. The Truffula Trees, as far as we can tell, belong to no one but themselves and the wildlife that thrives among them. The Once-ler stumbles upon them and takes all he wants, and the Lorax is powerless to stop him. Such a scenario is not entirely ahistorical: the Once-ler resembles the frontier spirit of U.S. history, folk heroes like Daniel Boone or Pa Ingalls who showed up in a new place, claimed it, and began bending it to their will. The Lorax plays the role of a Native American who lives on the land but gets no respect as an owner or decision maker from the new arrival.

Hearing this story, FME argues that the best answer would come not from convincing the Once-ler to listen to the Lorax out of the goodness of his heart but instead ensuring that the Truffula Trees are not a commons destined for tragedy. The best solution would arise naturally if the Lorax could do more than merely *speak for* the trees—in other words, if he actually owned them. With property rights backed by the rule of law and the threat of punishment, the Lorax would have the power to throw the Once-ler off his land and prosecute him for "stealing" his trees. In addition, he could sue for the loss of eco-tourism that depends upon the Bar-ba-loots and Swomee-Swans. Or, if the Lorax wanted to make a compromise and leverage his property for private gain, he could charge the Once-ler a mutually beneficial price for the right to cut down a few trees and make Thneeds out of the tufts. The Lorax could then use his profits to buy up more land or plant more Truffula Trees, ensuring plenty of bear, bird, and fish habitats, as well as profits, for years to come.

Of course, as critics of economic logic are quick to point out, people who own big swaths of land are not always tree lovers dedicated to defending wildlife. However, FME replies that even if the tables were turned and it was the Once-ler who owned the trees, it would be rational for him, too, to treat them more respectfully. If the Once-ler had clear and enduring property rights, he would have an incentive to take care of his assets, harvesting his trees sustainably rather than cutting them all down. Clear-cutting a forest may provide short-term gain, but an owner who expects to control the land over the long term has reason to keep the system healthy so that it provides wealth for years to come.[15] A quick boom of income from Thneeds is just fine, but with property rights and basic business sense, the Once-ler would understand that he could make far more money producing them sustainably, replanting as he went and spreading his income over decades. Meanwhile, he could run a lucrative side business selling tourists the privilege of observing the majestic Swomee-Swan in its native habitat.

In short, if *either* the Lorax *or* the Once-ler had property rights to the land, free market environmentalists are confident that reason and self-interest—that is to say, prudence—would quite naturally and effortlessly lead them to long-term Truffula forest preservation and a happier ending. Ownership breeds prudence and saves species by making us "care a whole awful lot." An example from the real world that free market environmentalists offer is the African elephant.[16] According to FME, the only way to ensure that African elephants are not hunted to extinction is to make them someone's property. As long as elephants belong to no one and are protected only by the government, they argue, no one is more than symbolically or abstractly invested in their survival. Even worse, hunting bans create perverse incentives for poachers to kill as many elephants as they can before the animals are extinct or the government cracks down. A far better solution, according to FME, is to turn the animals into economic assets, ensuring property owners have the right to control hunting on their land and thereby making it profitable to keep some around. Hunting will be managed sustainably because it will be in the self-interest of property owners to manage it that way.

Not only does private property preserve other species according to FME: it also teaches prudence. When people own an ecosystem, they have an incentive to understand it, to care for it, and to make wise and careful decisions about it. It is simply human nature to make more careful, practical decisions about private property than public, "because the wealth of the property owner is at stake if bad decisions are made."[17] In contrast, FME argues, governmental and other forms of communal ownership fail to foster discipline or to encourage the cooperation and innovation that emerge from the natural desire to improve one's own property and quality of life. Government ownership and management create a commons, essentially a free-for-all, which encourages rapid degradation while everyone tries to grab whatever they can before it is gone.

According to FME, the major flaw with traditional environmentalism is that it simply asks people to "care a whole awful lot" without offering anything in return, trusting in the goodness of human nature; or it makes "command-and-control" laws without creating the right kinds of incentives for self-interested humans. Free market environmentalists prefer to support organizations like the Nature Conservancy, which sometimes uses private funds to buy land in need of preservation rather than asking the government to publicly manage such areas and the species within them.[18] Property, in this view, is the *only* thing that truly incentivizes good stewardship.

The connection between private property and human reason is familiar in the Christian tradition. Around 200 C.E. theologian Clement of Alexandria insisted that "what is managed with wisdom, and sobriety, and piety, is profitable; . . . the Lord introduces the use of external things, bidding us put away not the means of subsistence, but what uses them badly."[19] A millennium and a half later, Pope Leo XIII put it this way: "Private ownership is in accordance with the law of nature. . . . Now, when man [*sic*] thus turns the activity of his mind and the strength of his body toward procuring the fruits of nature, by such act he makes his own that portion of nature's field which he cultivates."[20]

Despite Christian ideals of universal love, observation and common sense seem to indicate that human dignity demands at least some degree of autonomy and ownership—not to mention payoffs for sacrifices made. Humans, like all other species, have a natural bent toward self-preservation and, to this end, tend to take better care of their own things than those of others. FME asks even the most loving, idealistic Christians prudently to bear this in mind.

Wise as Serpents, Innocent as Doves

When it comes to conserving God's creation, one side insists that human self-interest is the root of the problem, while the other insists that harnessing human self-interest is the only solution. The virtue of prudence is about finding a golden mean, seeking a balance between naïvely selfless care and proudly self-interested ownership, between the story of the rich young man and the parable of the talents. Christians who care for the diverse species of this earth must somehow stand between these two extremes and learn what we can. The beginning of prudence is for environmentalists to admit that each side of this debate is right about something and each side is also missing something. Human altruism is not as all powerful as the Loraxes of the environmental movement seem to hope, and yet nonhuman species do have value beyond what the free marketeers attribute to them. To make the same point positively—prudent Christians are those who understand that our fates are wrapped up in those of other species and also know that God, not humankind, is the ultimate owner of all that is.

In the Gospel of Matthew, Jesus sends his disciples to preach the good news of God's reign, and he makes a point of asking them to leave their money behind—"Take no gold, nor silver, nor copper in your belts, no bag for your journey"—but assures them that they will be provided for in the towns where they preach, "for the laborer deserves his food." His final instruction is for his disciples to be "wise as serpents and innocent as doves" (Matthew 10:9-16). This verse offers a key to the golden mean between too much prudence and too little: Christians treat other species rightly and well when we can find wisdom from free market environmentalists who expect to be paid for their sacrifices, but also maintain the innocence of the Lorax who is willing to forgo wealth for the sake of the inherent goodness of other species.[21]

The Wisdom of Self-Interest

The first lesson of prudence is about the pervasive and unavoidable power of human self-interest. Free market environmentalists offer an important and helpful reminder that human beings are naturally motivated by our own bottom lines. This is what leads FME to worry about the tragedy of the commons—as long as there is profit to be made from taking more than one's share of fish from the common stock, cutting down unowned trees indiscriminately, or violating hunting bans on priceless elephants, people will do all of these things. So, one prudent solution is to make it profitable *not* to do these things: give fishers a reason to save their stocks, give loggers a reason to preserve and replant trees, and give landowners a reason to maintain a healthy population of elephants. Appeal to self-interest, free market environmentalists argue, and the natural result is that species will be saved in the long run.

This is an important lesson that the Loraxes of the world should learn. At its extreme, the wide-eyed innocence of the Lorax seems more than a bit naïve. He seems to be asking people to make fundamental changes in their lifestyles and social structures simply out of the goodness of their hearts, for no reason other than caring "a whole awful lot." While Christians are indeed called to act out of love and are defined by the love we show for our neighbors, FME reminds us that we are called specifically to love our neighbors *as ourselves*. This suggests that we are not expected entirely to forgo self-interest but are instead expected to learn from our self-interest about how to love prudently.

As it happens, there are many self-interested reasons to care about the diverse species with which human beings share the world. For example, those who eat other species—which is to say all of us—must remember that human food supplies depend upon the genetic diversity of animals and plants. Even a creature as humble as the common honeybee is responsible for pollinating one-third of what we eat.[22] A growing human population will be fed only by learning more about the food sources to be found on earth, some of which are in undiscovered and unexplored ecosystems. Humans who seek good health also need other species. Many of the most powerful medicines in use today are extracted, derived, or inspired by plants and animals, and new medicines for the future will be found in the same sources. In addition, humans who simply enjoy the beauty of the world need other species: the towering trees, trilling bird songs, and swaying prairie grasses associated with the majesty and splendor of nature depend on diverse ecosystems made up of many fragile species.[23] Finally, humans who seek to honor God the creator need other species. Psalm 148 tells us that God is praised by "sea monsters and all deeps" and "wild animals and all cattle, creeping things and flying birds." Christians learn to worship from and with other species; the God who is invisible, the God who is all knowing, good, and wholly other, has filled the world with evidence of God's work, the means for humans to see, hear, touch, smell, and taste God's goodness.[24]

It is clear, then, that caring for other species does not require human beings to be wholly altruistic, ignoring self-interest altogether. Human beings, now and for all generations to come, are thoroughly interdependent with other creatures in ways of which we are only partially aware. Humanity's fate is tied up with the fates of all God's other creatures, so it is only prudent that, for our own sake, we work to save the coral reefs, rainforests, and all the other ecosystems that support the species with whom we share this planet.

The Innocence of Caring

At the same time, prudence is not merely about serving self-interest, and FME is wrong if it goes to the extreme of prescribing that humans should *only* preserve other species when we can see some immediate economic benefit from it. Free market environmentalists too often take this perspective, as demonstrated in a basic textbook that asserts: "The environment's only value derives from human perceptions . . . the environment itself has no intrinsic value."[25] This takes the wisdom of self-interest too far, assuming that if people are inevitably self-interested (and since honeybees and elephants cannot speak for themselves), then prudence calls for *exclusive* focus on the interests of people. This way of thinking may be appropriate in the limited realm of abstract and highly simplified economic models, but it should be a red flag for anyone whose ethics allow for complexity, maturity, and nuance in the real world. Even Adam Smith, the father of free-market thinking, saw a crucial role for "sympathy," which he understood as the human quality of using imagination to put oneself in another's shoes.[26]

In stark contrast to FME, Christian tradition does not teach that value derives from human perception; it teaches that the ultimate source of all goodness is God. In the words of the psalmist, "The earth is the Lord's and all that is in it, the world, and those who live in it, for he has founded it"

(Psalm 24:1). The environment has value far beyond human measure, which comes from the God who created it and called it good. Prudence includes not just the wisdom to acknowledge that people need appropriate incentives; it includes also the innocence to admit that human beings are not the arbiters of the world's value and the humility to see that dangerous mistakes have been made by people who chose to give self-interest free rein.

In the final analysis, Christian environmentalists are called to care for the world because—regardless of whoever's name actually appears on the deed—it belongs to God. Private ownership may have much to recommend it, but it is theologically secondary to God as the owner of all that is and ever will be. Not every species has the cash value of a Truffula tree or an African elephant. Indeed, some endangered species might seem totally worthless in economic terms. Consider the snail darter, a tiny, confusingly named fish found in the Tennessee River, which is one of 150 species of darter and is now threatened with extinction. Science and economics do not (yet) know of any way these fish directly benefit human beings, but prudence asks believers to trust that God's creation is valuable and to seek to preserve the snail darter. The innocence of Christianity emphasizes that human beings are not the only judge of what matters; we are most prudent when we serve not only human interests but also the interests of all the others beloved by God.

In Dr. Seuss' story, it seems that the Lorax does not want anything from the trees or the other creatures in his neighborhood; he simply loves them and wants to see them happy and flourishing. So, too, Christianity encourages humans to be lovers rather than just consumers of the earth. This makes sense especially because we are not truly the owners of the earth but merely stewards of it on God's behalf. Pope Francis put this eloquently: "We human beings are not only the beneficiaries but also the stewards of other creatures. Thanks to our bodies, God has joined us so closely to the world around us that we can feel the desertification of the soil almost as a physical ailment, and the extinction of a species as a painful disfigurement. Let us not leave in our wake a swatch of destruction and death which will affect our own lives and those of future generations."[27]

Prudence calls for both the wisdom of serpents and the innocence of doves. Virtuous Christians will learn to treat other species prudently when learning to take human self-interest seriously but refusing to go so far as to believe that it is the *only* thing of any consequence in this world. Other creatures can be valuable as God's creation despite the fact that, in practical terms, human beings need incentives to care consistently. This golden mean will be difficult to master, and it will inevitably require ongoing self-correction and the ability to learn from mistakes. But the work of virtue is not about perfection; it is about practice.

Learning Prudence

Discussions of endangered species almost always come to rainforests, because the tropical rainforests are the most diverse places we know, likely containing at least two-thirds of all the land species on earth. One small area of rainforest, the Yasuni National Park in Ecuador, is only ten thousand square kilometers (smaller than the Dallas/Fort Worth metro area) but contains one hundred thousand different species of insect—about the same as the entirety of North America. In just one hectare (the size of a standard athletic track and field) of this park, researchers found 655 distinct species of tree, which is more than the total number of tree species recorded in the United States and Canada combined. The Yasuni is also home to at least twenty-three globally threatened mammal species, including breeds of otter, manatee, anteater, and tapir that might soon die out in the rest of the world. In short, the Yasuni is densely packed with a variety of endangered life.

The Yasuni also sits on top of an enormous reserve of oil, an estimated 850 million barrels, which is worth well over $7 billion. This money could do enormous good for the nation of Ecuador, where many people struggle with poverty and debt. Drilling for oil is a destructive business, though, and extensive exploration would destroy at least parts of the rainforest and much of its biodiversity. This left the government of Ecuador with a difficult choice between drilling and conservation: between the Once-ler's market forces encouraging profit and development on one hand and the altruistic voice of the Lorax speaking for the trees, otters, and manatees on the other.

In 2007 Ecuador decided to try a prudent middle course by not drilling in the Yasuni wildlife preserve but asking the world community to help pay for the lost profits. They proposed that foreign governments and donors contribute $3.6 billion—about half the value of the oil for which Ecuador would not drill. The government felt justified in asking for this, emphasizing that an intact rainforest benefits the entire world community not only by providing clean air and water and capturing carbon dioxide but also because its biodiversity has so much to offer and teach humankind. For example, they cited the discovery of a fungus that could potentially eat through the rapidly increasing plastic waste that currently chokes the oceans and other ecosystems.[28] Donated funds would be managed by the United Nations Development Program and would be restricted to transitioning the nation of Ecuador to clean energy sources, restoring natural areas, and assisting indigenous tribes that live in the Yasuni and other Ecuadorian rainforests.[29]

Some skeptics worried that Ecuador was unethically "ransoming" this rainforest for cash. They feared that Ecuador was merely delaying exploration in hopes that the price of oil would rise or that the government was insufficiently stable to ensure the safety of the rainforest over the long term.[30] However, Ecuador (home of the famous Galapagos Islands) has a history of caring for other species that is even codified in its constitution, which asserts that nature has rights and prohibits the extraction of nonrenewable resources in protected areas. The nation wanted to do the right thing for its species, but also for its people.

This approach was finally unsuccessful, and Ecuador's president dissolved the fund for the Yasuni in 2013, saying "the world has failed us" by not sufficiently investing in the intact rainforest.[31] Oil companies are now developing the infrastructure to extract oil from the rainforest. This conclusion is either a tragedy—showing that the prudent path of Ecuador's government trying to avoid destroying the rainforest was hopeless—or a sensible resolution (showing that market forces prudently deemed the land most valuable as a source for oil rather than a protected habitat). Either way, this demonstrates the complexities of trying to live prudently by balancing incentives and self-interest with altruism and responsibility. Regardless of what happens in the Yasuni, human beings must continue learning how to prudently manage our own lives while still treating other species with the dignity and respect of which they are worthy.

Christians seeking to treat other species prudently might decide to encourage smaller-scale solutions in their own neighborhoods, where parks are frequently put up against development and jobs are frequently thought to compete with environmental protection. The complexity of species extinction calls for creative and innovative solutions in the middle ground. A prudent approach to caring for the earth amid pluralistic societies and global ecosystems may mean that ideological purity is less important than practical results that help humanity progress toward more sustainable systems.

Prudence is no longer a stuffy and old-fashioned killjoy, nor is she an economically obsessed efficiency expert. She is the open-minded and practical voice of reason at the cutting edge of finding new ways forward, willing to listen to anyone with a reasonable idea. For Christians who hope to do good for the world while still taking care of ourselves, our neighbors, and the wild variety of life on God's earth, prudence is a virtue worth cultivating.

Questions for Discussion

1. What kinds of associations, if any, do you have with the word "prudence"? Where can you see the importance of practical reason in everyday life, apart from environmental issues?

2. Which do you think is more dangerous in the contemporary world: the innocent naïveté of those who want to inspire good behavior or the selfish calculations of those who seek to enhance profits? Do Christians need to work harder at being wise as serpents or innocent as doves?

3. The message of *The Lorax* and much environmentalist literature is that if people learn to "care a whole awful lot," environmental problems will be solved. Can people learn to care about distant ecosystems or faraway species? Can people learn to care for things that do not belong to them?

4. Free market environmentalist arguments about owning property are not explicitly Christian, but can they be framed in Christian terms? What does it mean to "own" property, given the theological belief that everything ultimately belongs to God? What does it mean to be a "steward"?

5. How does the story of the Yasuni National Park in Ecuador demonstrate the virtue of prudence? How does it demonstrate the absence of prudence? How do you think the rest of the world should have responded to Ecuador's proposal?

3

COURAGE
Between Fossil Fuels, Alternative Energies, and Sabbath Living

Be of Good Fortitude

For many of us, courage calls to mind traditional images of muscular warriors charging into battle with swords drawn. Or perhaps it reminds us of someone like Rosa Parks, who in 1955 famously refused to give up her seat on a city bus to a white man, thus helping to spark the Montgomery bus boycott. Courage is indeed required for these heroic acts of bravely insisting on what is right in the face of grave danger. But if we dig a little deeper, we might also remember that courage includes less conspicuous acts of fortitude: the habit of maintaining a courageous stance even when it proves unpopular, fruitless, or exhausting. This is the virtue of sustained action in difficult times, such as the thousands of Montgomery citizens who walked to work every day for over a year to protest racial segregation on the city's buses. Courage stands up for truth and justice, sometimes by charging head-on into danger, sometimes by persevering quietly and confidently over a long period of time.

Consider the exodus, a narrative filled with examples of heroic courage. The Hebrew midwives courageously lie to the Egyptian authorities about killing newborn baby boys. Moses' mother courageously puts her son in a basket in the Nile in order to save his life. Pharaoh's daughter courageously adopts a stranger's baby from the river. The baby's sister, Miriam, courageously offers her own mother to Pharaoh's daughter as a wet nurse.[1] Years later, Moses courageously answers God's fiery call to stand up to the Pharaoh, his people's oppressor. Most cinematically, he and the Hebrews courageously walk across the raging Red Sea to escape the pursuing Egyptian army. The exodus is nothing if not a story of heroism and derring-do.

But it is important not to forget that much of the story is about another kind of courage, the fortitude to persevere through difficult and less exciting times. Soon after their dramatic escape, the Israelites find themselves wandering in the wilderness with no clear direction and no reliable source of food. Lamenting their hunger, some wish they were dead, while others begin to long for the days of enslavement when at least they were well fed. God, hearing the complaining of these stiff-necked people, responds with a miracle. Quail appears around dinnertime, and each morning bread "rained from heaven" in the form of manna, small flakes of nourishment covering the ground like frost and tasting like honeyed wafers. There is one condition, however: God stipulates that there will be enough manna for all, but only just enough. They must gather precisely what they need for the day, no more. Only the sixth day is different: they may gather two days' worth to allow for Sabbath rest. "In that way," God says, "I will test them, whether they will follow my instruction or not" (Exodus 16:4). Of course, human nature being what it is (especially if the hoarders on reality TV are any indication), some of the Israelites do not listen. Inevitably, some want to gather more than just what they need for the day, perhaps to protect themselves against future want or to sell to lazy neighbors. But God is not to be disobeyed; the extra manna becomes foul and infested by worms upon its one-day expiration date. God teaches the people to be content with their daily bread, confident that they will be fed tomorrow just as they are today.

The Israelites wandered in the desert like this for forty years. Without fortitude—the courage of staying power—fear would have driven them to give up: to divide and go separate ways, to turn around and return to enslavement in Egypt, to fight among themselves for whatever scarce resources they could find, or simply to die in the wilderness. Contemporary Christians continue to find ways to let ancient biblical tales such as the exodus inform their behaviors. For example, in his book *Manna and Mercy*, Lutheran author Dan Erlander argues that God sent the Israelites into the wilderness and fed them with miracle food precisely to teach them the virtues required to be God's people. Erlander sums these virtues up in three lessons: God gives enough manna for all; everyone is fed when no one hoards; and everyone must keep the Sabbath and rest. These lessons, he argues, are the path toward "a universal manna society . . . where humans live in harmony with all creation, each part living for the good of the whole."[2] If we gratefully trust that God provides, if we share rather than hoard, and if we take proper rest and enjoyment, we will all be able to live well.

After some false starts, the Israelites proved their staying power. They faced their fears and kept moving forward toward the promise. In gathering just enough manna each day, they found not only daily bread but also the fortitude to live with uncertainty. They learned to persevere, trusting that the God who had led them into the wilderness would not abandon them. They could bravely endure hardship while making their way into a new kind of existence, living for something bigger than private self-interest or short-term gains. Against all odds, they faced their challenges, took resolute action, remained a community, and followed God's path. They would of course falter and face trials again (worshiping the golden calf comes to mind), but each time, they returned to the hard work of living out God's plan. They learned enduring courage.

Courage is about what we do in the face of threats and uncertainty. Aristotle defines this pivotal virtue as reason in response to fear and irascible passions. It takes courage to remain rationally virtuous when one is afraid; it takes fortitude to avoid irrational actions when provoked to anger or panic. The philosopher makes the vital point that courage does not banish fear; rather, the courageous person "will fear what is fearful; but he will endure it in the right way and as reason directs for the sake of acting nobly."[3] As with all the virtues, courage is classically understood as a golden mean between two extremes: cowardice and recklessness. Cowardice is a deficiency of courage, and the cowardly are those who cannot remain virtuous and thoughtful in the face of fear. But an irrational surplus of courage is also a problem; it can become recklessness or foolhardiness. To kill a person who makes you angry (as Moses did) may show a lack of cowardice, but it may then go to the other extreme and demonstrate foolhardiness rather than the virtue of fortitude.

And as with all the virtues, courage cannot exist alone. There is no courageous action without love, no persevering fortitude without a commitment to justice. At the same time, the other virtues require courage. As C. S. Lewis puts it, courage can be understood as "not simply one of the virtues, but *the form of every virtue at the testing point.*"[4] A person can be said to truly have any virtue *only* if she has the courage to persevere even when it becomes difficult to practice. Courage is the habit of considered action and resolution that allows human beings to follow through—and to keep following through—on what prudence, temperance, justice, faith, hope, and love show us we must do. We need fortitude to avoid panic, to try new things, and to be confident that we should act with virtuous reason even when we are not sure it will "work" in the short term or according to conventional wisdom.

The Israelites found a testing point for their virtues at the edge of the Red Sea and again as they were wracked by hunger in the desert. These trials taught them courage. Human beings in the twenty-first century, particularly those of us in industrialized cultures, find our virtues tested by energy-related fears and particularly by finding the difficult balance between fossil fuels, renewable resources, and reduced consumption; between having everything we want when we want it at the price we want and having an ecosystem that will be healthy for the long term. In order to respond courageously to the realities of energy in our time, we need to carefully examine the passions that currently condition the consumption of energy—both the world's and our own.

Energy Fears in the Twenty-First Century

Energy is a matter of the ground we stand on, the air we breathe, and the happiness we pursue. Fossil fuels are currently essential to the way of life of every person in the industrialized world. And yet they also offer many reasons to fear: fear of the pollution they cause, fear of the politics they nurture, and fear of the future of our economies if they are restricted or run out. In order to be truly courageous in response to these fears, to avoid both recklessness and cowardice, Christians must educate and shape our fears and passions according to reason. This requires, first, that we look the situation squarely in the eye.

It used to be that scarcity was the most prominent fear that came up in discussions of fossil fuels. Industrialized civilization is based upon the burning of oil, coal, and natural gas that formed over millions of years through geologic processes, and we are using these fuels much faster than they can be replenished. The idea that supplies would soon run out was actually encouraging to some environmentalists, who hoped it might "force us to undergo a virtuous transition" to clean energy. In recent years, though, that fear has been turned upside down, leading some to ask, "What if we never run out?"[5] Industry has proven tremendously adept at developing new technological capacities to find and extract oil and other resources and will likely continue to do so for some time. But even though imminent scarcity seems like less of a threat today, the scientific community generally agrees that industrial society will still need to transition away from fossil fuels sooner or later. The reasons for this transition, and the pace of it, are varied, growing out of distinct and sometimes conflicting fears.

Fear 1: Degradation and Pollution

Contemporary environmentalists worry that our use of fossil fuels is—not to put too fine a point on it—destroying the planet. This concern begins with what is done to the earth when fossil fuels are extracted. Coal, for example, is commonly mined through a process called "mountaintop removal." This is exactly what it sounds like: the surface of a mountain is blown off with controlled explosions to reveal underground seams of coal. These explosions not only turn mountains into bare, lifeless plateaus; they also send tons of polluting debris pouring into valleys and rivers below. Natural gas, meanwhile, is increasingly gathered through a process called "hydraulic fracturing" (more commonly, "fracking"), which uses enormous quantities of chemically treated water to push the gas from below the earth's surface so that it can be gathered and sold. Like mountaintop removal, hydraulic fracturing makes fundamental changes to local geography and may pose threats to nearby people and animals, particularly in the form of water contamination.[6] Oil drilling is also dangerous, as the public is reminded whenever blowouts and spills occur, such as the BP disaster in the Gulf of Mexico or the increasing instances of oil train explosions across North America.

However, it is not only the extraction, production, and transportation of these fuels that pollute. Perhaps more urgent is the fact that by burning these fuels we consumers produce not only energy for our use but also substantial pollutants—chemicals that cause acid rain, contaminate water and food supplies, and contribute to world-altering climate change. Fossil fuels contain hydrocarbon, heavy metals, and even radioactive materials, all of which are released into the atmosphere, ending up in our air, our water, and our bodies. Perhaps most poignant is the fact that people who pollute the least can sometimes suffer the most, such as breast-feeding mothers in the arctic, who have almost no ecological footprint but whose food supplies are among the most contaminated on earth.[7]

Fear 2: Political Injustice

If purely ecological fears are not enough, still more reasons to fear come from the politics of energy. The world's fossil fuels are not evenly distributed, and not all decisions about them are made justly or wisely. Much of the world's oil is located in places with authoritarian governments, and the lion's share of profits from that oil goes to the few richest people in those nations while doing little good for the poor. This fosters volatile political climates and contributes to international tensions.[8] The United States of America's "addiction to oil" has led to military and political engagements that have changed the shape of geopolitics for the worse, and to compromises that have changed the stature of the United States in the world for generations to come.[9] The fact that U.S. citizens use about 20 percent of the world's energy (and constitute the second-most polluting nation on earth), despite representing less than 5 percent of the world's population, has damaged our relationship to other nations as well as to God's creation.[10]

Energy addiction can also shape domestic politics in scary ways. For example, environmentalists complain that even in democracies, large energy companies and wealthy individuals with vested interests can buy disproportionate influence over elected politicians who are supposed to represent all citizens equally, regardless of wealth. These companies benefit from legislation that provides taxpayer-funded corporate subsidies, lax regulation, and shoddy oversight, often to the detriment of workers and other common citizens—not to mention the land and the rest of creation—who cannot afford such influence. This, too, is legitimate cause for fear.

Fear 3: Restriction of Freedom

While the first two fears are most common among liberal or left-leaning thinkers who conclude that the pollution and politics of energy call for a global shift toward wind, solar, geothermal, and tidal power, the other side of the political spectrum also has reasonable fears. Conservative or right-leaning thinkers tend to worry less about pollution and corporate influence and more that alternative fuels simply cannot provide enough power to maintain industrialized civilizations at the levels to which we have grown accustomed. Nor, they add, will alternatives be able to bring up the quality of life in poor and developing nations as rapidly as fossil fuels. According to this perspective, the great danger is not that humankind will continue to use fossil fuels or destroy the earth but that we will be forced to stop by some external authority before we have reaped the full benefits of the bounteous energy such fuels provide.

More than CO_2 and methane, these conservative thinkers fear government intrusions, regulations, and limitations that would prevent people from making what they see as private, voluntary, informed decisions about their energy consumption. Strong societies, they argue, are based on democratic structures that prioritize individual freedom. Libertarian environmentalists and businesspeople worry that "big government" will take away their lands, their money, and—most importantly—their freedoms by taking away their rights to use and sell fossil fuels. To the ideologically pure, it is dangerous to offer government subsidies for businesses that sell alternative energies or to place extensive taxes or regulations on oil, gas, and coal. The dangers exist not only for societies that are currently thriving with unfettered use of these traditional fuels (which, it must be said, have long enjoyed government subsidies) but also for those societies that have lagged behind in economic development.[11] The specter of history's centrally controlled economies, some of which have been crushed under their own respective weights, offer genuine reasons to fear any government that overreaches to the point of neglecting individual human freedom.

Fear 4: Global Slowdown

Closely tied to fears about governmental interference and liberty is the fear of economic recession and anything that might decrease the rates of growth in today's booming (or recovering) economies. Economic conservatives tend to assume that environmental interests stand in opposition to concerns such as jobs, profits, and growth.[12] Corporate leaders and investors worry that any laws restricting the use of fossil fuels will necessarily reduce profits and hurt economies. Meanwhile, property owners who believe that their private economic successes will eventually create broad social benefits (often referred to as a "trickle-down" effect) fear that bans on mining, drilling, and fracking will cause the value of their assets to plummet.

If economic growth requires a marketplace that is as free as possible from rules and regulations, then imposing restrictions on energy extraction and usage is indeed something to be greatly feared. If the "invisible hand" of the market is the best way to coordinate effective human responses to large problems, then the manipulative hand of government trying to solve energy problems from the top down can be at least as scary as the threats of pollution, scarcity, and international politics. Economic conservatives also argue that these fuels are vital, at least in the near term, for economic growth among those whose livelihoods depend upon fossil fuels—which is to say, everyone in the industrialized world. Perhaps even more importantly, they say, fossil fuels are essential to humanitarian projects such as feeding the hungry, caring for the sick, and educating children. Our neighbors in need can be helped through the fossil fuel economy, and so Christians have reason to fear anything that might impair that economy.

These four fears generally present themselves along a predictable political spectrum: liberals tend to worry most about the pollution and injustices
of energy while conservatives tend to worry more about individual liberties
and maintaining a growing economy. The sum of these interrelated concerns
reveals that, when it comes to the world's energy future, everyone is afraid of
something. As a society and as a civilization, most people in the industrialized world agree that we will someday move away from fossil fuels, but we
disagree about whether we have more to fear from those fuels themselves or
from a premature departure from them. We are in a wilderness of a kind, and
we cannot know exactly where we are going, how we will get there, or what
kind of manna will appear to help us survive along the way.

Christians are called to understand such fears and cultivate courage in
the face of them. The story of the Israelites can serve as an inspiration. Just
as our spiritual ancestors exhibited courage in following God into the desert and (eventually) resisting various temptations to act irrationally or panic,
we too can practice courage by seeing our situation clearly and then acting
boldly. Again, Dan Erlander's three lessons are useful here. In seeking a courageous energy future, we can trust that God will provide, we can remember
that hoarding is not necessary, and we can commit to a Sabbath trust that
the world does not require our constant work. These lessons will guide us
through a conversation between three distinct voices about what it will look
like to take on the issues of energy in the twenty-first century with courage
and fortitude.

T. Boone Pickens and the Courage to Use
Existing Energy Wisely

The most popular energy strategy in contemporary politics is frequently called
"all of the above" because it involves expanding research and development in
new energy sources while maintaining and even increasing current levels of
drilling, extraction, and burning fossil fuels. One advocate of this approach
is T. Boone Pickens, a wealthy business magnate and a prominent public
advocate for increasing the use of natural gas to supplement the current use of
oil. With a background in geology, Pickens made a fortune from oil drilling
before acquiring other energy companies throughout the 1980s, 1990s, and
2000s, during which time he became a billionaire investor. Pickens was not
only successful at business but also very active in politics, supporting many

popular Republican causes throughout his life and dedicating millions of dollars to George W. Bush's campaign in the 2004 presidential election.

The subsequent emergence of Pickens' "Energy Plan for America" therefore surprised many—both his supporters and his critics—with its environmental agenda. The plan has three parts, the first of which is to emphasize the need to move toward "energy independence," by which he means no longer importing fossil fuels from other nations.[13] He appeals to Americans' deep-rooted sense of independence and fear of foreign rule: "As long as we are dependent on other countries for oil, the very lifeblood of our nation," he says, "our security is at risk." He also cites the physical impossibility of continuing current rates of global oil consumption, given its scarcity: "The world has been turned upside down in the search for oil," and everything that is easily accessible has already been found.[14] There may still be oil for decades to come, but it will be harder to come by and therefore increasingly expensive.

Because the majority of oil imported into the United States is used for transportation, the second part of Pickens' plan is to find alternative means to power cars and trucks. He advocates natural gas, which he calls "the fuel of the future." It burns cleaner than oil and coal, and there are substantial supplies of it still accessible in the United States. If we hope to keep our economy growing while slowing climate change and finding fossil fuel energy within our own borders, natural gas will be vital. Not coincidentally, this step of Pickens' plan represents his largest personal investment: he has founded numerous gas-based companies, hoping to build and sell vehicles and distribution systems that use natural gas rather than oil.

However, Pickens recognizes that natural gas is still not perfect, and he does not propose it as a permanent solution. Rather, he assumes that sometime in the next century, the era of fossil fuels will be over. Having watched energy companies develop solutions to complex problems his entire life, Pickens is confident that this will not mean the end to civilization as we know it or even to long-term prosperity and wealth. The third step of Pickens' plan is to develop wind and solar power, which can offer clean and renewable energy for thriving civilizations well into the future. But so far he has invested less money in this work, because he sees it as a realm in which private enterprise cannot work alone. Calling for government subsidies and public investment in energy independence, he argues: "I would much rather [my government] subsidize solar and wind than spend billions on foreign oil, wouldn't you?"[15]

The theme of the Pickens Plan is that all possibilities should be included; all available resources should be put to work fueling our economy and pushing us into the future. He writes: "We're going to need everything. We're going to need all of the oil and gas we can find. We're going to need ethanol, natural gas, solar, wind, tides, biofuels, and nuclear. In an energy-starved world, our country is the hungriest."[16] In other words, while fossil fuels are imperfect, they still provide vital energy to get us where we need to go. So Pickens does not ask citizens to banish oil and coal but rather to allow the market to phase them out as natural gas and then renewable energies become more competitive. The courage to face the future can be found in the prudent use of all of our resources.

Critics are justifiably skeptical about whether a man who made over a billion dollars selling fossil fuels is fit to lead the nation away from dirty energy. Pickens' proposals would undoubtedly increase his personal wealth, and he significantly downplays the environmental hazards of natural gas extraction, particularly the still-experimental scaling up of hydraulic fracturing. But though it is important to raise questions about Pickens' ideas, it is also worthwhile to note that his business success may equip him with the expertise and power, and indeed the courage, to change business as usual. It takes courage for an oil magnate to say that oil is on its way out and to shift his investments away from proven sources. For better or worse, he reminds us that our energy system will change only when change becomes affordable and then profitable—when people are persuaded, in other words, that change is in their best interests.

While Pickens' public activism does not rely on religious language, his perspective subtly expresses manna's first lesson: God will provide. According to this logic, the end of oil is not the end of the world, particularly when substantial supplies of natural gas remain. Creation contains powerful stored energy in the form of fossil fuels, and it is not only sensible but responsible to use those fuels to advance human well-being until alternatives become economically feasible. God has provided, and it is our job to gather and to use. Even without divine guarantees, Pickens does not seem overwhelmed by fear. Instead, he persists with fortitude born of the belief that if humans learn to use our resources wisely, there will always be enough energy to get us through another day.

Bill McKibben and the Courage to Abandon Fossil Fuels

In 2012 the United States produced 79 percent of its energy from fossil fuels. The other 21 percent was divided between nuclear and renewable sources: water, sun, wind, and geothermal heat.[17] Nuclear power remains deeply controversial, so left-leaning environmentalists generally focus their attention on renewable energy sources, which they believe must quickly replace fossil fuels. From this perspective, humanity does not need "all of the above" to produce our energy; instead we need to embrace an entirely new approach right away, warding off disaster by powering communities with renewable systems arising from locally available resources. The fear that motivates this approach is not about scarcity or economic collapse but about ecological catastrophe; courage therefore consists of bravely turning away from dirty old energy in confidence that there is enough clean energy to fuel the necessities of human societies and economies and that humankind has all the creativity and innovation we need to access it.

Activist and journalist Bill McKibben, founder of the organization 350.org,[18] is one of the most prominent voices expressing this type of opposition to the continued use of fossil fuels. McKibben argues that the planet we currently live on has already been fundamentally changed by humans. This new world—renamed in the title of his book, *Eaarth*—is a world irrevocably shaped by human action that he and others refer to as the "anthropocene";[19] it is further degraded by every additional day of burning coal, oil, and natural gas. While extant reserves of fossil fuels might make some people rich or at least comfortable in the short term, they will also exacerbate fundamental and disastrous changes to the atmosphere and the planet that will affect everyone negatively in the long term.

For McKibben, the answer is simple: stop now. From its extraction to its use to its lingering pollution, "fossil fuel is dirty at every stage, and we need to put it behind us as fast as we can."[20] Moreover, the powerful industries that market this dirty fuel are also greatly to be feared: oil, gas, and coal companies are "Public Enemy Number One to the survival of our planetary civilization,"[21] because no matter how "clean" they claim to be, their success is ineluctably dependent upon the destruction of the soil, air, and water upon which all life depends. To facilitate the end of fossil fuels, McKibben advocates a movement of divestment in which universities, city governments, and religious denominations (not to mention private individuals and corporations) refuse to invest their money in oil, gas, and coal companies. This not only deprives those companies of funds in the immediate term; it also takes a resolute and public moral stance against extraction, burning, and pollution.

In direct contradiction to T. Boone Pickens, McKibben asserts that natural gas is no "bridge" to a cleaner tomorrow but instead "a rickety pier extending indefinitely to a hotter future." The problems begin with its extraction from the earth. McKibben fears that natural gas, when obtained as it increasingly is by hydraulic fracturing, poses disastrous threats to drinking water, air quality, and geological stability.[22] But even if fracking itself were perfectly clean, the use of natural gas does not fix our climate problems: it may be less polluting than coal or oil, but burning it still emits CO_2. If global energy consumption continues to increase exponentially, as it has done in the last century, natural gas will simply replace oil as the new number-one polluter. Leaks are a real danger as well, because the methane in unburned gas is even more potent than CO_2 in trapping atmospheric heat.[23] For McKibben, natural gas is not the best of the fossil fuels; it is simply another fossil fuel to be resisted.

Lest it seem that this approach is based solely on an emphatic "no" to fossil fuels, McKibben also adds a resounding "yes" to a world powered by clean, renewable energy. He courageously imagines an alternative future, confident that we can find the energy we need more safely and sustainably if we are willing to invest in renewables with the same level of creativity, wealth, and political power that we already have in fossil fuels. On this, he and Pickens seem to agree. However, unlike Pickens, he does not want us to wait for a gradual shift toward alternatives while giving global markets time to adjust. McKibben calls for "a green Manhattan project, an ecological New Deal, a clean-tech Apollo Mission" to develop new technologies.[24] He wants the world's leaders to use their authority to crack down on fossil fuel use immediately, making dirty energy much more expensive while making alternative technologies more accessible and appealing.

But despite his belief that governments must act, McKibben's ultimate hope is not for a world of large-scale "command and control" solutions. Echoing the rhetoric of local food advocates, McKibben argues that energy is safest and best when produced close to home. He does not call for miles and miles of centralized wind farms or desert solar arrays to power the entire nation. Instead, his ideal is smaller-scale production and local distribution, a shift that finds energy in "the wind and sun in our neck of the woods, not from that abstraction called 'the Middle East.'" Imagine New Orleans powered by local tides, Fargo powered by local winds, and Las Vegas powered by local sunlight. Under current conditions, when centralized power stations fail or run out of fuel, millions are thrown into turmoil, and only highly trained experts can help (think of the seven hundred million citizens of India who experienced long blackouts in 2012). By contrast, when the local power source for a small and tightly knit community is damaged, the community itself can band together, fix the problem, and ensure that everyone is safe in the meantime. Car travel requires global economic and political infrastructures to ship gasoline across the planet, while bicycles built from materials closer to home require only a small amount of collaboration and know-how. In contrast to the grand and sweeping Pickens Plan, McKibben hopes for a wide range of local clean energy projects, "myriad and quiet, not a grand few visible to the whole world."[25]

Not surprisingly, McKibben's critics dismiss his approach as untenable. Skeptics of renewable energy sources frequently note that these are difficult to scale upward. While a well-placed windmill or a few solar batteries can light a house or power a few small appliances, it is difficult to capture enough of the sun's energy to reliably power a large city twenty-four hours a day.[26] However, advocates see the decentralized character of renewable energy as a great advantage: diverse people in diverse communities will create and have access to their own power rather than depending upon a faraway corporate monopoly or a sprawling central government. For a villager in Bangladesh who currently lights her home with kerosene lamps, a small solar system with photovoltaic cells and a battery would be sustainable progress. It not only lights her home more cheaply and cleanly than kerosene; it also avoids the pollution and dependence created by a centralized power grid that many in the industrialized world take for granted.[27]

McKibben admits that local-scale energy would require immediate and sustained sacrifices from people in wealthy nations, who have grown accustomed to the concentrated and portable power of fossil fuels. Without them, we will travel shorter distances, use less electricity, buy fewer products, and have less access to the rest of the globe beyond our local communities. But McKibben argues that once we get used to it, this will ultimately be a better life, shaping us into better people. Our primary relationships will be to our nearest neighbors, a situation that, he points out, has worked for most of human history. Our lives will be more locally focused and slower paced. However, he also hopes that we will have enough power to keep global connections alive through the Internet, "the window left ajar in our communities so new ideas can blow in and old prejudices blow out."[28] This somewhat incongruous fondness for the Internet is reflected in McKibben's organizing strategy, which relies extensively on social media and web videos to nurture a global "Fossil Fuel Resistance" movement.

Like Pickens, McKibben seeks a kind of energy independence, but he is far more interested in the independence of communities and neighborhoods than of the nation-state. When McKibben calls for a courageous move into a better energy future, he asks people to face the fear that we cannot survive without fossil fuels, without jet travel, without an ever-growing global economy. Courage, from this perspective, involves imagining a different sort of life, hoping and working for a world where communities are bound together and inventive enough not only to keep themselves powered with the natural systems of the earth around them but also to thrive within those new limits. He asks us to avoid the foolhardiness of thinking that we can blindly continue on with our current excesses. We need fortitude to resist momentary, habitual, individual passions in favor of longer-term benefits for ourselves, our communities, and the earth.

This approach calls to mind Erlander's second lesson of manna in the wilderness: everyone has enough when no one hoards. We do not need large corporations to monopolize rare and dirty fossil fuels, parceling them out to get the best prices they can; we do not need national governments to keep large national oil reserves; and we as citizens do not need to stockpile fuel in our backyards. Instead, we need to develop diverse ways for every community to harvest the renewable energy that appears each day—the sun, the wind, the water. For McKibben and those like him, fossil fuels are a "curse" that encourages vicious hoarding, complete with its famines and wars. Because they are rare and nonrenewable, fossil fuels put power into the hands of the few who own mineral rights, drilling technologies, and political systems while impoverishing those who labor in their mines and who are at the mercy of their distribution channels. Fossil fuels tend to make a few people unfathomably rich while countless others remain jobless, hungry, or disenfranchised. The Israelites might have called this "Pharaoh's way," the way of the powerful hoarding and storing up rather than a community sharing and trusting God to provide enough to meet everyone's needs. The argument for neighborhoods powered by diverse, locally produced, renewable energies makes sense when understood in Christian terms as an expression of the story of manna.

Brayton Shanley and the Courage to Use Less

While much distinguishes them, Bill McKibben and T. Boone Pickens agree on one energy strategy: conservation. Given the reality of an uncertain energy future, virtually all environmentalists unite around the principle that, whatever else we do, we must cut back on how much energy we consume. Most trust that the best path to conservation is technological innovation: better insulation, smarter cars, new materials, and high-tech distribution systems could all greatly increase efficiency and thereby reduce consumption. One physicist estimates that the United States could use half as much oil and one-quarter as much electricity simply by applying existing conservation technologies more widely and wisely.[29]

However, a different and more controversial approach to energy conservation depends not on smart application of technology to increase efficiency but instead on something much more basic: actually consuming less. People in the industrialized world must simply give up most of the comforts and conveniences to which we are accustomed. From this perspective, what we should fear most is not government regulation or ecological destruction but the uncontrolled nature of our own all-consuming desire. People with excess wealth should learn to want less, to need less, and so to use less power. We should, in essence, rest from our anxious and incessant consumption.

This approach resonates with Erlander's third lesson from the exodus about keeping the Sabbath. The Bible says that God allowed the Israelites to gather just enough extra manna every sixth day so that the seventh could be a day of rest. Four chapters later, this is inscribed into a broader law as the fourth commandment: "Six days you shall labor and do all your work. But the seventh day is a Sabbath to the Lord your God; you shall not do any work—you, your son or your daughter, your male or female slave, your livestock, or the alien resident in your towns" (Exodus 20:9-11). By commanding rest in imitation of God's creation, God teaches the Israelites that "the world will not fall apart if they do not work all the time." By commanding that the Israelites also offer rest to their slaves, their guests, and their livestock, God creates a community-wide break in work, a rest from production, and—most importantly for this discussion—time away from energy consumption.[30]

Sabbath asks people to reflect upon their usual habits of consumption and to produce only what they truly need with at least one day away from work each week, thus requiring a prioritization between what is necessary and what is not. By demanding that humans slow down and cease working and worrying, Sabbath offers a path to consuming less energy. For example, ethicist Laura Hartman notes that, in contemporary Orthodox Jewish observations, the Sabbath forbids "igniting or extinguishing fire (which includes electricity and internal combustion engines)." Avoiding driving on the Sabbath not only saves gas one day a week, it also nurtures a sense of community, because all members of an Orthodox synagogue will live within walking distance from it. As Hartman argues, a holy day away from work is preparation for the reign of God on earth: "With its slower pace and deeper connections, its healthful conscience and social awareness, and its eschewing of stress and excess, [Sabbath teaches] the type of consumption that will characterize the world to come."[31] By practicing Sabbath, by trusting that we need not constantly work and toil, we learn what it is to have enough. We learn how to survive without consuming so much energy even as we learn to trust God rather than our own efforts.

An advocate of environmental conservation who demonstrates the radical energy conservation of a contemporary Sabbath practice is the activist and writer Brayton Shanley, cofounder of the Agape Community in western Massachusetts. The life he shares with that community, a center for nonviolence education and sustainable living inspired by the Catholic Worker movement, is characterized by deep commitment to energy conservation. They live in a heavily insulated and hand-built straw-bale house, use composting toilets, derive their electricity from the sun, and run the entire community without fossil fuels. In many ways, Shanley's view of an energy future is like Bill McKibben's: he advocates "urgent and immediate measures . . . to phase out all dependency on oil and to begin today to embrace alternative renewable energy—wind, solar, hydro, geothermal, vegetable oil for diesel engines, indeed, for any energy that is local, sustainable, kinder to the earth, and affordable." He goes even further than McKibben in his critique of oil, arguing as a pacifist that "petroleum is a warlike energy. First we must fight over it; then when we burn it, we do violence to the earth."[32]

Unlike McKibben, Shanley's arguments do not focus on technological change or a widespread social movement. Rather, he takes a more personal approach, advocating that each individual "begin to listen to the resonance of inner simplicity," to learn to live quietly with less. Shanley's deepest commitments are to a new kind of seeing, rethinking personal priorities based on a spiritual self-analysis that teaches him how much energy is truly necessary to live a good life. His household community ponders together hard questions about their energy consumption: "How many lights do we need? Two? Three? Ten? Fifty? How many watts per bulb are needed to see in the dark? How many gadgets—a DVD player, a computer in every room, phones ringing all day and night? How do we pump a running water system that is 'green' from our well? And how will we heat water and refrigerate our food?"[33] For Shanley, the most powerful answers to these questions are not technological innovations but personal, inward changes; he does not hope for tools that will make his life easier but instead seeks to adjust his life so that it requires no more energy than he and his immediate environment can provide. To live with less light, less refrigeration, hand-pumped water, and hand-chopped wood is to better reflect the Christian goal of peace with creation and, in his mind, to be more closely formed to who humans are meant to be.

Sabbath plays a central role in teaching Shanley to limit his needs and desires. He writes of a weekly commitment to "constant mindfulness" rather than endless work. Every seventh day, he resists temptations "to finish grinding the herbs, fulfill social obligations, return phone calls and e-mails." Instead of indulging these activities—all of which require external energy—he seeks to cultivate "stillness and quiet," and thereby learns to rest with what he has and what he has done rather than to hope for more. For Shanley, Sabbath is the alternative to a culture that teaches, "More is better. More is important. More is secure." These are claims of fear: energy is scarce, we do not have enough; energy will make us dependent, we must secure our own future. Instead, Shanley calls Christians to be Sabbath people, who cultivate the spiritual virtue of courage, of ordinary fortitude that comes with self-discipline and focus on God: "The still small voice is always 'just enough.'"[34]

While Bill McKibben organizes with the Internet and seeks to preserve it for the future, Shanley is suspicious of the physical and emotional energy such connections require. He tells the story of a group of students who came to the Agape Community and gradually put away their technological connections to the rest of the world, "relinquishing their frenzied ways for a slower, more mindful rhythm" that follows the lead of the earth, "observing that her bountifulness never hurries. We praised the perfect moments of the sacredness of it all."[35] These new rhythms take time and discipline to learn, but so did the rhythms of highways, jet planes, and social media. The only thing preventing us from change is our ability to imagine a different sort of life.

Shanley's proposal for responsible energy use includes no national or regional plan. His perspective is rooted in individual activism and in the church, drawing lessons from the earth, from the practice of Sabbath, and from Christian community about how to live with less, how to surrender the desires and the worries that lead us to want ever more energy. Emerging from a deep Christian commitment and requiring profound personal and familial change, this approach is unlikely to solve the energy problems of the whole world. It certainly will not change things rapidly enough for the tastes of Pickens or McKibben and perhaps not rapidly enough to stave off widespread destruction from climate change. But, as Brayton Shanley's life and witness demonstrate, the courage to envision something different for ourselves—radically to align our desires with the life God has made possible on this earth—can change individuals and foster slow social change by serving as an example to all.

Christian Courage

There is no easy conversation to be had among the three perspectives just outlined, no simple compromise that arises. To embrace and advocate T. Boone Pickens' plan requires lobbying for the continued use of fossil fuels, while Bill McKibben asks us to oppose the burning of fossil fuels altogether. Both ask us to get on the energy-hungry Internet and spread the word about our future to broad social networks while advocating better technologies for the future.[36] By contrast, Brayton Shanley encourages us to step back from such fast-paced global engagement in order to enter into the stillness and quiet of our immediate surroundings and of a Sabbath community lifestyle. The differences among these three approaches illustrate how Christians face difficult choices in responding to the complex problem of energy in the twenty-first century.

To a certain extent, these choices may be more or less courageous depending upon the facts: for example, we must learn as much as we can about the processes by which natural gas is mined and how much its leakage is a danger before we can decide whether it is as safe as Pickens and others in the natural gas business claim. Early evidence suggests it is not.[37] The facts we find, the voices we listen to, and the questions we choose to focus on will all make a difference in what we fear, what we find appropriate, and what action we decide courage requires. Apart from the facts, the choices we have before us also come down to questions of faithfulness: Christians must decide whether we are called to separate ourselves from the tainted ways of the world, as Shanley strives to do, or to get our hands dirty by fully participating in the culture around us, even if it requires compromising with the worst examples of human greed and materialism.

The virtue of courage provides a valuable tool for discerning a Christian approach to energy in the twenty-first century. First and foremost, while Christian courage is informed by fears, it cannot be wholly defined by them. Natural worries about scarcity, pollution, politics, government intervention, and economic upheaval are justified, but as Christians our vision and our actions should not merely react against fear but should instead arise from a clear and positive understanding of the good, of where we want to go, and of who we want to be—namely, people who love God and love our neighbors as ourselves. Only when we have our goals laid out before us will we have the fortitude to continue on when things get difficult, as they inevitably will.

This leads to a second, complementary claim: Christian courage must be educated and shaped by Christian faith, which has never preoccupied itself exclusively with worldly concerns such as unlimited economic growth, technological progress at all costs, or a life full of material creature comforts. Christian teaching emphasizes fidelity to God, forgiveness of debts, and love of all humankind that begins with our nearest neighbors and moves outward from there. None of these concerns—much like taking up the cross—has ever been easy for humans, and it will take fortitude for us to put them into practice in contemporary life, and in energy policy in particular. But we should learn from the story of manna in the wilderness that God provides enough for all. It takes courage not to hoard, not to get all we can right now for ourselves and our few favorite people. The willingness to share—with everyone, including the stranger—is part of the courageous life to which we are called.

Finally, it is important to remember that none of the virtues is truly virtuous on its own; courage must be informed by its six counterparts. Pickens' version of courage leans heavily toward prudence—it is simply good business to move away from oil—but lacks significant consideration of justice, especially for the earth and those harmed by our current systems of fossil fuel use. In contrast, McKibben's public presentation of courage leans heavily toward justice—it is simply unfair for people alive today to leave the earth in ruins for future generations to deal with—but lacks explicit attention to the faith or hope that God is alive in the workings of the world, even when things seem dark. Meanwhile, Shanley's version of courage leans heavily toward temperance—it is simply not good for our souls when we gluttonously consume as much as we do—but lacks a prudent sense of how we might actively bring about systemic change in ways that would demonstrate concrete love for our suffering neighbors. These observations are not meant to downplay the contributions each thinker makes, but they remind us that when conversing about what it means to be courageous, we look not only for the golden mean between foolhardiness and cowardice but also for a synthesis of all the virtues.

Courage is the testing point of virtues, and energy policy—production, distribution, and consumption—puts all of our virtues to the test. Our prudence, temperance, justice, faith, hope, and love will shine through in the ways we think about and behave around fossil fuels and their renewable alternatives. Eco-virtue is a way of being human that seeks the elusive golden mean between old and new energy, between growth and conservation, between climate change and human need. Thinking about energy can be frightening. We do not know where our energy will come from in the future or how the energy we are using today will impact our atmosphere, our water, and our health. We do not know how to free our politics and our international relationships from the dynamics of power and money created by oil and other fossil fuels. Such fear, born of uncertainty, is healthy insofar as it pushes us to respond, but it can also be dangerous if it leads us to seek easy, quick answers or to turn a blind eye to problems rather than respond with our best reason. Courage is the habit of finding healthy ways to act when we are afraid, taking the wisest step forward even when our passions seek to get the better of us, when we cannot be certain of every outcome. It is the distillation of the lessons taught by manna in the wilderness: God will provide, there is enough for everyone, and occasional rest from our labors and consumption will do us all good.

Learning Courage

Founded in 1992, the Seattle-based nonprofit Earth Ministry was one of the first organizations systematically to connect Christian faith and environmental stewardship, and it is one of the nation's leaders in bringing a religious voice to environmental activism.[38] In 2010 Earth Ministry partnered with other environmental groups to move the state of Washington beyond coal-generated electricity. They set out to close the TransAlta plant in Centralia, Washington, the last coal-fired electricity generator in the state.

Even to set this goal required courage. Conventional wisdom said that closing a coal plant would be impossible during a recession, that the promise of jobs and income at the plant would drown out any environmental concern, and that Washington's divided politics made the state incapable of courageous action in difficult times. Facing such fears of deadlock and controversy, Earth Ministry nevertheless moved boldly forward. And they succeeded. In April of 2011, Governor Christine Gregoire signed a bill that requires TransAlta to take one of its boilers offline by 2020 and the other by 2025, scheduling an end to the industrial burning of coal in Washington state.

The law also requires TransAlta to develop a fund to clean up contaminated land and help workers transition to new jobs, and its delaying the closure of the plant will allow most of the older workforce to retire as planned. This was part of Earth Ministry's approach: to build a diverse coalition of faithful citizens who could work together and make a deal to end coal burning rather than to pit ecological and economic interests against one another. When Earth Ministry's program and outreach director went to Centralia, she took the time to meet the manager of the plant over coffee at his Lutheran church. As the executive director prepared to lobby for the plant's closure at the state capitol in Olympia, she spoke with plant workers in order to incorporate their concerns into her testimony.[39] This careful attention to the human beings who depended on jobs at the coal plant was not only strategic but also a reflection of faith: "Driven by Jesus' call in the Gospel of Mark to 'love your neighbor as yourself,' [Earth Ministry] wanted to ensure that the transition to a clean energy future would create jobs and a healthy economy for the local community."[40] Such listening required courage: while other environmentalists took an absolute stance against coal power and coal companies, Earth Ministry sought a different path.

Such activism is one example of courage and effective action, and it offers important lessons in virtue. Earth Ministry demonstrated a courageous political stance, and the three authors discussed above would likely all celebrate the accomplishment. But, of course, any good lesson in virtue raises as many questions as it answers. In addition to celebrating, T. Boone Pickens might ask whether more might have been accomplished with courageous entrepreneurial innovation in addition to political organizing. Bill McKibben might ask whether the plant could have been closed sooner, preventing over ten years of pollution still to come. Brayton Shanley might ask about the energy burden of all the organizers' driving (not to mention phone calls and e-mails) between Seattle, Centralia, and Olympia and might encourage a more personal commitment from everyone involved to move off the energy grid entirely. Virtue is always a work in progress, and the work of courageously standing up for what is right and persevering in its pursuit is never simple.

Earth Ministry's example calls other Christians to practice courage, the habit of finding healthy ways to act in response to fears and taking the wisest step forward even when the outcome is uncertain. Such courage is built upon hope that God will provide, upon love of our neighbors that ensures there is enough for everyone, and upon faith that, once in a while, we truly can rest from our labors.

Questions for Discussion

1. Consider the distinction between "courage" and "fortitude." How are these aspects of virtue relevant to the exodus narrative about Israel in Egypt and later in the wilderness?

2. Christians often pledge allegiance to the Ten Commandments, but the fourth commandment about ceasing all work on the Sabbath (which the Bible indicates is from Friday at sundown to Saturday at sundown) is often treated as optional. Why do you think some Christians do not take the Sabbath as seriously as the commandments about adultery, theft, or lying?

3. When it comes to questions about fossil fuels, which fear do you most relate to: fear of dependence on foreign oil; fear of ecological destruction; fear of government intrusion; or fear of economic downturns? Why do you think this fear troubles you more than the others?

4. Which approach to the future of energy is most attractive to you: innovation in pursuit of an "all of the above" approach (like T. Boone Pickens); a large-scale radical shift away from fossil fuels toward alternatives (like Bill McKibben); or a small-scale radical reduction in your own energy consumption (like Brayton Shanley)? How is your preference related to your most troubling fear?

5. What facts do we need to know about energy in order to make wise, virtuous decisions about the ways we consume in our own individual lives, as well as about how we engage with society and the world?

6. What do you think of Earth Ministry's political campaign to close the last coal plant in Washington? Was it a valid goal, and did it pursue the most appropriate strategy? What might a similar effort look like in your community?

4

TEMPERANCE
Between Communal Production and Personal
Consumption of Food

Toward Responsible Enjoyment

In the classic Danish film *Babette's Feast*, a French refugee lives with two elderly sisters in an isolated seaside village among their very small, pietistic Christian sect.[1] Babette works in the sisters' modest house as their cook, dutifully serving up austere mashes of pickled fish and stale bread for years. When she wins the lottery and decides to spend her new wealth on ingredients for a gourmet feast for the sisters and their fellow church members, the pious Christians are horrified, overcome with fear that too much gustatory pleasure will turn their souls away from God. Not wanting to offend Babette, though, they vow to eat every last bite and sip every last pairing of French wine without comment. Much to their surprise, the overwhelming generosity and exquisite delicacy of Babette's lavish gift turns out to be an occasion for divine grace. Over the many courses of the long meal, their quarrels are resolved, their regrets laid to rest, and the mysteries of life are briefly revealed. In the end, for this particular community, it turned out to be a surplus of self-denial—rather than a surplus of desire—that most threatened their relationships with God and one another.

To eat well is to exercise the virtue of temperance. In light of environmental challenges, right eating is that which brings humans' natural desires for food into conversation with the limits of healthy living, healthy neighbors, and a healthy earth. But temperance is also about Babette's lesson that the good life entails taking pleasure in food and the communities it creates. Christianity has generally affirmed that food is a great gift of God, a bounty of creation, and one of the great pleasures of living in this world. Even the straitlaced Protestant reformer John Calvin, who is normally associated with

Puritanism rather than bodily delight in earthly things, believed Christians are called to enjoy their food.[2]

Thomas Aquinas suggests a balanced approach to food by teaching that temperance is the virtue focused on "the emotions regarding desires and pleasures of the senses."[3] In case this is too vague, he goes on to add: "Temperance in the strict sense concerns the pleasures of food and drink and the pleasure of sex."[4] It is the virtue that prevents overindulgence: "Excessive sense desire," according to Thomas, is a "childlike" sin;[5] it is to be expected of babies or adolescents who are still essentially "slaves"[6] to their impulses but is shameful in adults who should know better. Temperance, then, is the virtue of mature responsibility, the ability to control urges and to think through the implications of one's temptations before acting, rather than immediately indulging every infantile desire.

Like all the other virtues, however, temperance is a golden mean, a balance between two extremes rather than a rejection of just one sin. While indulging gluttonous desires too readily is problematic, it is also wrong to take too little pleasure in the senses. Aquinas notes that it is natural and good to eat as well as to breed: "Natural order requires that human beings use such pleasures as much as they are necessary for human welfare, whether regarding preservation of the individual or preservation of the species."[7] While too much of a good thing should definitely be avoided, failure *ever* to indulge one's desires can also be understood as another kind of sin—a rejection of the embodied life God has given to all human beings and declared good. Temperance thus means that a crusty old prude must temper his tendency to kill the buzz, just as a careless adolescent must temper her tendency to gratify every whim. Temperance is the virtue of responsible enjoyment: it is a matter not of eliminating desire for all sensory pleasures but rather of ordering desire toward God's purposes for humankind and creation.

Aquinas suggests that the way to learn temperance is to pay careful attention to natural desires, to consume what we need but never more than is good for us. This virtue "takes the needs of this life as the rule governing the pleasurable things one uses; namely, that one should use them insofar as the needs of this life require their use."[8] Christians should therefore temper our approach to food based on how much and what kinds of food we need, as well as how much and what kinds of food our neighbors need. Such "need" goes beyond simplistic calorie counts because food nourishes not only our bodies but also our spirits, cultures, and relationships. Some foods sustain cultures by playing central roles that cannot be simplistically quantified in nutritional terms—think of a plate of barbecue in Texas or a lobster roll in Maine. A simple bowl of rice or a cup of tea might mean very little to some of us, but it can mean the world in a culture that revolves around these as symbols of hospitality and shared enjoyment. Temperance is thus about enjoying food appropriately and ensuring that others can do the same.

Anyone who wants to think seriously about food needs the virtue of temperance, because society, politics, business, and the media are saturated with conflicting data and messages from competing interest groups. As one social critic notes: "One minute, we're bombarded with images of food, advertisements for restaurants or the latest sweet or fatty snack, with recipes and cooking tips. A minute later, we're reminded that eating is tantamount to suicide, that indulgence and enjoyment equals social isolation and self-destruction. And someone is making money from both sides of our ambivalence about and fascination with food, diet, gluttony, and starvation."[9] Most of the messages in popular discourse tend to emphasize individual eaters' relationships to food, but this disguises the ways in which food inevitably connects people to one another and to the world. Responsible enjoyment means finding a balance between competing messages, between nutrition and pleasure, between feasting and fasting, between individuals and ecosystems.

Food Is an Environmental Issue

For those of us who grew up eating food that seemed magically to appear on the supermarket shelf or in the drive-through window, debates about food production and consumption may not at first seem relevant to the environment. Food may seem like a simple matter of personal preference or, quite literally, of taste. But growing, distributing, and consuming food are in fact some of the most powerful ways humans interact with the earth and our neighbors. Food might even be considered the clearest single connection that exists between individuals, public health, and the health of other creatures and ecosystems. Everyone who lives must eat, so thinking about responsible and virtuous enjoyment of food requires us to look beyond mere preference. It requires a prudent understanding of environmental processes and a courageous acknowledgement of the ways other people and other creatures may suffer so that we can eat what we want.[10]

Acknowledgment 1: Food Comes from the Earth

The most obvious connection between eaters and the earth is the fact that every last morsel of our food originates in the ground—even meat, fish, and dairy products come first from plants eaten by herbivores. But given the intricate and global systems that supply most of us with our food, that connection can be well hidden from eaters who live in urban and suburban areas. As Christian thinker, farmer, and poet Wendell Berry worries, most Americans do not think or know enough about what they eat. They will tell you, he says, "that food is produced on farms. But most of them do not know what farms, or what kinds of farms, or where the farms are, or what knowledge or skills are involved in farming. . . . For them, food is pretty much an abstract idea—something they do not know or imagine—until it appears on the grocery shelf or table."[11] Berry sees this ignorance as a problem not only for farmers, whose economic and environmental interests are often misunderstood or neglected, but also for the farms themselves, which are delicate ecosystems that require careful stewardship. Consumer ignorance can lead to careless and intemperate eating, but it is not only eaters who need to cultivate temperance. Those who grow and produce our food also need this virtue, because the careless treatment of land and creatures can cause serious ecological harm. For both the eater and the producer, a lack of attention to the environmental costs of food can be dangerous, even sinful. Virtue is a matter not only of counting our own calories but also of attending to the earth that gives us those calories.

Food choices also have profound effects that extend to what may be the most pressing of all environmental issues: climate change. The majority of farms in the developed world today are industrial operations—essentially food factories—that require substantial inputs of fossil fuel and electricity to operate. Animals raised for meat produce a substantial portion of the world's greenhouse gases through their digestive processes, and the system that ships meat across continents and oceans produces even more climate-changing emissions.[12] Of the energy spent on food, only one-fifth is used in actual production on farms. The rest comes between the farm and the eater—in transporting the food as well as processing, packaging, marketing, and preparing the food and then moving the waste to landfills. Environmental organizations work to call attention to these facts, noting that "getting food from the farm to our fork eats up 10 percent of the total U.S. energy budget," and that "the U.S. food economy uses as much energy as the entire economy of the United Kingdom."[13] Temperance calls Christians to wake up to the many ways in which food is an environmental issue and to respond actively to those realities.

However, while some are called to greater responsibility, others are called to greater enjoyment. Christian virtue is not a simple matter of scrupulous abstinence: no meat, no fast food, no pesticide-soaked produce, no refined sugar, no alcohol, no matter how much it hurts. Temperance must say "yes" as often as it says "no." To those with time to spare and access to land, temperance might teach the skills of growing food.[14] For those with disposable income, temperance might call for the added expense of ensuring that their food is organic and local. For others who cannot put their hands into soil and cannot afford more expensive foods, this virtue would still insist upon the importance of understanding the connection between food and land. Temperance teaches people to love food so that we enjoy what we have while also ensuring that our neighbors have enough to eat, that the earth's bounty is sustained for future generations, and that all God's creatures thrive, today and in the future.

Acknowledgment 2: Food Can Cause Suffering

A second environmental aspect of food is the impact it has on living creatures, both human and nonhuman animals, who are an inherent part of God's interconnected creation. Christian environmentalism is about responding to the travails of our neighbors, and recent data has brought to public consciousness the disturbing ways our contemporary food system causes great suffering. Four companies now produce 81 percent of cows, 73 percent of sheep, half the chickens, and 60 percent of pigs in the United States, and they do so primarily by confining animals to small spaces, connecting them to machines, pumping them full of antibiotics, and paying little attention to their comfort. Even if one believes that God and nature have granted human beings dominion over other animals, including using them for things such as food or wool, it is difficult to make a persuasive case (on the basis of anything other than profit margins) that the prevailing model of factory farms represents responsible or virtuous management. Furthermore, these farms are highly technical operations where machines act as go-betweens for human beings and the animals they process. As one critic puts it: "The corporate farmer is the absent farmer, the stranger on his own property, too important to worry about little details like whether a pig has room to turn or straw to sleep on. . . . Factory farming isn't just killing: It is negation, a complete denial of the

animal as a living being with his or her own needs and nature."[15] In treating
fellow creatures cruelly or negligently, humans also run the risk of dehumanizing ourselves.

Humans' relationship to other animals is a highly controversial issue,
even in churches. Although most Christians throughout history have eaten
animal products, historians of theology point out that the tradition has
always exhibited, at the very least, "a persistent awareness of the problematic
nature of meat."[16] Christians of good conscience will disagree over where
to draw the line on eating animals. Vegetarians will note that, according
to Hebrew scripture, meat was not part of God's original plan for creation
(Genesis 1:30, 9:3), or may cite the story in which Daniel resolves to eat
only vegetables and is blessed with both health and "knowledge and skill and
every aspect of literature and wisdom" along with insight into all visions and
dreams (Daniel 1:8-17). Others, however, may cite the fact that Jesus himself
was known to eat fish, even after his resurrection (Luke 24:41-43). What
seems certain is that Christian virtue does not allow for the immoderate and
inhumane treatment of animals, even for the sake of cheap Buffalo wings
or Greek yogurt. If animals were mere bits of inanimate machinery, rather
than members of the interdependent community of God, God would not
have commanded a day of rest for them too (Exodus 23:12). Christians are
called to be conscious and deliberate about our consumption, always guard-
ing against mindless self-indulgence at one extreme and joyless abstinence at
the other. Imitation of Christ calls us to reflect carefully on how we treat the
animals that nourish us.[17]

In addition to the role it plays in animal suffering, the industrialized
food system is also complicit in the acute suffering of human beings, most
obviously in the fact that far too many people face starvation on a daily basis
and many others are only a few days or a single paycheck away from hunger.
Eight hundred seventy million people in the world do not have enough to
eat, which means that one in eight human beings on earth will go to sleep
tonight without basic nutrition. This trend contributes to the deaths of 260
million young children each year.[18] Most of these are in developing nations,
particularly in Asia and the Pacific, but not even the food-rich United States
is immune to hunger. About one-fifth (22 percent) of American children live
in "food-insecure households," meaning that while they may not be hungry
at any given moment, their household's income is below 130 percent of the
poverty line, and so they are at risk of serious long-term malnutrition.[19]

Meanwhile, anywhere from 30 to 50 percent of the food produced world-wide never actually gets eaten, ending up rotting in fields, storage containers, and landfills.[20] One report offers the staggering statistic that "the average American consumer wastes 10 times as much food as someone in Southeast Asia, up 50 percent from Americans in the 1970s."[21] Waste occurs not only in our kitchen, but throughout the process of food production and distribution, beginning on the farm, where much of the food that is grown is never harvested for reasons that range from weather to market prices to labor costs.[22] After harvesting is completed, the chain of waste continues: much of what is picked rots in storage while waiting for a buyer; some gets purchased by processors, who throw away up to half of it (e.g., turning whole carrots into "baby carrots"); and even more is discarded by those who fail to sell it by its expiration date. Wasted food that is not composted goes into landfills where it emits methane, contributing to global warming. Recall that as this food goes to waste, one in eight of our fellow human beings is malnourished. In short, our current methods of food distribution fail to relieve the vast and horrible human suffering of starvation and malnutrition. The fact that so many people are denied the joy of life because of empty stomachs is not just a social issue; it is an environmental issue because it reveals problems in the ways we as human beings relate to God's creation.

Other people suffer more directly from the food system oriented at delivering quick food cheaply. Best-selling books and popular film documentaries such as *Fast Food Nation* and *Food, Inc.* highlight "the most dangerous jobs" that are often filled by undocumented workers and others who are without better employment options.[23] They suffer scarred lungs from breathing in toxic cleaners, broken bones and dismemberment from heavy and sharp equipment, and cumulative trauma from repetitive motions on high-speed assembly lines. Meat packing is particularly hazardous. Consider this troublesome case of one slaughterhouse worker's injuries over twenty years, during which time he

> was struck by a falling 90-pound box of meat and pinned against the steel lip of a conveyor belt. He blew out a disc and had back surgery. He inhaled too much chlorine while cleaning some blood tanks and spent a month in the hospital, his lungs burned, his body covered in blisters. He damaged the rotator cuff in his left shoulder when a 10,000-pound hammer-mill cover dropped too quickly and pulled his arm straight backward. He broke a leg

after stepping into a hole in the slaughterhouse's concrete floor. He got hit by a slow-moving train behind the plant, got bloodied and knocked right out of his boots, spent two weeks in the hospital, then returned to work. He shattered an ankle and had it mended with four steel pins. He got more bruises and cuts, muscle pulls and strains than he could remember."[24]

This is an extreme case but represents the kinds of damage that can be done to those who work in this industry.[25] We who partake in the products of their labor are culpable for their suffering.

The pain of human and nonhuman animals cries out for active, appropriate, and immediate responses that ensure everyone can enjoy the fundamental gift of a satisfying and humane meal. Temperance means knowing where our food comes from, how it impacts the earth's ecosystems, what creatures have suffered to bring it to us, and which of our neighbors are not getting what they need. Genuine virtue requires attention to every aspect of the systems of food supply and demand in which we participate, beginning with global methods of production and continuing all the way down to the specifics of our personal diet.

Producing Temperately: Between Human Ingenuity and Earth's Natural Limits

It is important to begin by considering how food—and how much food—is grown and manufactured, because everything we eat has social and ecological impacts long before it reaches our plates. This is by no means a new concern. Indeed, the eighteenth-century parson and political economist Thomas Malthus became famous in his time (and remains so in ours) for his concern that food production could not possibly keep up with the rate of human reproduction. His argument was, at its roots, mathematical: he predicted that the earth's population would continue to grow exponentially, while food production could increase only arithmetically, making widespread starvation inevitable.

Malthus was wrong, at least in the short term. He underestimated the power of human ingenuity: better technologies, fertilizers, seeds, pesticides, transportation, and factory farming have made possible incredible strides in the production of food over the last centuries. Perhaps the most famous of these innovations is the "Green Revolution" of the mid-twentieth century, a series of agricultural innovations credited with feeding over a billion starving people through the expansion of irrigation techniques, the development of high-yield grains, and the wide distribution of chemical fertilizers and pesticides.

However, Malthus was right to observe that the earth is finite, its resources have natural limits, and there is an upper limit to how many people this planet can feed sustainably.[26] Thus, neo-Malthusian predictions about the impact of human population tend to emphasize not simply the scarcity of food but more importantly the devastating ecological costs of food abundance. The benefits of the Green Revolution came with concomitant costs in the consumption of fossil fuels, the loss of wilderness and traditional agriculture, and fundamental changes to soil, water, and air quality. Such costs beg the question as to whether or not industrial agriculture is genuinely sustainable on the scale necessary for billions of human beings. But although technological progress has its obvious drawbacks, it is also unclear that moving backward to more traditional agriculture, powered by human hands on a smaller scale, can meet the growing appetites of humanity. As one author asks, "Why had countless individuals worked so hard and for so long to create our globalized food supply chain if things were so great when most food was produced and consumed locally?"[27]

This debate plays out vividly in discussions of chemical agricultural products, including fertilizers, antibiotics, and pesticides.[28] According to the fertilizer industry, around fifty-five million tons of fertilizer are used annually in the United States.[29] The production and distribution of these fertilizers is powered by fossil fuels, and the entire process is indispensable to maintaining and growing our current food economy. "Without it," writes a *National Geographic* journalist, "human civilization in its current form could not exist. Our planet's soil simply could not grow enough food to provide all seven billion of us our accustomed diet."[30]

Other manufactured chemicals are also essential to the way most of us in the industrialized world eat. The Food and Drug Administration reports that around 9,000 tons of antibiotics are given to livestock (especially those kept in highly concentrated factory settings) to treat and prevent illness each year. Meanwhile, additional pesticide is required for keeping fertilized plants unmolested by hungry creatures. The Environmental Protection Agency reports that a typical year sees 438,000 tons of chemicals applied to deter and destroy insects, rodents, weeds, and fungus in the agricultural sector.[31]

Those who support "better living through chemistry" are likely to celebrate factory-produced agricultural aids as impressive technological accomplishments that feed billions of people. But those who are suspicious of highly technological food systems see 54.9 million tons of fertilizer, 9,000 tons of antibiotics, and 438,000 tons of pesticide as disturbing numbers, suggesting that our food system has blown past nature's limits and is leading us into disaster.

One of the most famous spokespersons for the latter perspective is Michael Pollan, whose best-selling books, such as *The Omnivore's Dilemma*, emphasize the need to return to a simpler, more local, more traditional food system. Pollan worries that mass-produced fertilizer and pesticide have encouraged monocultures, making the average diet in the industrialized world less biodiverse and less secure while also separating people from their cultural roots. He argues that the fossil fuel energy required to manufacture fertilizers and pesticides has grown vastly out of proportion; "a system that in 1940 produced 2.3 calories of food energy for every calorie of fossil fuel energy it used" has been transformed "into one that now takes 10 calories of fossil fuel energy to produce a single calorie of modern supermarket food. Put another way, when we eat from the industrial-food system, we are eating oil and spewing greenhouse gases."[32] Meanwhile, the massive use of antibiotics on livestock not only allows for overcrowding and inhumane treatment of animals but also contributes to "the evolution of new antibiotic-resistant 'superbugs'" that increasingly affect humans as well.[33]

Pollan's proposed alternative is a return to diverse, traditional food ways that arose around the globe over millennia tested by generations of trial and error and local wisdom. Healthy livestock, given space and nutritious food, need fewer antibiotics. Their manure can be used to fertilize a diverse set of crops, which can be planted in rotation to reduce the threat of pests and the need for artificial fertilizer. His ideal is not a few large-scale farms with tractors and technology but thousands of smaller gardens and local farms feeding their neighborhoods. Such growing methods will benefit not only the environment, Pollan emphasizes, but also human health and community. He believes people will flourish when they eat "real food" rather than that which is grown and processed with chemicals. He encourages everyone to eat only what "your great grandmother would recognize as food" and to be very cautious of chemical ingredients that you cannot pronounce.[34]

Critics dismiss Pollan as romantic, elitist, and naïve. Blake Hurst, a Missouri farmer, defends large-scale agriculture that depends upon industrial chemicals, arguing, "We have to farm 'industrially' to feed the world, and by using those 'industrial' tools sensibly, we can accomplish that task and leave my grandchildren a prosperous and productive farm, while protecting the land, water, and air around us." Without artificial fertilizers and the other tools of industrialization, Hurst argues, there will be no way to feed the world's current population or avoid utterly depleting existing soil. Hurst dismisses critiques of technology in farming, asserting that he is "tired of people who wouldn't visit a doctor who used a stethoscope instead of an MRI demanding that farmers like me use 1930s technology to raise food."[35]

Hurst goes on to argue that the popular alternative to large-scale chemical application is brutal work for human beings: "Lots of hired stoop labor doing the most backbreaking of tasks." He worries that the logical implications of Pollan's ideas will mean more and harder work for those with the least ability to demand fair wages and healthy conditions. Similarly, he argues that it is essential to supplement the use of traditional fertilizers with chemicals, saying that producing enough manure to fertilize all the farms in the world would require five billion additional cows—an impossible number that would create a disastrous need for grain and an enormous increase in greenhouse gases. For Hurst, Pollan is simply too optimistic about what he thinks of as "traditional" farming and too pessimistic about the wisdom of modern farmers who use industrial tools.

Michael Pollan also comes under attack for his critique of processed foods. Journalist David Freedman accuses Pollan and his "Pollanite" disciples of promoting food solutions that work only for "trim, affluent Americans" and thus offering no real response to the crisis of obesity and undernourishment among the poor of the United States and of the world. Freedman argues that the best way to reach such eaters is through the scientific tools of "Big Food" that are so often critiqued—namely, chemical additives that can replace fat and sugar to satisfy cravings without sacrificing flavor. With proper incentives, he suggests, industrial food processors will make hamburgers and soft drinks healthier, impacting far more people than a farmer's market or a new kale smoothie recipe ever could. Like Hurst, Freedman worries that Pollan is more "pleased by images of pastoral family farms" than he is truly informed about farming; Freedman, too, marvels at Pollan's fears of technology: "In virtually every realm of human existence, we turn to technology to help us solve our problems. But even in Silicon Valley, when it comes to food and obesity, technology—or at least food-processing technology—is widely treated as if it *is* the problem."[36]

With so many opposing voices involved in today's food debates, it is difficult to discern who offers the most virtuous solution. Temperance would seem to demand moderating the indiscriminate use of industrial machinery, given the harm it does to soil, water, and creatures. But temperance also calls attention to the costs of such a change and the importance of using all available methods to feed the world's hungry. In other words, temperance offers a reminder that both paths have costs; when it comes to food policy, there is no such thing as a free lunch.

Producing food locally and without chemicals, limiting the efficiencies of mass production and specialization, has costs that translate into higher prices for consumers. "Biology works more slowly than a nitrogen factory," and the speed and power of industrialism have their benefits.[37] On the other hand, industrially grown food shipped across the world comes with costs in fossil fuels, pollution, and vulnerability—costs that are not always borne by the one who pays low, low prices at the store. Likewise, the antibiotics that make concentrated livestock operations possible come with the cost of drug-resistant diseases that increasingly kill human beings. In short, all food has costs, and someone is always already paying.

Christian temperance begins with awareness about our food and how it is produced, processed, and brought to the table. Pollan, Hurst, and Freedman all promote the responsible enjoyment of food, but they come to different conclusions about what responsible enjoyment looks like. For Pollan, it means reducing our environmental footprint and learning to enjoy locally grown, natural foods. For Hurst and Freedman, enjoyment means responding to the world's demand by producing the most, best food for the most people. Christians are called to listen carefully to all accounts and temperately examine each claim while not shirking our duty of loving God and neighbor. Virtuous Christians must be creative in seeking out new, productive models between the extremes for a thriving future on God's earth.

Eating Temperately: Between Private Enjoyment and Public Responsibility

In 2013, shortly after his fiftieth birthday, New Jersey governor Chris Christie underwent weight-loss surgery.[38] The governor explained that he felt his family deserved a healthier husband and father, emphasizing that this was a private decision. However, after years of political opponents mocking his size and pundits asking whether he was "too fat" to run for president, it was difficult for many observers *not* to believe that fat shaming had played at least some role.[39] In the public imagination, being overweight often signifies something more than just a particular aesthetic or a set of DNA. It comes with moral associations of intemperance, with many people believing that obesity indicates a lack of self-control. In our culture, fat can be understood to mean, "among other things: lazy, ugly, gluttonous, rude, careless."[40] For a politician whose livelihood depends upon public confidence, being overweight may therefore be more than just a personal hurdle.

Society also offers criticism to those deemed too slender. A cultural fascination with thinness, especially for women, feeds ravenous media speculation over which celebrities are suffering from anorexia.[41] Film, television, and music stars from Portia de Rossi to Mary-Kate Olsen to Lady Gaga have had to answer publicly for their appearances and eating habits. Some are willing to speak about struggles with eating disorders, but more often these stars ask the public to respect their privacy, to let them make decisions about food and weight without a critical audience. Despite such pleas, media figures suggest that because female celebrities are in the public eye as role models to girls and young women, their health is not simply a private matter. Stars set an example that others will follow, so they have a responsibility to project good health.

These stories demonstrate some of the ways that choices about diet are very personal—everyone makes individual decisions about what and how much to eat—but also very public (others notice what we eat and what it does to our bodies). Balancing these two dimensions of eating requires temperance. On one hand, temperance calls Christians to note that, as individual adults, we must take responsibility for ourselves. On the other hand, it also requires us to consider our own eating in a broader social and cultural context that none of us alone creates.

Multinational food corporations spend billions of dollars influencing human desires, conducting research and development, and advertising to ensure that eaters buy their products. Government subsidies, originally designed to prevent food insecurity, now primarily seem to enhance the profits of large corporations that produce a few commodity crops.[42] These trends make it ever easier to ignore temperance and to overly indulge natural human cravings for sugar, fat, and salt.[43] For some thinkers, given a corrupt or intemperate context, the healthiest response is to remove oneself from these factors, to make private decisions about food rather than allowing corporations and the government to determine what is healthy and expedient. Temperance, from this view, is about purifying one's own diet, eating according to God's teachings, and expressing love for God's creation in daily, private decisions. It is about getting one's own plate in order.

Consider the fourth-century monk Evagrius Ponticus, who lived much of his life in the Egyptian desert as the leader of a monastic community. His famous manual for ascetic life, *The Praktikos*, emphasizes that monasticism is about learning to focus on prayer despite all distractions. Evagrius lists gluttony as the first temptation that calls monks away from prayer with temptations of food and fullness. The task of a monk is to train himself to eat less, to overcome frivolous desires in favor of prayer and discipline: "When the soul desires to seek after a variety of foods then it is time to afflict it with bread and water that it may learn to be grateful for a mere morsel of bread," he writes. He goes even further to suggest that "limiting one's intake of water helps a great deal to obtain temperance."[44]

Evagrius did not seek to banish all pleasure from monks' lives, and he did not deny that food and water should be enjoyed. He worried not so much about "the sinfulness of the act of eating itself" but instead about "the wider nexus of desires and social commitments which that act signifies: variety, satiety, security, fellowship and health."[45] In other words, Evagrius cautioned monks to limit their eating because he connected food to the temptations of the secular world. The act of eating enticed monks to find solace somewhere other than in God, so the job of the monk was to control his appetite rather than be controlled by it. For these reasons, despite being a member of a monastic community and a participant in that social and cultural system, Evagrius emphasized that temperance is something an individual monk ultimately learns in the privacy of his own cell.

Fourth-century Egypt certainly posed different problems and challenges than those faced by twenty-first-century citizens of the industrialized world, but it is easy to imagine an Evagrian call for contemporary Christians to turn away from irresponsible and uninformed eating, to seek simple foods in order to avoid distractions, and to dedicate our lives to the service of God rather than the service of the food-industrial complex, the ideal weight, or the healthiest body. It is also easy to see parallels in environmentalists' calls to turn to local, vegan, or organic food in service to God's creation. When people decide to remove factory-farmed meat or corn syrup from their diets, they frequently use the same language of purification and self-control that

Evagrius used to overcome gluttony. The task of Christian eating, in this per-spective, is to separate oneself from the sins of the broader culture.

Insofar as it emphasizes private choices, this approach is not about con-trolling or changing the ways *others* in wider society relate to food. Caution-ing against vainglory and pride, Evagrius would likely discourage Christians from passing judgment on Chris Christie or Lady Gaga (meat dress aside) for their eating habits. The goal of purification is about taking care of the plank in one's own eye, not about preaching to others about the specks in theirs. The focus is on eating well oneself, not on creating social or political pressures to change the global food system. The Christian response to a sinful world, for Evagrius, is to learn self-discipline through deliberate separation.[46]

On the other hand, food is always wrapped up in environmental and social ethics, and so it is bigger than any one person. Strains of hepatitis nor-mally found only in North Africa and the Middle East sicken eaters of frozen berries in Colorado and California. Chinese consumers eat corn from India, while Japanese people consume American wheat. Growers of organic pro-duce sue the manufacturers of genetically modified foods when new strains of crops appear unbidden on their farms.[47] In the global marketplace, no one ever eats alone, so temperance demands thinking together as communities to discern the interconnections and interdependencies that inform every dietary choice each of us makes.

Speaking for this social perspective is the contemporary theologian Jen-nifer Ayres, whose book *Good Food* insists that Christians should take respon-sibility for eating in ways that engage and improve the global food system. Ayres emphasizes that many Christian communities are founded on a liturgy of eating together in a weekly or monthly Eucharist: "In shared meals, God's presence is revealed. . . . Within every meal—and in the paradigmatic meal of the Eucharist—is embedded an invitation to both divine encounter and moral responsibility."[48] God calls Christians to gather around a table and to be inspired and changed by the sacred exchange of bread and wine. Thus, Christians should not only seek to understand the global food system and the complexities of production and distribution but also commit to practices that transform that system into something more just and sustainable. Christians who seek to responsibly enjoy food must work toward a world where people, the places we live, and the planet we share can all thrive together.

Like Evagrius, Ayres calls Christians to resist the dominant culture of food. Mainstream culture encourages people to approach food as "ratio-nal choosers," seeking the best possible deal and making most transactions anonymously, with no attention given to where food was grown, how it was grown, who worked to grow it, or in what condition the land was left. However, unlike Christians who might hear Evagrius calling for a purifying disconnection from society, Ayres insists that the appropriate and faithful response to a broken food system is to engage and connect as deeply as possible. She calls Christians to "re-member" the intricate details of our food, and to thereby "embody the responsibility of *membership* in an interdependent universe."[49] When an eater intentionally chooses a vegetable grown on local soil rather than a processed chip of unknown origin, she is more fully a member of her bioregion. When meat is intentionally purchased from a local farmer who raises animals in a humane and sustainable way, the eater is more fully a member of an interspecies community. Potatoes and pork chops are no longer simply commodities and calories; they become connections that bring people of faith into communion with God's creation. Thus, Ayres' resistance to mainstream food practices is not about what we avoid but rather about where we belong, about what we commit to, and where we put our energy and attention.

A practical theologian, Ayres insists that the gift and obligation of membership in God's creation require action. She cites Warren Wilson College in North Carolina, which embeds sustainable agriculture into its liberal arts curriculum with a fully operational mixed crop and livestock farm that covers 275 acres of campus. Students at this Presbyterian school spend time caring for a sick pig between classes, applying research on soil health to their farm, and fulfilling their commitment to the school by cooking and cleaning in the dining hall. The farm provides locally grown meat and produce to the campus community and to neighbors in the region. In producing and eating local food, the students at Warren Wilson become self-conscious members of the community and, through it, God's creation.[50]

Christian practices are not only about local places, though. Ayres also tells the story of Christians brought from the United States to the Mexican pueblo of Cuentepec by the Chicago Religious Network for Latin America in order to better understand the global food system. Hand-making tortillas with an indigenous corn farmer, the visitors gain an understanding of how essential this process is to the local culture and draw inspiration to challenge the industrialization and commodification of corn that makes local grain and homemade tortillas increasingly hard to come by. By practicing their membership in a global food community, these Christians learn to invest time and energy in communities of the poor and marginalized who are too often denied secure and self-directed access to healthy foods.[51]

The students at Warren Wilson and the pilgrims in Cuentepec consciously recognize the communities with whom they are eating—the indigenous peoples of a neighboring nation or the livestock raised on local land. This demonstrates Ayres' primary lesson about temperate Christian eating: we never eat alone, so responsible enjoyment of food calls for a public engagement in a broader community. By contrast, an Evagrian approach stresses that Christians must separate ourselves from the destructive and corrupting aspects of a wider food system; temperate eating here is a private act of aligning oneself to God's commands separate from—perhaps even in spite of—the wider community.

The contrast between these two approaches should not be put too starkly—Evagrius does not teach Christians to ignore the world or its structures, and Ayres does not encourage Christians to pridefully tell others what and how to eat at every opportunity. However, there is enough difference here to warrant a conversation, a discussion of the proper balance between a private quest for purification and a public attempt to change systems. Food consumption is deeply private, but it is also undeniably public and socially conditioned for regular citizens as well as for famous politicians and celebrities. All people must make their own choices about what and how to eat, but temperance is necessary to help them make those choices responsibly—that is to say, *in response to* the realities of our social contexts, food systems, and environmental challenges. To eat ethically is not a simple task of cutting back on high-fructose corn syrup or shopping at Whole Foods. Balancing private and public responsibility, balancing discipline and enjoyment, are tests of virtue undertaken with every bite.

Temperance in Action

In food production, temperance calls for a balance between industrial agriculture and simpler methods. In food consumption, temperance calls for a balance between individual responsibility and social engagement.

It is also important to be temperate when engaging in conversations about a topic as complex and emotionally powerful as food, since this is an inevitably personal issue in which all people are involved in many ways. Accusatory statements can alienate others and inspire defensiveness rather than dialogue.

Overstatements can invite sharp criticism and feed the kind of cynicism that reduces motivation to seek solutions.[52] There are different reasonable views about how humans should use technology and engage tradition and about how to balance the personal and the political. Despite the difficulties of this topic, however, there is no denying that human hunger, inhumane treatment of animals and human workers, and the environmental degradation caused by immoderate agricultural practices are important problems that should concern everyone who eats.

There are reasons to hope that food systems in the United States are gradually changing for the better, as citizens and consumers become ever more aware that issues of waste and hunger exist side by side. Partly in response to consumer awareness, Wal-Mart—the country's largest food retailer—has committed to increasing the amount of fresh, local produce available to its customers. Meanwhile, even politicians are sensing shifts in public opinion, for example adjusting the level of subsidies offered to America's farmers in 2013's federal Farm Bill. Farmers' markets and CSAs (community-supported agriculture) are on the rise across the country, and many American recipients of food stamps (Supplemental Nutrition Assistance Program) are now able to use their benefits to purchase local, fresh produce.[53]

Despite hopeful developments, there are also signs of continuing intemperance. The explosion of packaged and processed foods, pushed upon consumers with slick advertising, invites quick and super-sized consumption without reflection or genuine enjoyment, followed by mountains of trash. Legislators, hoping to save money (or benefit donors in their home districts), often represent food choices as purely private matters for individuals to solve alone. And everyday people continue to make questionable choices against our better judgments, choosing convenience and familiarity over foods that will protect land or sustain the livelihoods of environmentally conscious farmers. Consumers too often fail to ask how the cow that produced their half-and-half or hamburger was treated, or neglect to engage fellow citizens in the political challenge of feeding the hungry.

The global food system, and the food available to any one individual, is flawed. It will always be so. The system is as complex as humankind, as complex as the ecosystem, and as such can never be perfect. Food systems will change. Most citizens of the industrialized world eat in ways completely different from how our great-grandparents ate; this means that our great-grandchildren will likely eat in completely different ways than we do. The choices we make today steer our cultures, however subtly, toward that future, so temperance means taking responsibility for our choices and their short- and long-term impacts; it means taking responsibility to make whatever small changes are within our power to make—individually, politically, or both—in faith that the seeds diligently planted today in small choices will bear fruit somehow, somewhere, sometime. Although the food system is bigger than all of us, each of us has an important role to play. Christian virtue requires conscious, careful eating for the sake of a better future.

Learning Temperance

In 2013 the Philippines completed trials on a strain of genetically engineered rice that it began permitting for production and sale. This "golden rice" was designed to contain substantial vitamin A, which does not normally occur in rice but is often missing in the diets of very poor and malnourished people. Because such people tend to eat only the most accessible and cheapest grains, the government of the Philippines and an international community of development professionals hope that including a vitamin A supplement in rice will help to quickly and efficiently increase the health of the most vulnerable people in that nation.[54]

If golden rice works to combat vitamin A deficiency, it will do substantial good: the World Health Organization estimates that, globally, between 250,000 and 500,000 children go blind every year because of this deficiency, and half of these children die within a year of losing their sight. A lack of vitamin A also weakens the immune system of all who suffer from it and particularly poses dangers to pregnant women. Currently, this problem is treated with vitamin A supplements, which work but have so far not been deployed widely or efficiently enough to meet the needs of the world's poor.[55] Developers of golden rice hope that it will be easier and cheaper to distribute, preventing thousands of cases of blindness and death wherever it is approved and implemented. They argue that this is an elegant and vital solution to the serious problem of malnutrition: to give the hungry more nutritious food is to heal them in the most direct way possible.

Although golden rice has existed since before the year 2000, the Philippines is the first nation officially to sanction distribution. Approval of this rice has been held up for many years by critics concerned that genetically engineered food poses serious environmental and economic dangers. For example, Indian activist Vandana Shiva argues that these new organisms' impact on ecosystems is not yet fully understood and is therefore a "Trojan horse" that should be approached with extreme caution. She also argues that producing seeds in an industrial lab ignores the traditional wisdom of farmers across the world while disguising the true causes of malnutrition: the greed of wealthy people who prioritize the increase of their own profits over the just distribution of food. Shiva worries, moreover, about the fact that golden rice is a consumer product, designed to make money; it will not be distributed freely to farmers in poor nations but will instead be sold by profit-seeking companies. Because it is engineered and patented, even the seeds that result when farmers grow the rice on their own farms will be considered the private property of a corporation rather than the property of the farmers. She argues that the answer to malnutrition is not a single crop but a broad diversity of foods. For example, in her native India, people used to grow a leafy green vegetable called Bathua, which is rich in vitamin A among other nutrients, but farmers were encouraged to stop their traditional practices by Western development agencies, which encouraged them to focus on (Western-produced) grains instead. Shiva rejects the idea of genetically modifying an organism to solve a problem that could readily be solved by a more diverse, traditional, and just agricultural system.[56]

A Christian response to golden rice requires temperance, balancing the very real promise of this technology with its very real risks. This issue reminds those of us who can afford sufficient food and nutrition that we are blessed and called to care for our neighbors, especially our neighbors who suffer the tragedies of starvation and nutritional deficiencies. But discerning how to help these neighbors reasonably and responsibly is more difficult. Those who advocate traditional agricultural methods are likely to reject golden rice as an intemperate and unnecessary extension of human power and economic forces into nature's fundamental structures. This is a sensible argument: technology is not an unmitigated good, and temperance requires that human beings not do things simply because we can, not leap too quickly into new behaviors the long-term results of which we have not considered, lest we cause worse problems than those we were trying to solve.

However, as the beginning of this chapter emphasized, temperance does not automatically mean saying "no" to new things or unfamiliar foods. Those who celebrate the accomplishments of industrial agriculture may well see golden rice as a logical extension of humanity's current successes. They might, moreover, remind critics that responsible enjoyment of this world should include helping to make food more nutritious and more widespread for others, as well as to heal human diseases as efficiently as possible. Developing the habit of temperance means careful consideration of whether golden rice's rewards are worth its risks. Environmental questions almost always inspire more than one reasonable answer; healthy directions for our future depend upon our considerations and actions being as temperate and virtuous as they can be.

Questions for Discussion

1. When it comes to the mean of temperance, which extreme comes more naturally to you: too little enjoyment or too much? What is one practical step you could take toward "enjoying responsibly" in the way you eat and drink?

2. Conversations about transforming how humans eat involve a balancing act between changes in one's own diet (as Evagrius Ponticus modeled) and conscious transformations of business, politics, and cultural food structures (as Jennifer Ayres proposes). How do you balance these two goals in your own life? How would you like to?

3. Questions about food production often center on how much industrialization and technology should be involved in the production of food. What do you think is the proper balance between producing enough food for billions of people (as Blake Hurst argues) and producing food in ways that are not harmful in the long term to the world's soil, water, and air (as Michael Pollan argues)?

4. Do you think golden rice is a good solution to the global problem of vitamin A deficiency? Why or why not?

5. Aside from food, what other areas of contemporary life do you think would benefit from the virtue of temperance?

5

JUSTICE
Between Revolution and Reform in the Fight
against Environmental Injustice

The Challenge of Environmental Justice

The reservation of the Skull Valley Goshutes, a Native American tribal nation, sits on the edge of the Great Salt Lake Desert in Utah. The Goshutes have lived in the Great Basin Desert for centuries and traditionally survived through adaptive hunting and gathering that depended on careful understanding of the harsh conditions in their arid homeland. However, as European Americans began to settle Utah in the nineteenth century, the Goshutes' way of life became increasingly threatened and limited. Beginning in the 1860s, the Goshutes signed a series of treaties with the U.S. federal government to create two reservations in Nevada and Utah. The Skull Valley reservation was created in 1912.[1]

The eighteen-thousand-acre reservation is not on prime real estate. To the southwest are the Dugway Proving Grounds, where the U.S. Army tests and implements chemical and biological weapon defense systems. This is the site of an infamous release of nerve agents that mysteriously killed over six thousand sheep in 1968, which were later buried on reservation land by the U.S. Army without the Goshutes' knowledge or permission.[2] To the northeast is another U.S. Army site, this one devoted to storing and maintaining ammunition. To the northwest are two hazardous waste incinerators, a hazardous waste landfill, and a disposal site where Tooele County, Utah (which surrounds the reservation), buries all of its low-level radioactive waste. The Skull Valley Goshutes receive no payment or benefits from any of these projects and had no say in their location. Yet these storage facilities and incinerators just outside their borders make agriculture and economic development within the reservation difficult.

One industry that was willing to come to the reservation was nuclear waste disposal. In an effort to support their population economically, Skull Valley Goshute leaders signed a 1997 agreement with a consortium of eight utilities from around the United States that use nuclear power. Under the plan, the reservation would have stored forty thousand metric tons of high-level nuclear waste, which is currently on sites near the nuclear reactors that produce it. At one point, Leon Bear, the tribal chairman who negotiated the deal, predicted that the project could provide a dividend of $2 million to each of the roughly 130 enrolled Skull Valley Goshutes, about a third of whom live on the reservation.[3]

The plan met resistance. Utah state politicians opposed it vocally, worrying that the "temporary" storage on the reservation would become permanent and that their state would essentially be forced to host nuclear waste for the entire nation. While these politicians had no authority over the reservation, they emphasized that the waste would have to travel on public roads and railways to get there and argued that such material is fundamentally unsafe. Furthermore, some members of the Skull Valley Goshutes even opposed the move from within, citing the same concerns about the dangerous nature of the waste and uncertainties about how long it would remain. But when Leon Bear was reelected as chairman in the year 2000, he interpreted this as a mandate to continue pursuing the deal.[4] After substantial debate, the Nuclear Regulatory Commission approved the plan in 2006, but the U.S. Bureau of Indian Affairs refused to sign off on the agreement between the tribe and the corporations, while the Bureau of Land Management refused to allow transport of the waste. Legal battles continued until 2012, when the consortium of energy companies finally abandoned the project.[5] This is far from the last word, however, since nuclear energy continues to be touted as a popular alternative to fossil fuels. Indeed, as of this writing, another band of Goshutes are looking to have a nuclear power plant built on their land.[6]

Nuclear waste is an environmental issue of profound importance and controversy. While the actual production of nuclear energy is relatively clean and has little impact on climate change, it nevertheless depends on mining and consumptive technologies to produce power. More alarmingly, nuclear waste in its current form remains dangerously radioactive for tens of thousands of years, and the nation has no long-term plan for how to store it safely. Some argue that technological innovation and continued processing will eventually remove this threat, while others believe that the existence of such waste is reason enough to cease the use of nuclear power entirely.[7] In the context of eco-virtue, the story of the Skull Valley Goshutes calls special attention to another environmental issue and the focus of this chapter: environmental justice.

Environmental justice has to do with how hazards such as nuclear waste are distributed across the human community; it also concerns who gets to participate in making decisions about such waste. Whether or not the Goshutes should store nuclear waste on their own land, their story demonstrates the ways in which marginalized peoples—people of color, people who are economically poor, and people who are victims of historical oppression—bear an unfair share of the burdens created by environmental hazards. The Goshute reservation was already surrounded by toxins beyond the Goshutes' control, and the decision about storing nuclear waste on their own land was, ultimately, also denied them by those outside the reservation with greater political leverage.

Sadly, there are countless examples of such environmental injustices across the world. Other Native American communities face disproportionate threats from mining, climate change, and population control efforts.[8] Low-income people in Louisiana have dubbed an area along the Mississippi River "Cancer Alley" based on disproportionate levels of the disease in their communities, which they attribute to the many industrial plants surrounding them.[9] The issue is also international: laws designed to protect the profits of corporate seed manufacturers deny traditional farmers in India the right to save and replant the seeds from their crops.[10] Environmental victims in developing nations argue that their experience of climate change—brought on largely by the consumption habits of wealthy nations—constitutes a form of "terrorism" by rich nations against poor.[11] These are all examples of environmental injustice: in each case the poor and marginalized are deprived of full participation in environmental decisions while also being exposed to an unfair share of environmental hazards. Christians, learning from Jesus' special care and attention to those who suffer the most, are called to wake up to environmental injustice and fight against it.

Liberation theologian James Cone powerfully raises the core issue of environmental injustice in his seminal essay "Whose Earth Is It, Anyway?" He argues that most pro-environmental organizations pay inadequate attention to social justice, speaking as though they are defending the earth for *all* humanity but tending instead to advocate disproportionately for the interests of wealthy and white people—people who already enjoy relative safety in their food, water, and air and who therefore have time to think about the importance of wilderness or the needs of polar bears. For Cone, environmentalism is incomplete unless it first includes a careful analysis of the injustices between human beings, in particular the legacy of racism and segregation that unfairly and systematically divides people based on arbitrary distinctions. He calls Christian environmentalists to "deepen our conversation by linking the earth's crisis with the crisis in the human family. If it is important to save the habitats of birds and other species, then it is at least equally important to save black lives in the ghettos and prisons of America." Cone's argument offers an important corrective not only to the environmental movement that has too often ignored race as if it were irrelevant but also to racial justice movements that have too often ignored the environment. "The fight for justice," he insists, "cannot be segregated but must be integrated with the fight for life in all its forms."[12]

After offering a more complete definition of justice as a virtue, this chapter takes up Cone's challenge by learning from two movements for environmental justice: one to protect urban communities from the disproportionate burden of toxic waste and the other to protect migrant farm workers from harmful pesticides. Each case demonstrates the complexity of environmental justice and the importance of noticing and acknowledging injustice, interrogating the roots of such injustice, and considering multiple perspectives on how to create a better future for everyone.[13]

Justice as Community Integration

North American Christians seeking to understand the virtue of justice can find great insight in the prophetic teaching of Reverend Dr. Martin Luther King Jr. As a Christian leader, King could be associated with many of the virtues: he demonstrated hope with his famous dream for an integrated and equal nation; he modeled courage by standing up against segregation and hatred in the face of violent threats; he practiced love by insisting that protests be conducted nonviolently in hopes of saving rather than defeating his opponents. Connected to all these other virtues, justice is at the center of King's legacy, grounding his work in a commitment to respecting the dignity of all people as children of God and members of a single community of equality.[14] While there was some debate surrounding the exact wording of a quotation engraved upon the 2013 memorial built in his honor in Washington, D.C., no one questioned that King was, first and foremost, "a drum major for justice."[15]

While he was a deeply reflective Christian with an extensive theological education, King's understanding of justice was formed primarily through struggles in the courtrooms, streets, and jail cells that defined the civil rights movement in the United States. He trained himself and all those who protested with him in the virtue of justice, insisting that all people deserve fair treatment. He was committed to respect for everyone he encountered, whether they were for or against his cause. For King, this was not only a Christian virtue but also an American virtue, because he understood the United States to be founded on an "amazing universalism" reflected in the Declaration of Independence's assertion that "all men [sic] are created equal." He wrote: "It does not say all white men, but it says all men, which includes black men. It does not say all Gentiles, but it says all men, which includes Jews. It does not say all Protestants, but it says all men, which includes Catholics."[16] All people deserve fairness, King asserted, and this meant to him that segregating laws giving white Protestant human beings better schools, better government, or better treatment than other human beings could not possibly be just. Justice for King meant a fair and equitable distribution of society's common resources.[17]

In addition to distribution, justice is also a matter of participation. King struggled not only for equal access to resources but also for an equal place at the decision-making table, most explicitly in his work on voting rights. In his famous "I Have a Dream" speech, King insisted that he could not be satisfied "as long as a Negro in Mississippi cannot vote and a Negro in New York believes he has nothing for which to vote."[18] His ultimate goal was not merely to end segregation but to establish genuine "integration," which he defined as "a real sharing of power and responsibility" that meant not only a vote for all but also a genuine community where diverse voices were heard and respected.[19] For King, such participation extended beyond the mere inclusion of African Americans into white-dominated politics or spaces, to the integration of all races and classes of people into a single community.

This integration was more important than any borders, and King's interest in justice extended beyond the United States. Indeed, in response to various struggles for independence in Africa and wars in Asia, he also called for an integrated foreign policy that viewed all people as full members of the human community who should be heard and attended to. Justice for him was about the entire world: "Injustice anywhere is a threat to justice everywhere. We are caught in an inescapable network of mutuality, tied in a single garment of destiny. Whatever affects one directly affects all indirectly."[20] Though he lived in Atlanta, King could not ignore the violent segregation in Alabama. Though he lived in the South, King could not ignore the economic disparities in Chicago. Though he lived in the United States, King could not ignore what he saw as the grave injustice of the Vietnam War. An integrated virtue of justice requires a recognition of the interconnectedness of all human communities and a commitment to hear and support struggles against oppression everywhere.[21]

King's expansive view of just distribution and just participation were ultimately grounded on his faith in God's justice. A preacher raised in the black Baptist church, King did not seek respect and integration for merely democratic or political reasons, but for theological reasons—because he saw every human being as a child of God and believed that God was pushing the entire world toward integration and justice. He reassured his activist colleagues with an appeal to this belief: "When our days become dreary with low-hovering clouds of despair, and when our nights become darker than a thousand midnights, let us remember that there is a creative force in this universe, working to pull down the gigantic mountains of evil, a power that is able to make a way out of no way and transform dark yesterdays into bright tomorrows. Let us realize the arc of the moral universe is long but it bends toward justice."[22] When King sang "We Shall Overcome" with protestors, he sang with confidence because he had faith in a God who was guiding the world toward justice. When King was arrested for breaking unjust laws, he walked boldly and publicly into the jail cell because he had faith in the higher justice of God, who allowed worldly authorities to crucify Jesus but then resurrected Christ. Justice, for King, included the conviction that human beings are most closely aligned to the purposes and plans of the divine when we respect all others as members of a single community and as children of God.

Inspired by King's witness and his wisdom, the virtue of justice can be defined in distributive, participatory, and divine terms. Justice is the ability to treat all people fairly, to include all people in community decisions, and to work toward God's vision of an integrated and equal future for the human race. This virtue—the habit of seeing others as children of God regardless of their differences from ourselves or their distance from our positions—is not only a matter of interpersonal or political relationships. It is also absolutely essential in the context of environmentalism, especially when considering the distribution of hazards or wrestling with the moral challenges of toxic wastes and pesticides. Such questions have to do not only with the earth itself but with the human beings who live together on it.

Fighting for a Healthy Neighborhood: Environmental Justice in the City

Martin Luther King was assassinated in Memphis in 1968. He had traveled there to aid a group of African American garbage workers who were striking to demand equal pay and better working conditions. While King would not have used the term, this was an obvious manifestation of environmental injustice in that the workers were demanding fair compensation and bodily safety as they handled the hazards of their neighbors' waste.[23]

Following in King's footsteps, many Christians continue to participate in the movement for environmental justice. For instance, in 1987 the United Church of Christ's Commission for Racial Justice produced the first national study that correlated the locations of toxic waste dumps with demographic data. They found that race was the single most statistically significant factor in determining where hazardous waste sites were placed—more significant than income level, home ownership level, or land values. Throughout the country, zip codes with lower percentages of white people were far more likely to contain the type of toxic waste that can leak into water supplies or contaminate soil and air. While it is tempting to hope that such environmental racism is ancient history, an update of that report twenty years later, using a more precise methodology, found that racial disparities have continued into the twenty-first century.[24]

Environmental justice is desperately needed in minority neighborhoods across the United States. Communities of color are more likely than white communities to house central stations for diesel buses that release asthma-causing exhaust, such as the predominantly African American neighborhoods of northern Manhattan, which contain six out of the island's eight bus depots.[25] In addition to living with a disproportionate share of the nation's pollution and toxic waste, these neighborhoods have also historically enjoyed less legal protection from the harms that arise from living near such waste. Violations of pollution laws in such communities are less likely to be investigated than violations in white communities, and investigations that do take place among minority communities tend to move more slowly and result in smaller fines for the offenders.[26]

While the wastes produced by industrialization are more plentiful in the neighborhoods of the poor and marginalized, the benefits of that technology are conversely more difficult to find. Sources of fresh and healthy foods, for example, are notably scarce in neighborhoods of color across the nation; they contain disproportionately few supermarkets, such that most of the food available is from convenience and specialty stores that sell fewer healthy foods and charge more for them.[27] Living in a healthy environment is, all too often, a luxury only for those with both money and political clout; in the United States, these are privileges still most often associated with high incomes and white skin.

Because of the close connection between race and unhealthy environments, the environmental justice movement has often seen itself as an extension of the civil rights movement, using tactics of organized protests aimed at gaining attention in order to influence the decisions of local, state, and federal governments.[28] Like the civil rights movement, the environmental justice movement insists that the most serious problem is not *deliberate* racism or prejudice but rather the even more insidious forms of invisible racism, such as neglect and unintended consequences of well-meaning people who are ignorant of or willfully blind to injustices.

For example, traditional, predominantly white environmentalists have tended to focus their efforts on preserving wilderness—wide open spaces to which wealthier folk can escape on weekends or vacations—rather than focusing on the health of cities, in which the majority of human beings spend their daily lives.[29] Meanwhile, those with political and economic power generally want to keep pollution out of their neighborhoods and tend to succeed, while those with less leverage are then burdened with hazards not necessarily of their own making. Employing arguments scarcely more sophisticated than "not in my backyard," privileged Americans repeatedly push environmental hazards toward those who have the least clout, leading to a disproportionate burden of environmental problems in poor neighborhoods of color across the nation that do not have the organization, knowledge, or wherewithal to prevent it.[30] Environmental justice thus means waking up to the significance of cities and the people who live in them, particularly the poor and marginalized who have historically been denied a voice in decisions about environmental hazards that directly affect their well-being.

An example that illustrates such injustice is Chester, Pennsylvania, a small city that once housed Martin Luther King's alma mater, Crozier Theological Seminary, but has in more recent decades experienced many of the challenges of environmental racism. Only fifteen miles from Philadelphia, Chester is 75 percent African American in a county that is 20 percent African American, and it has higher poverty, unemployment, crime, and infant mortality rates than the rest of the area. It is also far more polluted, containing four waste processing plants as well as being neighbored by oil refineries, an infectious medical waste treatment facility, and a plant for burning contaminated soil. The most controversial of these sites is an enormous incinerator that processes over three thousand tons of industrial waste per day, accepting deliveries from trucks at all hours of the day and night despite its location next to a residential neighborhood. Soot and dust cover many parts of the town, and visitors invariably comment on noxious odors in the city. Residents experience stress from the noise and smells of their community, and they fear the long-term health consequences, particularly for children, of the exhaust and other byproducts of the industries that surround them.[31]

Chester residents have responded by demanding environmental justice. With fortitude, they have committed to the difficult long-term work of participating in the political process to change the direction of their city. Chester residents repeatedly organize and speak at public hearings and meetings with local government and company officials to protest the pollution and dangerous industries near their homes. Church and community groups have formed to help coordinate these actions, including Chester Residents Concerned about Quality of Life and the Chester Environmental Partnership, both chaired by local clergyman Reverend Horace Strand.[32] These efforts eventually bore fruit in the form of legal settlements with two local facilities that had violated the Clean Air Act, gaining funds for a community-run lead poisoning prevention program. But when political advocacy has not succeeded, Chester residents have not given up; they have turned to other methods of protest and civil disobedience, such as one effort to block delivery trucks on their way to the incinerator by standing together in the middle of the street. In a film from this protest, one resident emphasized that their quarrel was not with the economics of the facilities but with environmental conditions that threatened the survival of the people: "We are not against profit or gain, but we want to gain in our own areas. . . . We want to live."[33]

Another threat to the lives of Chester's residents is severe food insecurity due especially to a lack of access to healthy foods and supermarkets in an area where few people have private transportation. This means that many residents of Chester and other poor communities primarily eat the high-calorie and low-nutrition processed foods available at convenience stores. From 2001 to 2013, there was no grocery store in the entire city until the organization Philabundance opened a nonprofit store in the city's downtown with help from government and foundation grants.[34] In the meantime, Chester residents banded together to form a food co-op, which theologian Mark Wallace describes as "a beacon of light and hope," because it is a place where members create justice by providing fresh food, a sense of community, and a way for residents to take control of their own health. Wallace argues that steps like these are a vital model of justice for Christians today, who are called "to follow in Jesus' steps and care for the marginalized and forgotten in a world hell bent on unsustainable agricultural and economic policies."[35]

Chester demonstrates multiple aspects of environmental injustice, beginning with the fact that its mostly African American citizens bear the burden of environmental hazards far more heavily than do their white neighbors in other parts of Pennsylvania and across the country. This is a failure of distributive justice. The city also represents a struggle for participatory justice, as citizens must work—in the absence of economic clout—to make their voices heard politically, to play a role in shaping and revitalizing their home town, and to live with dignity and good health in a safe and thriving community. Finally, Chester reminds Christians about divine justice: God's plan for creation certainly does not call for the most vulnerable humans to be directly and dangerously exposed to pollution and toxins by their more influential brothers and sisters. Christian environmental justice calls for a world in which everyone has a say in how environmental benefits and hazards (if indeed there must be hazards) are distributed.

Fighting for Safe Working Conditions: Environmental Justice in the Fields

Human beings need safe environments not only where we eat and sleep but also where we work. Agricultural workers, who currently face some of the most severe environmental risks that the U.S. economy has to offer, offer another vitally important and disturbing case of environmental injustice.

While everyone in the world lives by consuming the products that agricultural workers plant, cultivate, and harvest, those workers often find themselves standing alone on the front lines of agriculture's chemical pesticides.

In the early 1960s, Rachel Carson first drew the nation's attention to the dangers of pesticides, particularly DDT, a highly toxic chemical that was harming not only insect pests but also birds. She further explained that DDT could cause serious neurological problems and birth defects in human beings. The Environmental Protection Agency did not ban the use of this chemical until 1972, but a local ban had already taken effect in 1967 when the United Farm Workers—founded by César Chávez and Dolores Huerta in 1962—persuaded California grape growers to stop using the chemical. Chávez, the union's president, had focused attention on pesticides throughout the five-year strike that led to that contract and insisted that careful assessment of pesticides was not only a legal issue but was the industry's moral obligation: "As producers of food you must be aware of your social responsibility to the workers and consumers to insure their health and safety. Surely, California table grape growers are not so interested in profit from the sales of grapes that they would willingly do harm to unsuspecting workers and consumers."[36]

In a later campaign, Chávez called for a similar ban on the powerful pesticide methyl parathion, another nerve gas that causes severe illness and potentially permanent brain damage. Chávez cited evidence of worker deaths, as well as an EPA report that found parathion to be highly toxic even to those wearing protective clothing and using the chemical as directed.[37] This pesticide was not banned in most food crops until 2000 and is still allowed on cotton and wheat.

Methyl parathion and DDT—together with the 438,000 tons of other pesticides and herbicides that the EPA reports are still used in U.S. agriculture each year[38]—should be of concern to everyone who consumes food produced by U.S. farmers. However, these chemicals pose a far more serious threat to those who grow and gather food than it does to those of us who eat it. These farm workers, a high percentage of whom are poor people of Latin American descent, tend to have very little control over their working conditions and face severe threats from pesticides. These chemicals raise pressing issues of environmental justice for agricultural workers and the people who live in agricultural areas.

Pesticides are chemicals designed to be toxic—they discourage or kill rodents and insects by poisoning them. When human beings are exposed to these poisonous chemicals in large or repeated doses, they almost always cause health problems—including temporary problems such as headaches and vomiting, more serious issues such as skin disease, and catastrophic problems such as cancer, miscarriages, sterility, birth defects, and neurological disorders. Farm workers are directly exposed to these chemicals when they apply them to crops or when they work with irrigation or other farm equipment that has been contaminated. The vast majority of their exposure comes in one of two forms: drift (when sprayed pesticide is blown by the wind onto neighboring fields or homes) and residue (when workers handle produce that has been sprayed and are thus exposed through their skin). Sadly, these threats extend to workers' children, who are sometimes brought to the fields when no childcare is available or are exposed to residues on the clothes and shoes of their parents.[39]

Because farm worker populations tend to be migratory and have little access to health care, and because many farm workers are undocumented and afraid to ask for help, the problem of pesticide-related health problems is not well understood. For example, in California, over four thousand farm workers reported pesticide-related illnesses and injuries to their work supervisors or doctors between 1982 and 2010, but this number likely represents only a fraction of the problem because many workers do not report their health problems.[40] Even if workers want to appeal to local, state, and federal authorities, there are many cases in which existing laws do not protect them. Almost half of reported illnesses from pesticides in California, for example, occurred with no violation of rules or regulations.[41]

For this reason, farm workers frequently seek to make their work safer not through lobbying the government but through labor organizing, including the formation of collectives and unions. The most prominent such effort is the United Farm Workers union (UFW), which still advocates for corporate transparency and limitations on the use of agricultural pesticides for the sake of laborers. Its co-founding president César Chávez, a Christian activist inspired by Martin Luther King Jr., appealed directly to the Christian virtue of justice and the universal dignity of all human beings. In response to agribusinesses that paid their workers as little as possible in order to maximize their profits, managers who sprayed products and people with dangerous and untested pesticides, and consumers who gave no thought to where their food came from, Chávez asserted the dignity of the human beings who grow and harvest food for the rest of us.

In a 1984 speech reflecting on his career to that point, Chávez said, "All of my life, I have been driven by one dream, one goal, one vision: To overthrow a farm system in this nation which treats farm workers as if they were not important human beings."[42] As with King's approach to civil rights, another essential aspect of Chávez' work involved teaching his fellow workers to respect themselves and their opponents. He believed that the farm workers could best prove they were worthy of dignity by treating their opposition as human beings worthy of respect and dignity.

Another aspect of farm workers' campaigns concerned calling national attention to their working conditions. In the last years of his life, Chávez argued that "protecting farm workers and consumers from systemic poisoning through the reckless use of agricultural toxics" was even more important than raising wages. He told stories of grape workers' children who died of cancer at age five or were born with no arms or legs, tragedies he argued were directly caused by exposure to pesticides.[43] In 1988 Chávez undertook a thirty-six day "Fast for Life," eating no food and drinking only water, to call attention to the union's demands for new limits on pesticide usage. The growers did not respond and refused to change their policies, but Chávez garnered national attention and emphasized to audiences across the nation that he was doing penance and praying not only for farmworkers and their children but for all who were exposed to these poisons in their food. In his statement ending that fast, Chávez called pesticide usage a "cycle of death that threatens our people and our world."[44]

César Chávez passed away in 1993, but the problem of pesticide exposure among farm workers remains deathly serious and little understood in the United States and around the world.[45] The movement for environmental justice in farming continues, and it follows the model of other environmental justice struggles by working for two goals: first, it seeks to reduce environmental harm, calling for limitations on pesticide usage, protections for workers and their children, and the development of alternative agricultural methods. Such regulations would naturally increase food prices, thereby distributing the cost of food more fairly among workers, consumers, and owners, rather than asking workers to pay with their lives simply because they have no other job options. Second, it seeks to increase participation in integrated communities, both locally and around the world, empowering marginalized farm workers to raise their voices in broader debates through unions or nongovernmental organizations.[46]

Perhaps the most obvious solution to the unfair distribution of pesticides and toxic waste would be to stop using them altogether; if there were no toxic waste to distribute, there would be no unfair distribution or environmental injustice. While this may seem an impossible dream on this side of the eschaton, it is nevertheless something Christians should bear in mind as we strive against "the powers and principalities" of this world (Ephesians 6:12). Until such a time as seven billion people can be fed without the use of pesticides, Christians who seek to cultivate the virtue of justice are called, at the very least, to attend to how environmental hazards are distributed and who is participating in shaping the world we all share.

Paths toward Justice: Revolution or Reform?

The pollution and waste produced by the industrialized world's current patterns of consumption is daunting and disturbing. But we cannot comfort ourselves by simply looking the other way. The first steps toward environmental justice are to recognize the problems and try to see them clearly; to pay attention to the realities of injustice in the agricultural system that feeds us, which does not always protect its laborers from toxic chemicals; and to learn about conditions in cities where low-income people and people of color are dealing with more than their fair share of the pollution we, too, help create. These problems exist across the country and around the globe, and Christians must learn to be awake to such issues, particularly paying attention to the injustices in our own neighborhoods and the injustices to which we contribute with our own choices.

But awareness by itself is not enough. Injustice calls for change, even sacrifice. Virtuous people must be willing to push against injustice before there will be significant movement toward a vision of a just environment where all God's people are treated fairly and fully included. The virtue of justice requires action, beginning with the difficult process of choosing what kind of action to take—whether revolutionary attempts to reorder social and cultural institutions from the ground up or more modest reforms to include more people in currently existing political and economic structures. What follows are descriptions of these approaches by those who sought justice through revolution and reform.

Radical Injustice Calls for Revolution

In 1991 a group of activists gathered for the first National People of Color Environmental Leadership Summit in Washington, D.C., and adopted seventeen principles of environmental justice, many of which spell out a vision of justice of the sort discussed in this chapter.[47] The second principle affirms distributive justice and calls out environmental injustice, insisting "that public policy be based on mutual respect and justice for all peoples, free from any form of discrimination or bias." The seventh principle insists upon participatory justice by affirming all citizens' "right to participate as equal partners at every level of decision-making, including needs assessment, planning, implementation, enforcement, and evaluation." Such principles do not come across as particularly radical; instead they simply call for greater integration in the system as it already exists.

Other principles, however, indicate that the summit's participants believed true justice would require a much more profound change in social institutions. The sixth principle, for example, calls for a fundamental restructuring of the modern economy, demanding "the cessation of the production of all toxins, hazardous wastes, and radioactive materials." In a similar vein, the fourteenth principle calls contemporary capitalist economic structures into question when it "opposes the destructive operations of multi-national corporations." But it is not only corporations that are called to radical restructuring; the tenth principle demands that the U.S. government also subject itself to external authorities, labeling "governmental acts of environmental injustice a violation of international law, the Universal Declaration on Human Rights, and the United Nations Convention on Genocide."[48] Such principles do not merely ask for minor reforms or broader participation; they suggest that injustice must be pulled out by its roots, not just trimmed and pruned. In this view, the only way to move toward genuine justice in environmental matters is for society to make profound changes.

In this revolutionary perspective, the roots of environmental injustice are every bit as deep as the roots of racism. The mindset that thinks farm workers have no right not to be poisoned by pesticides ("no one is forcing them to work there") or that poor people have no right to clean water or air ("they should just move away") rests on a callous dehumanization of the poor. It can be traced back to the mindset that gave birth to colonialism and American slavery: a disregard for much of human life alongside an utterly instrumental view of ecosystems as commodities. The only way to solve a problem with such deep roots is to make radical changes, dismantling the very economic systems that made environmental degradation and injustice possible (perhaps even necessary), and restructuring the power dynamics that have made human oppression seem normal. Some activists insist that environmental justice will be possible only after a decisive move away from capitalism's destructive celebration of profit, growth, and exploitation at all costs.[49] Others argue that the root of the problem is a culture of individualism, calling for a widespread transformative awareness of the interconnectedness of all people and creatures.[50] What these perspectives share is a belief that there is no small change that will create environmental justice. The evil must be torn out at its source and the entire system rebuilt from the ground up.

At its core, the movement for farm worker safety that César Chávez stood for was a revolutionary one. In an early statement, he and other leaders of the movement noted that, as American persons of Mexican heritage, they were children "of the Mexican Revolution, a revolution of the poor seeking bread and justice. Our revolution will not be armed, but we want the existing social order to dissolve; we want a new social order."[51] Of course, many of the protestors marching with Chávez were likely more moderate than their leaders, but the voices at the head of their movement were calling for something radically new. Environmental justice, from this perspective, requires sweeping and comprehensive changes, away from an individualistic system that rewards a powerful and fortunate few and toward a holistic system designed to benefit everyone touched by the system's processes.

A Decent System That Needs Reform

While there are many people of goodwill who wish things were different, some are skeptical about the practical value of dramatic proposals to overthrow capitalist markets or imperfectly democratic processes. They worry that if environmental justice is impossible without a complete revolution, then it will never occur. From this perspective, the project of making the world more just calls for creative adaptations and applications of existing social structures. Environmental justice requires working within the system to make incremental changes, which can then make environmental benefits more accessible while seeing a decrease in and a better distribution of environmental hazards.

Some of the most developed arguments along these lines defend market mechanisms as the best means for increasing environmental justice.

For example, economists Spencer Banzhaf and Eleanor McCormick insist that markets are the most effective tools by which human beings distribute resources and make communal decisions: "The market is a remarkably efficient machine. It provides goods, including local environmental amenities, to those who demand them most—and who have the resources to pay for them." Based on this faith in markets, Banzhaf and McCormick conclude that the best thing for oppressed and marginalized peoples "is to empower them, strengthening their position within the market system."[52]

Consider the case of an impoverished community whose property values have been driven down by toxic waste or polluting industries. A revolutionary approach might insist that industrial pollution be declared altogether illegal, but this is often impractical and perhaps even undesirable, given the jobs and serviceS that such industries create. An alternative revolutionary approach might demand that the neighborhood be cleaned up at any cost, along with providing victims of injustice the medical care they need to restore their health. But Banzhaf and McCormick argue that this would do nothing to redress the disenfranchisement that led to the problem in the first place—poverty. Indeed, cleaning up the neighborhood could actually make things far worse by attracting wealthier residents who then gentrify the neighborhood until it is too expensive for its original residents.

A better solution, they suggest, is simply to put a price on the injustice that has been done and pay victims in cash, whether by charging the polluters or taking the funds from government coffers. Then affected people could decide for themselves whether they would be best served by cleaning up their neighborhood or by moving away. A market system, according to these economists, gives people freedom and options. In other words, the path to environmental justice is paying victims in cash for their suffering, thereby enabling them better to use the market system to redress their situations in the ways they deem most suitable. If polluters pay for the harm they cause, or if income is redistributed to those who suffer injustice, then markets can be an essential part of the path to environmental justice.[53]

While not everyone is comfortable with the idea of "paying to pollute," there are many Americans who trust the power of existing political structures to effect real change or of existing cultural institutions to empower people here and now. From this perspective, environmental justice requires not revolution but a pragmatic and wise use of existing institutions to solve concrete problems, as well as a careful legislative shaping of economic systems.

The citizens of Chester, Pennsylvania, demonstrated this approach when they faced the environmental injustices in their area. Rather than seeking to revolutionize the national food system, they responded to food insecurity by securing grants for a supermarket and coming together to form a co-op. Rather than outlawing pollution, they employed the existing court system to prosecute and extract fines from corporations found to have violated the Clean Air Act; they then used those fines to make their community healthier. While some residents of Chester would undoubtedly have preferred a revolution, the main strategy of the community has been one of incremental change based on well-established channels of political power.

Solidarity for the Sake of Reform or Revolution

There are strong arguments suggesting that true environmental justice will require revolutionary change, that the poor and marginalized of the world will never receive their due under current market conditions that consistently favor those who already have power and wealth. However, there are also strong arguments suggesting that the wisest course of action is reform: making gradual adjustments to the systems we currently live in and tweaking existing institutions so that the poor and marginalized can more fully participate in the benefits that privileged people already enjoy. But any community-wide, statewide, nationwide, or worldwide reform is necessarily a long-term, large-scale undertaking. As such efforts continue to take shape, Christians must also begin, here and now, to shape a more just world.

This requires, first and foremost, seeing things as they really are. We cannot blissfully eat cheap grapes without a care for the worker who was poisoned while harvesting them. We cannot thoughtlessly throw away our garbage without a care for those who will suffer from asthma when it is burned near their homes. Justice declares that farm workers do not deserve to be poisoned in the fields, even if they consent to do that job in order to support themselves and their families. Justice declares that the urban and rural poor do not deserve to be poisoned in their homes, even if they "consent" to live in dirty neighborhoods.

Once Christians in the industrialized world become aware that our behaviors may harm our neighbors near and far, we must look for ways to be in solidarity with them. Of course, there is no simple way for privileged people—white, educated, middle class—to be in genuine solidarity with those who risk their lives to come to the United States, live in crowded apartments, and do back-breaking labor for little money. (Nor can we even relate very well to those who were born in the U.S. but are nevertheless treated as second-class citizens.) But we can seek ways to support farmworkers striking for better working conditions, urban dwellers organizing for neighborhood cleanup, or farmers lobbying for higher clean water standards. Meanwhile, if possible we might also make personal sacrifices—paying more for pesticide-free grapes, assisting migrant workers and their families in our home towns, donating more than is comfortable to environmental organizations, refraining from buying disposable items that we do not absolutely need, or spending time lobbying our legislators for cash payments to the victims of injustice.

In addition to such individual actions, however, the virtue of justice also calls for work toward social change, whether revolutionary or reforming. Martin Luther King Jr. pointed toward revolution when he said God was "working to pull down the gigantic mountains of evil," and he also pointed toward reform when he spoke of helping people to "make a way out of no way and transform dark yesterdays into bright tomorrows."[54] A virtuous Christian actively participates in God's ongoing creation—through reform or revolution and beginning with small personal choices—to help build a more just world. We seek a just world not only for those we know and love and who think and act just like us but for all human beings who share equally in God's image.

Learning Justice

This chapter ends where it began: in the Skull Valley of Utah on a Native American reservation, which is legally sovereign but has been denied the right to decide for itself about storing nuclear waste. Whatever one thinks of the outcome of the case, the treatment received by the Skull Valley Goshutes demonstrates the reality of injustice. Their land is surrounded by weapons-grade chemicals and dumps for hazardous and radioactive waste, which makes economic development very difficult on the impoverished reservation. The citizens of Utah seem willing to unfairly distribute the burden of their environmental hazards to the Goshutes, who have no effective voice in the regulations and policies that should protect them from such wastes. When the tables are turned, however, the state of Utah asserts its rights to prevent the Native Americans from using their own land as they see fit. The Goshutes have experienced a denial of both distributive and participatory justice.

A market-driven reformist approach to this case might emphasize the concrete rights of Native Americans to their own land. If their reservation is truly their property, then they have the same rights as their neighbors to use it as they see fit. If the reservation is a sovereign entity within a nation that legally produces and stores nuclear waste, then it is difficult to see why it should not be legal to store nuclear materials on the reservation, even if it is surrounded on all sides by another state.[55] In addition, insofar as the economic development of the Skull Valley Goshutes is impeded by Utah's surrounding industries, reformers might suggest that justice entails their right to receive damages—to be paid for the financial loss caused by the negative consequences of Utah's air, water, and land management. If the Goshutes were to be compensated for the damage to their property, perhaps they would not need to consider storing nuclear waste on the reservation. This might then create avenues for more sustainable and community-enriching business opportunities in Skull Valley.[56] From this view, the path to justice lies in reform, such that the Skull Valley Goshutes can benefit fully from existing political, legal, and economic structures.

A more revolutionary approach might call into question the entire system governing Native American reservations, which currently have status in the United States as "domestic dependent nations" rather than as states or sovereign nations. This means that, while tribes have limited authority to determine the laws within their borders, they nevertheless remain under the "guardianship" of the United States, specifically the Bureau of Indian Affairs (BIA). The result of such guardianship is that they are not truly in control of their land, such that "Native Americans have largely been excluded from the American economy."[57] The lack of genuine sovereignty experienced by the Skull Valley Goshutes is reflected in other reservations across the nation, such as among Navajo peoples in Arizona and New Mexico, whose land has been mined for much of the uranium used in nuclear power plants under leases negotiated with the BIA rather than with the Navajo themselves.[58] A revolutionary perspective would assert the sovereignty of native peoples more broadly, perhaps calling for the dissolution of the BIA and demanding an expansion of Native American lands as partial reparation for all that the U.S. government has taken from them. George Tinker, an enrolled member of the Osage Nation and an ordained Lutheran minister, emphasizes that genuine environmental change of this sort must be grounded in sovereignty, including restoration of native land. "In the United States alone," he writes, "it is estimated that Indian nations still have legitimate (moral and legal) claim to some two-thirds of the U.S. land mass. Ultimately, such an act as return of Native lands to Native control would have a significant ripple effect on other states around the world," as more people experience the dignity of land ownership and sovereignty.[59]

Another radical approach might call on the United States—together with its domestic dependent nations—to forgo nuclear power altogether, along with other toxic industries.[60] From this view, the path to justice lies in recognizing the folly of nuclear power and every other destructive and unsustainable source of energy; it would call for a wholesale rethinking of American energy consumption, rather than just fighting over who gets to store dangerous waste.[61]

For the Skull Valley Goshutes, the residents of Chester, Pennsylvania, and so many other peoples across the world, environmental justice is an urgent concern. It should therefore be an urgent concern for Christians who are committed to justice for these neighbors. Such justice is of primary concern to the God of the Bible. A well-loved verse says that what is "good" is not burnt offerings or other religious rituals, but "to live justly, to love mercy, and to walk humbly with your God" (Micah 6:6-8). Elsewhere, God reminds Israel that holiness excludes those who "trample on the poor" and "push aside the needy in the gate"; God calls instead for "justice to roll down like waters and righteousness like an ever-flowing stream" (Amos 5:11-12, 24).

Environmental justice, like all forms of justice, requires action. To live justly begins by hearing the voices of suffering people. To live justly is also to see all people as God's children, regardless of how different or distant they are from ourselves, and to struggle to achieve God's vision for the entire earth community. But living justly cannot end with seeing and hearing. Genuine justice will drive Christians—both individually and in groups—to give everyone his or her due, to treat all people fairly; indeed, to treat them as the children of God that they are.

Questions for Discussion

1. In addition to justice, what other Christian virtues are required to respond to the disposal of toxic waste? What virtues are needed for dealing with the creation of toxic waste in the first place? What would it take to achieve a world without such waste?

2. What lessons do you take from the work of Chester's residents to advocate for their own environmental health? How could this apply to the work of making your own community healthier?

3. What lessons do you take from César Chávez' approach to justice for farm workers? How do you think it applies to your own life in the twenty-first century?

4. Which approach to justice—reform or revolution—appeals to you most? Why do you think you prefer this approach? How do you think your preference might be different if your own life circumstances (racial-ethnic, socioeconomic, geographical, national, etc.) were different?

5. What would justice look like for the Skull Valley Goshutes? Is it more important to defend their sovereignty to use their land as they choose or to discourage the production and storage of nuclear waste?

6. What constitutes environmental justice when it comes to Native Americans? Can there ever be real justice, given the United States' colonial history, including genocide against North America's earliest residents? If perfect justice cannot be attained, is partial justice a good alternative?

6

FAITH
Between Personal, Political, and Technological Responses to Climate Change

A Worldly Virtue

German theologian Dietrich Bonhoeffer once recounted a long conversation with a French pastor named Jean Lasserre about what they would do with their lives. They were both in their early twenties and wanted to devote themselves to God. Lasserre declared that he would like to be a saint, but Bonhoeffer said that he "should like to learn to have faith." Reflecting years later, he wrote, "For a long time I didn't realize the depth of the contrast," but he finally learned that "it is only by living completely in this world that one learns to have faith. One must completely abandon any attempt to make something of oneself, whether it be a saint, or a converted sinner, or a churchman (a so-called priestly type!)." Bonhoeffer equated faith with living fully in the world: "By this-worldliness I mean *living unreservedly in life's duties, problems, successes and failures, experiences and perplexities.* In so doing we throw ourselves completely into the arms of God, taking seriously, not our own sufferings, but those of God in the world—watching with Christ in Gethsemane."[1]

Bonhoeffer's statement about faith carries particular power because of where he wrote it: in the Tegel military prison in Germany in 1944, where he was locked up for subverting Nazi policies and plotting against the Third Reich. His international connections had given him many chances to flee Germany and its turmoil, but he chose to stay and try to make things better in his disastrously troubled nation. Authorities later discovered that he had participated in a plot to assassinate Hitler, and he was put to death for his crimes shortly before the war ended.

Dietrich Bonhoeffer experienced many challenges that could have distracted him from the sufferings of God, he had many opportunities *not* to live fully in the problems and perplexities of the world, and he must have been tempted to separate himself from all the travails he saw around him. But he nevertheless maintained a deep and abiding fidelity to God's presence and purposes in the world. That faith kept him grounded in what he called "this-worldliness."

In everyday conversation, "faith" is often treated as synonymous with "belief," and Christian faith is often treated as shorthand for the affirmation of God's existence, summed up as "I believe in God" or "I accept Jesus as my personal lord and savior." However, this is only one small part of the classical definition of faith. The virtue of faith—also sometimes translated as fidelity or faithfulness—is not merely about intellectual assent to a precept but more broadly about commitment and engagement. Faith is the habit of committing ourselves entirely to God and God's purposes. Bonhoeffer insightfully captures this definition of faith in his letter from prison, noting that faith is not about what we believe or become but rather about "unreservedly" committing to the world in which God has placed us, come what may.

This is not to say that faith has no intellectual component of belief or understanding. Indeed, for Bonhoeffer, faith was a matter of seeing the suffering around him as God's suffering, a belief that quickly turned into resolve to do something about that suffering. This is a concrete interpretation of one of Jesus' harder teachings, "Whatever you did not do for one of the least of these, you did not do for me" (Matthew 25:45). In Bonhoeffer's life, the most urgent suffering calling for his resolve was the murderous and destructive work of Adolf Hitler and the Nazi regime. He remained faithful as he stood up against these horrors—even to the point of testing his own pacifist commitment never to kill another human being—and he demonstrated to Christians who came after him that the virtue of faith is more than simple belief; it is fidelity to the reign of God on earth, right here, right now.[2]

Twenty-first-century Christians face different kinds of challenges arising from the suffering we see around us. We are called, however, to the same kind of faith and commitment as Bonhoeffer was, to throw ourselves completely into the arms of God, into this-worldliness, into the sufferings of the world with which Jesus so closely identified. As a virtue, faith entails belief in the goodness of God and God's creation, fidelity to fellow creatures in the midst of their suffering, and faithfulness to God's purposes even when change seems politically unlikely or economically impossible.

A Global Problem

Just as Bonhoeffer's understanding of faith developed through his struggle for the soul of Germany, the virtue becomes clearer today when put into conversation with the contemporary environmental challenge of climate change. This problem severely tests every virtue we might exercise in relation to God's world, to other people, and to the future. But while climate change is widely discussed and is quite possibly the single most urgent issue facing the human species today, it is still not widely understood. While some thinkers are all but certain that "the apocalypse is coming,"[3] others cite human beings' repeated failures to predict the end of the world as reason to ignore such concerns. "After millennia of falsely predicting the apocalypse," writes one author, "humanity has become understandably flippant."[4]

At a March 25, 2009, hearing of the U.S. House Subcommittee on Energy and Environment concerning climate change, Representative John Shimkus de-emphasized the importance of thissue by quoting God's words to Noah after the epic flood that destroyed the whole earth: "I will never again curse the ground because of humankind, for the inclination of the human heart is evil from youth; nor will I ever again destroy every living creature as I have done. As long as the earth endures, seedtime and harvest, cold and heat, summer and winter, day and night, shall not cease" (Genesis 8:21-22). As Noah's ark touched land, God promised that the world would never again be flooded. Representative Shimkus argues that these Bible verses have something to teach those who are unduly worried about climate change, and he followed the quote with this statement of belief: "The Earth will end only when God decides it is time to be over. . . . This earth will not be destroyed by a flood."[5] This demonstrates an admirable willingness to relate faith and politics, and Shimkus is right to raise some suspicion about apocalyptic "doomsday" scenarios that predict the end of human civilization or all life because of climate change. Such nightmares about the end of the world are neither helpful for environmentalists nor authentic expressions of Christian faith.

However, insofar as Shimkus implies that Christians do not have to worry about climate change, he is wrong. Many of our neighbors know this all too well; climate change is *already* causing suffering across the world, a fact that one can ignore only with willful blindness. Christian faith, as Dietrich Bonhoeffer modeled it, is not about denying the real problems of the world but instead about diving into those problems and their perplexities without reservation. While climate change may not signal the end of the world, it is undeniably a challenge facing anyone who wishes to live fully and whole-heartedly in God's world in the twenty-first century.

Committing to faithful this-worldliness in a time of global warming requires, first, getting basic facts straight. A good place for such facts is the Intergovernmental Panel on Climate Change (IPCC), a collaboration of thousands of scientists who report to a coalition of national governments about the state of knowledge on this issue. In their 2013 scientific report, the IPCC notes that while some changes in climate are natural, there is "unequivocal evidence" that contemporary changes are largely caused by the greenhouse gases emitted by human beings in industrial cultures.[6] The most important of these gases is carbon dioxide (CO_2), which is released in substantial quantities every time human beings burn fossil fuels. Atmospheric CO_2 is measured in "parts per million," and there were 280 parts per million before the industrial revolution. In February of 2013, there were 398. These molecules capture the sun's heat in the atmosphere, thereby contributing to warmer average temperatures. The effects of this warming are clearly evident: the first twelve years of the twenty-first century were among the warmest years ever recorded. These rising average temperatures do not just mean we will have to turn up the air conditioner in the summertime; they cause the world's sea level to rise as oceans expand and ice melts, which in turn releases even more gases that have been frozen for thousands of years. The IPCC reports that climate change is already having serious impacts on both natural and human systems: glaciers are shrinking, nonhuman species habitat is shrinking and pushing some species toward extinction, agriculture is becoming more difficult in many parts of the world, extreme weather events are increasing, and the health and well-being of poor, vulnerable, and marginalized human populations are particularly threatened.[7]

The full reality of climate change is highly complex, but the basics are these: the average temperature on earth is going up because of industrial human activity; weather is becoming less certain and, at least in some places, less hospitable to human and other forms of life. God may have promised Noah never to destroy all life and to maintain the seasons forevermore, but human beings are making life more difficult for many creatures and changing the character of the seasons. For Christians to be faithful, to commit to this-worldliness, we must not presume that God will simply deliver humanity from the mess we have made. We must instead accept these facts as part of the world God has called us to care for, and we must use our God-given reason to address it.

Faith also requires a particular commitment to identify and respond to suffering in the world. Climate change is already causing human suffering, and it will cause more in the future. The citizens of New York and New Jersey suffered when Hurricane Sandy hit their shores in 2012 and caused tens of billions of dollars' worth of damage to people's homes and livelihoods. Without a doubt, flooding was more severe because the sea level in New York Harbor is one foot higher than it was in 1900 due to erosion and climate change.[8]

The citizens of Bangladesh are also suffering from climate change: not only is their nation frequently beset by worsening tropical cyclones; they also find it slowly disappearing because so much of it is so close to sea level. Much of the land that is left is becoming too salty for habitation and agriculture. This has important social implications: poverty increases, and women and girls often cannot go to school because they have to spend their days walking to find clean water for their families.

In 2013, Typhoon Haiyan, the most powerful typhoon ever to hit land, killed thousands of people in the Philippines. Most experts agree that climate change is increasing the frequency and severity of such storms and so is partly responsible for that suffering. If Christians are committed to loving our neighbors, if we follow Bonhoeffer's example of seeing God's suffering right here in the world, then we cannot turn a blind eye to the human costs that are already being wrought by climate change. This is not just a far-off problem that will affect the world of our children or grandchildren someday; it is happening now and has been happening for over a century. As activist and journalist Bill McKibben puts it, "Forget the grandkids; it turns out this was a problem for our parents."[9]

After faithfully committing to take climate change seriously, there are different ways to act on it, such as purifying one's own life by shrinking one's carbon footprint, seeking international agreements and sweeping political solutions, or trusting in technological innovations and human creativity to find solutions. The path of eco-virtue is to seek a golden mean among all three of these options, each of which raises vital questions such as, *In what or whom should we place our faith? To what or whom should we be faithful?* These questions offer the keys to finding sensible and virtuous responses to the complex problem of climate change.

Faith in Individuals: Solving Climate Change
One Person at a Time

If climate change is caused by choices about transportation, food, and consumerism made by individuals in industrial societies, then it makes sense to look for solutions in our own lives. This perspective places faith in the potential of individual human beings to inspire global change through responsible choices and the power of example. A representative figure for this approach is Colin Beavan, who named himself "No Impact Man" when he and his family spent a year faithfully trying to eliminate all of their own negative environmental impacts.

Beavan, a new father, was driven to this radical lifestyle experiment by anxiety over climate change and the world his daughter would inherit. He had known about global warming for years, but one day its reality set in and shook him to his core: "We burn too many fossil fuels, the sky gets blanketed with carbon dioxide and other greenhouse gases, the planet warms up, the ice caps melt, the polar bears can't get to their food, they eat each other's babies."[10] Beavan suddenly realized that his own consumer habits were causing others' suffering. He was also troubled by the realization that this wanton consumption was not, in fact, making him or his friends and neighbors any happier. Quite the contrary—they were stressed, cynical, and depressed about their lives much of the time, despite their wealth and privilege.

In response to the world's suffering and his own unhappiness, Beavan had to fight against deep feelings of helplessness. In the past, he had shrugged his shoulders about the environment, feeling concern but not knowing what he could do about it. He had lacked any confidence that he could take action, had no basic sense of agency. The solution he finally found was to change the one thing he could control: his own way of life. For his No Impact year, Beavan approached climate change not as a top-down political problem to be solved by policies or institutions but as a problem to be solved at the grassroots by a concerned individual, making different choices about his consumption, immediately and every day. "I was coming to think my political views had too often been about changing other people," he writes; "I made the mistake of thinking that condemning other people's misdeeds somehow made me virtuous." He decided, instead of preaching to others, "Maybe I ought first to worry about changing myself."[11] Christians might hear an echo of Jesus' advice: "First, take the plank out of your own eye, and then you will see clearly to take the speck out of your brother's eye" (Luke 6:42).

As No Impact Man, Beavan and his family committed themselves to removing the planks from their own eyes: creating no garbage (apart from what could be composted in a worm bin), eating food grown within a 250-mile radius, using no electricity, and even living without toilet paper. He gave up long-distance travel because of the incredible amount of CO_2 that airplanes release into the atmosphere: "Short of setting up an oil refinery in my bathroom, flying . . . is about the most carbon-intensive thing my family and I can do."[12] However, Beavan's story does not primarily emphasize such sacrifices. Instead, he focuses on the unexpected rewards he discovered. He lost weight, got more sleep, and felt healthier; he spent more quality time with his friends and became a better parent. Such behaviors and habits changed him, and by the end of his year of no impact he was a new, happier person.

Beavan's project demonstrates faith in the individual human capacity for change. He believes that people have the power to make themselves better and to improve the world one by one. In this approach, the decision about how to respond to climate change is primarily a decision for individuals. Moreover, he actually trusts human beings to do the right thing once they are aware of the situation, rather than throwing caution to the wind and "partying like it's 1999." He writes: "I suppose we could decide to burn hot and short. We could be the Hunter S. Thompson of species. I'm just suggesting that we should at least wake up long enough to make it an active decision. And yes, it's our decision. It's a decision that belongs to us. Not to the government. Not to big business. It belongs to us."[13] While Beavan acknowledges that humans do often behave in destructive ways, he is confident that we are not helplessly destined to do so. He has faith that individuals who really want to change the world can do so, beginning by changing themselves.

Of course, Colin Beavan knows that global environmental change will require collective action in the form of government regulations (he went so far as to run for public office in New York in 2012) and new technologies. But he does not put his faith primarily in institutions or inventions. He puts his faith in the goodwill of individuals. Transformation must begin, as his did, with people asking themselves "meaning-of-life questions" about who they are, what they want, and whether their habits are moving themselves and their world in the right direction.[14] The keys to long-term environmental health and human flourishing are thoughtful and engaged individuals, faithful to their values and committed to living them out. These, according to No Impact Man, are the best tools available for fostering cultural change in the face of climate change.

Faith in Institutions: Solving Climate Change with Politics

Not all climate activists share Colin Beavan's faith in the power of individual conscience and personal action. Others believe the urgency of the situation calls for immediate, large-scale solutions, so they turn instead to governmental institutions and legal processes. These systems, if they work well, can motivate (or force) whole societies to cut back on their consumption, to redistribute the burden of climate change away from the poorest victims, and to mobilize the entire human race for the monumental work of adapting to the changing world. From this perspective, solving a global issue such as climate change primarily requires changing the minds of voters and drawing the attention and commitment of political leaders with the authority to do something about it.

One advocate in this category is the progressive author and activist Naomi Klein, who regularly defends governmental initiative and regulation against conservatives and neoliberals who advocate smaller government and economic freedom. For Klein, the steady rise of global temperatures and the increase in extreme weather events reveal basic and profound flaws in libertarian economics, because the "blindingly obvious roots of the climate crisis" can be found in "globalization, deregulation, and contemporary capitalism's quest for perpetual growth."[15] The free market caused this problem, she asserts, so the free market cannot solve it. Unchecked capitalism has created apparently infinite consumer demand and has recklessly expanded consumption without any regard for the limits of nature's finite, closed systems.[16] Furthermore, she argues, the free market best serves the interests of the rich rather than the poor, which exacerbates the problem because it is the poor who are "on the front lines" of climate change.

Given the inability of markets to solve climate change in a timely fashion, Klein believes that the best response to this challenge is strong government action designed to restrict harmful economic activity: higher taxes on polluting industries and higher price tags on fossil fuels, nationalization of some corporations, as well as a return to long-term planning to ensure that communities are prepared for changing climate conditions. As Klein admits, these goals are unabashedly liberal, putting faith in the possibilities of constructive government action: "Climate change supercharges the pre-existing case for virtually every progressive demand on the books, binding them into a coherent agenda based on a clear scientific imperative."[17]

Opponents of "big government" might offer a knee-jerk critique of Klein's "socialist" agenda, but it is important to note that she is not advocating strictly centralized government. While she believes in the need for a strong legislative authority, she does not hope to banish private enterprise. Rather, she understands government as a necessary check on the otherwise unlimited power of international corporations; without government, corporations are at liberty to extract resources, manipulate people into exploitative working conditions, encourage excess consumption, and avoid responsibility for the climate change that they have helped to bring about.[18] While she does not seek to establish a single world government, she does hope for increased international agreements about climate change, because only coalitions of nations can properly regulate and monitor the excesses of international corporations.

Klein hopes that governmental action can empower individuals and local communities to control their own lives. She envisions "community-controlled renewable energy, local organic agriculture [and] transit systems genuinely accountable to their users." The job of politics, as Klein presents it, is not to take away individual agency; it is to enhance the control that people exercise over their own lives, which becomes all the more important in a world of changing climate and extreme weather.[19]

Naomi Klein's argument reveals much about the faith implied by political approaches to climate change. Her basic commitment is to democracy, the bottom-up development and control of communities and nations by their citizens. She believes global capitalism has caused and exacerbated climate change because it ceded power to giant corporations, giving control over the future to corporate boards rather than citizens, structuring the economy for short-term profits and rapid growth to benefit the few rather than for a healthy, sustainable future for all. Democratic politics is the answer, she thinks, because it is a sphere in which—at least ideally—everyone has equal power. Unlike in markets where one person can hold exponentially more buying power than another, the ideal of democracy means one person, one vote.

Klein rightly believes that addressing climate change will require big changes in economic systems, and it will require the biggest sacrifices from those who have benefited the most from extracting, selling, and burning fossil fuels. Such change will be possible only if everyday citizens band together to take political action, the substance of true democracy. Political solutions to climate change require faithfulness to the ideals of democracy, including the equal weight of all voices regardless of wealth and a genuine trust that people empowered with such decisions can and will make good decisions.

This faith in democracy characterizes many climate activists who seek to stir the hearts of citizens on the ground in hopes of motivating their elected leaders. The organizers at 350.org ask people across the world to produce photos and videos that will embolden those leaders who consider carbon taxes and international commitments at meetings in Kyoto, Rio, and Copenhagen.[20] The mayors of over one thousand U.S. cities signed an agreement to reduce the carbon emissions of their cities as a way to motivate Congress to change national laws. Student environmental groups at colleges and universities lobby their presidents and deans to purchase carbon offsets for campus power consumption and to design efficient new campus buildings to reduce their schools' impact.[21] These are political solutions, citizens responding to climate change not merely by avoiding this or that product or voting for this or that person but by committing to institutional change, putting their faith in the democratic process in order to have a positive impact upon the earth.

Faith in Innovation: Solving Climate Change with Technology

Beavan's and Klein's personal and political approaches to climate change share a sense of urgency, a belief that this issue is not merely an abstract problem down the road but an imminent crisis calling for the restructuring of lives and societies right now. However, there is another perspective that raises skepticism of this assumption, putting faith in innovation rather than in governmental institutions or individual altruism. Such skeptics have confidence that emerging technologies will best address our problems without the need for either Klein's political upheaval or Beavan's drastic personal sacrifice.

Danish statistician Bjørn Lomborg became famous as "the skeptical environmentalist" when he released a book of that name in 1998. Lomborg agrees with other environmentalists that human beings must recognize problems and make changes in the ways we relate to the rest of the world. However, he is dubious about dire predictions or demands for drastic changes. This skepticism shapes Lomborg's approach to global warming. He accepts scientific evidence that climate change is real and caused by human beings but says that this is no reason to make drastic social or political changes. In a book provocatively entitled *Cool It: The Skeptical Environmentalist's Guide to Global*

Warming, he cautions against "hysteria and headlong spending on extravagant CO_2 cutting programs at an unprecedented rate."[22] If climate change is understood as drastic and urgent, he worries, people will ignore the costs and unintended consequences of their imprudent responses to it while neglecting other vital problems such as poverty, disease, and hunger. Lomborg argues not only that these other issues are more threatening to human life than climate change but also that our societies are better equipped to solve them in the near term. In other words, he would rather fix what can be fixed than waste time and money on something that is beyond our current capacities.

Lomborg worries about approaches like Naomi Klein's, which call for enforced drastic cuts in carbon emissions, because he fears that the benefits of such cuts are far outweighed by the "staggering amount" by which they would reduce the global economy. He believes the world would lose $40 trillion by 2100 if it followed popular political proposals to limit climate change,[23] and he fears that a less prosperous human race would be less equipped to deal with all its problems, climate change included. Referencing the international Kyoto accords that seek to reduce worldwide carbon emissions, Lomborg writes: "I hope that in forty years we will not have to tell our kids that we went for a long series of essentially unsuccessful command-and-control Kyotos that had little or no effect on the climate but left them poorer and less able to deal with problems of the future. I also hope we will not have to say that we focused monomaniacally on global warming, neglecting most or all of our other challenges."[24] People's primary responsibility to future generations, Lomborg argues, is to ensure that they are as wealthy and as healthy as possible. So the best solution to a problem like climate change is to ensure that the economy is growing.

Lomborg's faith is primarily placed in technological innovation. He is confident that human beings in a healthy economy can invent solutions to whatever problems we face. He not only believes in the power of creativity but is also faithfully committed to promoting, enabling, and fostering it. While Colin Beavan emphasizes the negative impacts of human beings on the earth, Lomborg believes that our net effect on the planet is positive. Contemporary societies "are actually leaving the world a better place than when we got it." As technology and civilizations have developed, human well-being "has vastly improved in every significant measurable field and . . . it is likely to continue to do so."[25] One can hardly imagine a more devout statement of faith in human innovation.

In keeping with this faith, Lomborg edited a collection of essays entitled *Smart Solutions to Climate Change*, emphasizing that the response to this global problem should involve more research and development of new technologies rather than more government rules or personal sacrifices. The authors in his book explore large-scale engineering projects that capture and sequester carbon dioxide, ways to increase the efficiency of existing machines, and strategies to strengthen new energy sources that do not require fossil fuels. The book suggests that the most beneficial and efficient response to climate change might be something called "marine cloud whitening," which involves creating numerous artificial clouds over the ocean to reflect the sun's heat back into space and potentially offset the heat trapped by greenhouse gases.[26] This proposal to engineer the climate would be appalling to those who do not want humans to change the workings of the natural world, but it makes perfect sense to those who have faith in the power of human innovation to make the world a better place.[27]

Climate change is a real problem, but advocates of technological innovation caution that it should not be used as an excuse to limit the human capacity to creatively solve problems. Lomborg trusts that when human beings work together, carefully and diligently calculating the costs and the benefits of our actions, we can solve problems. Climate change calls for new ideas, and Lomborg is certain that such ideas will come in plenty of time, as long as our personal and political choices do not get in their way.

Faithfulness to God: The Virtue of Commitment

In response to climate change, some put their faith in individuals, others in institutions, and still others in innovation. Christians, of course, are primarily called to faith in God. Our ultimate commitment is not to personal transformation or politics or technology; it is rather to the God who makes each of these things possible. Our faith is not in human structures, human decisions, or human creations; it is in the God who created humanity. However, as Dietrich Bonhoeffer demonstrated, the virtue of faith is not simply about pledging allegiance to God. Faith is about people choosing to live their lives fully committed to the world in which God has placed them; it is about how people respond to the problems and perplexities of that world, about what people do in response to the very real suffering all around them. A Christian concerned about climate change cannot simply substitute belief in God for belief in technology, politics, or personal change. Rather, Christians must transform the ways we engage all three. A faithful response to climate change, a faithful effort to live fully in the world of global warming, requires commitment to political, personal, and technological transformation.

Commitment to Conversion: Faithful Personal Transformation

Christianity has traditionally been a religion of conversion, built on stories about lives changed when Jesus called a fisherman to come to shore, when the apostle Paul was blinded by the light, and when people like Dietrich Bonhoeffer decided to put their lives on the line for their neighbors. This faith is about transformation of the self, about repenting for—which is to say "turning from"—the past and being reformed for a better kind of life.

In this spirit, Christians should find much to resonate with in the story of No Impact Man. His, too, is a story of conversion: he recognized that he was doing wrong, repented of his old habits, and committed to a new kind of life; that new life transformed him in ways he could not have predicted. Colin Beavan suggests that climate change is a call to conversion. The struggles of polar bears in the arctic, the struggles of the poor in Pakistan, and the perils facing future generations should inspire people to a new life today. Furthermore, Beavan offers a reminder that conversion is not just a turn away from sin but also a movement *toward* something better: committing to less consumption and less negative impact on the environment means not only losing the familiar comforts to which people in the industrialized world have grown accustomed. It also means finding new joy in our families and local communities, in life's simple pleasures, in free time and quiet, in a life well lived. Beavan's conversion gave him courage to engage in more widespread political action instead of merely whining and hand-wringing over cappuccinos.

Faith in God and faithfulness to God's world require conversion, and conversion helps Christians to align more fully with the world God wants for us. Those concerned about climate change might read Beavan's account of his secular conversion alongside the thirty-second Psalm, which tells a similar story. The psalmist reports that life in sin is painful and unsatisfying: "While I kept silence, my body wasted away through my groaning all day long." But then the psalmist admits to sin and finds forgiveness, addressing God: "I said, 'I will confess my transgressions to the Lord,' and you forgave the guilt of my sin . . . you preserve me from trouble; you surround me with glad cries of deliverance" (Psalm 32:3-7). Similarly, those who seek deliverance from the scary implications of a changed climate must begin by recognizing our own transgressions. Faith in God means admitting to one's failings and repenting of them; Christians must admit that most of us have thus far failed to understand, to take responsibility for, and to deal with our impact upon the climate of God's earth.

Conversion truly based upon a faith in God has the potential to accomplish even greater transformation than just one individual's life. Conversion is something individuals do, but it also happens in communities: Christ called his disciples to convert and then to preach to "all the nations" to form an enduring Christian community. Dietrich Bonhoeffer learned from his church what it meant to commit to the Christian faith and spent years training future pastors to create nurturing faith communities.[28] Faith in God means not just individual change but also a new kind of community. Christian conversion to live more responsibly on earth should therefore involve communities, seeking not only to reduce our own negative impacts on the earth but also to inspire our churches and our neighborhoods to conversion as well. A Christian response to climate change must indeed have faith in the power of individuals to change but must not stop at private virtue.[29]

Commitment to the Poor: Faithful Engagement in Democracy

Naomi Klein's faith in politics offers one way to change communities as well as individuals. Klein expands the call from personal conversion to repentance on a global scale, asking for basic changes in the ways political structures regulate and tax CO_2 and other greenhouse gases and demanding democratic reform to ensure that everyone can more readily make responsible decisions toward a better future.

Perhaps the most important insight from Naomi Klein's perspective on climate change is that this problem is having the most impact on the poor, the people "on the front lines" of climate change. The world's poor tend to have contributed the least to climate change but are, unjustly, the most likely to be driven from their homes and livelihoods by rising seas and extreme weather events. Christians should take this very seriously, because our faith calls us to serve Christ by serving the poor, to recognize their suffering as the suffering of God. If climate change is hurting the poor in particular, then it demands a particular response from Christians.

Ecumenical Patriarch Bartholomew, the most prominent figure in Orthodox Christianity, regularly makes this point when he speaks about environmental issues: "The ecological problem of pollution is invariably connected to the social problem of poverty; and so all ecological activity is ultimately measured and properly judged by its impact upon people, and especially its effect upon the poor."[30] Christians are called to respond to climate change, if for no other reason than because it hurts the poor. Individual and small-scale charity is not enough; faith means addressing systems that leave poor people paying the price for climate change while the rich draw benefits from burning fossil fuels and freely emitting CO_2. This is a systematic and institutional injustice, undemocratic and cruel, that cries out for political change.

People of faith can therefore join enthusiastically with Naomi Klein by committing to a new kind of politics in which all voices are heard and all people's concerns are taken seriously. Social and governmental institutions should be reformed to give people more control over their own and their family's lives, to prevent multinational corporations from unduly influencing national policies, and to empower communities to produce energy renewably and grow food responsibly. Behavior will change when regulations, taxes, and incentives encourage it to do so. Global climate change, in other words, requires global political change.

However, not all Christians will go as far as Klein in embracing left-wing politics. Not everyone believes that the response to climate change is necessarily an affirmation of "virtually every progressive demand on the books." Christians must be open to ideas and initiatives from all sides of the political spectrum. Faith in God means moving beyond an unquestioning trust in any single political party or agenda; it means testing all ideas against our love for God and for our neighbors. The question for Christians is not whether a political solution fits into a human agenda but rather whether it helps to alleviate the sufferings of God and God's people in the world.

Openness to a wide range of political solutions is particularly vital in the face of a complex global problem like climate change and in the pluralistic world of diverse nations and peoples. Again, Ecumenical Patriarch Bartholomew offers a helpful insight, noting that as the world warms, "We are all in this together. . . . Let us listen to one another; let us work together; let us offer the earth an opportunity to heal so that it will continue to nurture us."[31] Working and listening together is a brave political act. Anyone who cares about the suffering of the poor and wants to live faithfully and fully in God's world should at least listen generously to Klein's political views, as well as to the views of those who disagree with her, seeking enough agreement to take political action together.

Commitment to Humanity: Faithful Use of Technology

Finally, faith in God should also influence Christians' confidence in technological solutions to climate change. When engineers propose creating artificial clouds to counterbalance the warming caused by CO_2 and other gases, our response must be faithful. Of course, there is no single faithful answer to such proposals. Christians may be thrilled by the notion of acting as "co-creators" with God, using the ingenuity and care imbued by the Creator to modify the world, or they might dismissively compare such engineering projects to the heights of hubris and the Tower of Babel.[32] There is room in Christianity both to celebrate human innovation and also to be suspicious of it. Somewhere in between lies a golden mean.

Christians should take Bjørn Lomborg and others like him seriously enough to realize that technological innovation truly has helped to do good things like feed the hungry and heal the sick. It has also helped to reduce the environmental impact of concerned people. There are many reasons to be hopeful about efforts to develop renewable energy sources; to create more efficient ways to transport people, food, and necessities across the world; and to prevent emissions from continuing to alter the earth's climate. However, the danger of such inventions and efficiencies is that they encourage us to use more: our lightbulbs are more efficient than they were thirty years ago, but now our total energy use has increased; airplanes are more efficient than they used to be, but that has made flying cheaper so more people can do it more often.[33] Technology, in other words, both solves and creates problems.

Christians must not dismiss technological innovation, nor must we pledge unconditional fidelity to it. If our faith is in God, then we must admit our climate-changing behavior and the harms it has done, and we must use all available means—including technology but also political and social institutions and individual initiative—to help the poorest people who suffer for our sins. Technology cannot solve all our problems and does not deserve our unquestioning faith. All the technology in the world will not save us if we are not also committed to the pursuit of the life-giving reign of God.

Dietrich Bonhoeffer, the German theologian who offered this chapter's definition of faith, offers a guide for faithful approaches to technological innovation. Ten years before he was imprisoned, Bonhoeffer observed that there are two ways to treat technology: to be ruled by it or to rule it. He makes the interesting observation that when people allow technology too large a place in their lives, they become its servants. At our worst, he writes,

"Human beings are made prisoners, slaves" of technology. When this happens, the earth is "no longer *our* earth, and thus we become strangers to the earth."[34] This is the opposite of faithfulness, the opposite of living completely *in this world*. Faithful use of technology, by contrast, recognizes that human beings are created to "rule over" the things that we make. Human beings are not supposed to be defined by our creations; we are instead defined by our creator. When people treat technology as a tool with which to serve God in this world—by helping the poor, by healing ecosystems—we come closer to living out God's intention. The faithful person learns, with Bonhoeffer, that "in my entire being, in my creatureliness, I belong completely to this world. It bears me, nurtures me, and holds me."[35] Technology is not itself a virtue; human beings should not serve it nor cultivate it for its own sake. Instead, human beings should be creatures of God who use technology only in order to live more fully in the world.

Throughout the twenty-first century, human beings will have to consider hard questions about technological innovation, balancing an increase in energy production with the reduction of the human footprint on earth, or discerning whether the creation of artificial clouds is the most responsible and wise approach to our problems. These will be challenging discussions. Christians can engage them faithfully if we act as wise servants of God rather than blind servants of technology.

There is no obvious solution to climate change. It is an enormous problem with diverse causes that calls for diverse responses. Christians facing this issue must have faith, and being faithful means committing ourselves every day to living in God's world, throwing ourselves into God's arms, and joining God's work of reducing suffering. Christian faith calls us to commit to the earth, to the poor, and to our own conversion.

Faithfulness is required to live on a warming planet, to love neighbors as the world grows even more dangerous, and to serve God. Christians do not yet know how to live unreservedly in the duties, problems, successes and failures, experiences, and perplexities of climate change. We will continue to struggle to balance technological innovation, institutional reform, and individual commitment in responding to this problem. But by recognizing that climate change calls for fidelity to God, and by acting to alleviate the suffering in God's world, we can nurture the virtue of faith that will allow us to move in the right direction.

Learning Faith

In February of 2013, the members of the Quaker meeting in Dover, New Hampshire, made the decision to divest the church's money from energy companies dealing in fossil fuels. "Because of our deep concern over the changing climate," they wrote to their investment agency, "we could no longer in good conscience remain invested." Withdrawing their investments from all fossil-fuel-related stocks, they then wrote to other Quaker groups asking them "to take a similar step toward a future which will eventually allow us to tread more lightly upon the Earth." They urged their peers to "look now to investing in the future, rather than in the past."[36]

Quakers, a common name for the Religious Society of Friends, are a congregational Christian denomination with a long history of social activism. In the United States, Quakers were among the most prominent voices opposing slavery from colonial times up to the Civil War. The Dover Friends Meeting appealed directly to this history when they wrote to their investment company: "John Woolman, a Quaker from Mount Holly, New Jersey, traveled to Friends Meetings in frontier regions of what became the United States, and in England, urging fellow Quakers to stop participation they had in the slave trade, and abolish slavery. . . . It is our belief that a modern day John Woolman would urge his fellow Quakers to divest from any stock or fund that contains shares of fossil fuel companies."[37] The same spirit of faith that animated antislavery activism also animates this appeal not to support companies that profit from harmful energy production and consumption.

These Quakers are one example of a broader international movement using divestment as a strategy to bring about positive change. If the use of fossil fuels is damaging the world we all depend upon, this movement argues, then the only virtuous thing to do is to stop funding fossil fuel companies while investing proactively in other kinds of industries and alternative energy technologies. Furthermore, just as the Friends in Dover traced their move to the antislavery activism of the past, the international divestment movement compares its work to political movements in the 1970s and 1980s that divested from South Africa in order to protest its unjust conditions of apartheid.[38]

Divestment attempts to create widespread institutional change by exerting consumers' economic pressure and changing public opinion. Of the approaches to climate change discussed in this chapter, it resonates most with Naomi Klein's. Unsurprisingly, Klein celebrates divestment and has argued most passionately for environmental organizations to join in the trend and divest from fossil fuel stocks. She writes: "One would assume that green groups would want to make absolutely sure that the money they have raised in the name of saving the planet is not being invested in the companies whose business model requires cooking said planet, and which have been sabotaging all attempts at serious climate action for more than two decades."[39]

The basic logic of Klein's argument and the Quaker meeting in Dover is sound: to fight climate change, one should first ensure that one is not actively contributing to the problem. But an activist focused on individual reform, like Colin Beavan, might point out that divestment by itself is not enough: whether or not Christians reflect privately on divestment or discuss it together, they are complicit in climate change every time they drive to church or turn on the lights and heat in the building once they get there. As long as environmental organizations are printing their inspiring calendars and annual reports on paper (most of which end up in recipients' trash or recycling bins), they are using energy and perpetuating a destructive system. To truly separate from the causes of climate change requires far more than a simple investment decision.

Another critique of the divestment movement might say that in fact it goes too far, creating a divisive atmosphere in which energy companies are driven into a defensive posture rather than encouraged to collaborate and innovate with those concerned about climate change. An activist like Bjørn Lomborg, who places his faith in technological change, might encourage environmentalists to stay invested in energy companies so that they can continue to profit from fossil fuel industries while also having a seat at the table to influence new directions for those industries. If the solution to climate change will come from new technology, *engaged* investment is a far more reasonable and productive strategy than divestment.

Faith is about commitment to the world, to other people, and to God. Investments reflect commitment as well, and it is appropriate for Christians to ask, out of faith, what we should support with our money. This is a question that most personally affects those individuals with enough resources to make private investments, but it is also a question for anyone who is part of a church, a denomination, a university, a business, or an organization with funds to invest. In a world of climate change, faithful investment is a challenge, and the Quakers in Dover have demonstrated one faithful response. The choices we make about our investments, like all other choices, shape our ability to commit ourselves virtuously and faithfully to God's world.

Questions for Discussion

1. How does it change your understanding of faith to think about it as "faithfulness" or "fidelity" rather than just "belief"?

2. Do you agree with Bonhoeffer's idea that engagement with the world's "problems and perplexities" is the best way to genuine Christian faith? Why might some Christians seek to keep their distance from the world?

3. Why do you think the idea of human-influenced climate change remains so controversial, despite years of widespread agreement in the scientific community? What kinds of evidence do you think people need in order to take this problem seriously?

4. What are the strengths and weaknesses, costs and benefits, of each approach to climate change: technological innovation (Lomborg), institutional change (Klein), and individual repentance (Beavan)? Which one appeals to you most readily, and which ones are harder for you to support?

5. If you are part of a church or school with investments or endowments, or if you yourself have any investments, do you know to what extent those funds are invested in fossil fuel stocks? Would you support divestment from such stocks? What is one other concrete action you believe individual Christians and/or Christian communities should take in response to climate change?

7

HOPE

Between Despair and Presumption about Human Fertility

Population Bombs or Fruitful Multiplication?

You're not actually mammals. . . . Every mammal on this planet instinctively develops a natural equilibrium with the surrounding environment but you humans do not. You move to an area and multiply, multiply until every natural resource is consumed. The only way you can survive is to spread to another area. There is another organism on this planet that follows the same pattern. Do you know what it is? A virus. Human beings are a disease, a cancer of this planet, you are a plague.[1]

While this dramatic soliloquy by Agent Smith in the film *The Matrix* is a product of science fiction, the sentiment that it contains is not merely imaginary. It finds echoes in the voices of real people in the early twenty-first century who are concerned about global population growth. "We are a plague on the earth," said Sir David Attenborough of humankind.[2] Organizations such as Population Matters or the European Population Alliance, not to mention China's former "one child" policy, are evidence of a widespread fear that there are too many people—more human beings than the earth can sustain. This can be especially true with regard to Americans, the greediest consumers of the world community, whose individual babies will use up exponentially more natural resources than individual babies anywhere else in the world. "My carbon footprint," writes one American journalist, "is more than 200 times bigger than an average Ethiopian's, and more than 12 times bigger than an average Indian's, and twice as big as an average Brit's."[3] Concern over the effects of her consumption drove this particular journalist to choose not to become a parent. "Far and away the biggest contribution I can make to a cleaner environment is to not bring any mini-me's into the world." She is not alone in her reluctance; in recent years, so many people in the industrialized world are having fewer children that it has led to declining birth rates and worries about a "baby bust."[4]

On the other hand, Christianity has traditionally maintained at least a tenuous connection to the command God gave to the first humans in the Hebrew scriptures: "Be fruitful and multiply, and fill the earth and subdue it; and have dominion over the fish of the sea and over the birds of the air and over every living thing that moves upon the earth" (Genesis 1:28). The God who created humankind "in our image" also declared us "very good," so for Christians to look on human beings as a plague upon the earth would be to exhibit faithless despair with regard to the goodness of God's creation. Of course, not too much later, this very same God was reportedly "sorry that he had made humankind on the earth" (Genesis 6:6), but God nevertheless saw fit to preserve Noah and his family in order that human beings could start anew.[5] For Christians, by far the most important sign of God's regard for humankind is Jesus: God saw fit to be born of a human being, to take on human flesh, and to die a human death. Despite humanity's many flaws and weaknesses, the incarnation has traditionally been interpreted as a crystal clear declaration of the goodness of being created human.

As of this writing, the earth is home to more than 7.2 billion (7,200,000,000) people, and that number grows by over eighty million people each year.[6] The United Nations estimates that there will be between nine and ten billion people on earth by 2050. Perhaps the most famous response to the fear of such numbers was China's one child policy, which generally limited urban families to one child and rural families to two in the most populous nation on earth. Parents who exceeded the limits were charged "social fostering fees" to offset society's costs in educating extra children.[7] Begun in 1979, the policy is now being phased out, but the Chinese government credits it with keeping the nation's population down to the modest 1.3 billion that it is today, avoiding the perils of famine that occurred all too often in the twentieth century.[8] But China's policy was always deeply controversial; critics worried that it created a shrinking labor force, a surplus of boys (and now men), and involuntary sterilizations, abortions, and even infanticide. They argue, moreover, that it was unnecessary. China's population growth had begun to slow even before the policy was implemented because of an economic-demographic shift: as people grow more prosperous, they tend to have fewer children, even without dangerous legal limits on reproduction.

In thinking about population, Christians must balance two legitimate fears—a fear of too many human beings consuming more than the earth can sustain and a fear of too much coercion limiting human freedom. However, as in the cases of courage and faith, fear should not be the primary motivations for people who believe in God and hope for the future signaled by the Gospel of Jesus Christ. Christianity is about hope, recognizing what is possible. The virtue of hope thus represents an ideal place to begin exploring the environmental question of population.

What Is Christian Hope?

"The object of hope," writes Thomas Aquinas, "is a future good, difficult but possible to obtain."[9] We might hope for some things that we can attain by ourselves through our own efforts and natural abilities—a new bike, a fruitful garden, a friendly relationship. But for bigger, ultimate thing,s Thomas says we must lean on God. In particular, "the good which we ought to hope for from God properly and chiefly, is the infinite good which is proportionate to the power of our divine helper . . . eternal life, which consists in the enjoyment of God Himself."[10] In other words, Christian hope is not merely about wanting and willing good things in finite matters but about clinging to the source of ultimate and eternal goodness.

As with all of the virtues, hope should be understood as a golden mean between two extremes. The more obvious of these two extremes is despair, an absence of hope fed by fear. Despair is the sense that we cannot work against fate; it surrenders to future catastrophes that exist only in our imaginations. To despair is to give up on the idea that God intends good for humankind. As such, Thomas argues, it is very dangerous. Despair sees only impossibility, thus making humans "rush headlong into sin, and [they] are drawn away from good works."[11] Despair abandons the belief that anything could be any better than it already is, leading to slothful inaction. Perhaps worse, despair can lead to a stoical detachment, "the most profound alternative to Christian hope,"[12] which discourages us even from caring about the creation God gave us. To believe that the food system of the industrialized world is beyond repair, for example, or that the human race is already doomed to imminent extinction are forms of despair that discourage hopeful action.

At the opposite end of the spectrum from despair is presumption, a perversion of hope. This is not simply a *surplus* of appropriate hope—for indeed, how can one hope too much in God's infinite goodness?—but a *misplaced* hope. This might take the form of hoping that "things will work out" in the natural course of things, without any effort on our part, or it might be blind optimism that we will find a simple and straightforward answer to every problem we face. Genuine hope, according to Aquinas, is not about things simply working out. It must, instead, be tempered by fear, which is a "gift of God." As he puts it, "fear and hope cling together, and perfect one another."[13] It is only by moving through fear—by seeing the outcome one hopes to avoid—that one can develop and work toward an appropriate and meaningful hope. It is only by seeing the future we do *not* want, and committing to work against that future, that we can fully understand the world we do want and figure out how to work toward it. For example, to believe that the proper balance between fossil fuels and renewable energy can be found with absolutely no sacrifice or struggle is a dangerous form of presumption arising from fearless complacency. Because hope emerges and develops in times of trouble or lack, rather than during times of abundance and happiness (there will be no need for hope in eternity, Thomas tells us),[14] fear and suffering are necessary precursors for this virtue.

Thus, to cultivate hope as an environmental virtue is to walk the line between despair and presumption, to learn from our fears and problems but also to recognize that we have the power to address them. Unlike optimism, which simply *expects* a good outcome, hope is a habit of reaching toward a future good: seeing what is wrong, seeing the possibility of good, and then working to make the good a reality.

While Aquinas teaches that hope is ultimately focused on God, this is not an exclusively otherworldly virtue about heaven to the exclusion of earth. Much to the contrary, Aquinas understands the hope of heaven to require provisional hopes along the way, many of which concern the people around us: hope for good instruction from parents, teachers, and pastors to help us attune ourselves to God; hope for good friends and communities to assist in the work of living a good life; hope for the ability and the opportunity to serve God by serving our neighbors.[15] When facing the realities of environmental degradation, we should add hopes for the rest of creation: hope for healthy ecosystems to nurture ourselves, our human neighbors, and other species; and hope for the diversity of creation to reveal God's glory. Because hope implies a lack, especially a lack of final happiness, it will always be with us in this life. But far from being a vision of "pie in the sky," hope—like faith—is deeply rooted in *this* world, with all of its beauties and difficulties, right here and now.

Hope is a vital virtue for any Christian consideration of population. On one hand, the growth in human population is a reason to hope: every birth brings a child of God into the world, and this is rightly reason to celebrate. Every person born offers another possibility to help make the world a better place. On the other hand, population growth is also reason to fear: the increasing number of people on earth means more mouths to feed, more potential to create pollution and consume energy, and more competition for the already stretched resources of the planet. Humankind—as scripture, history, and experience can attest—is a mixed bag. So hope has room to celebrate human fertility but also to fear it, and we learn virtue from seeking the right balance between these two responses.

Seven Billion Is Enough: Fear of Too Many People

The contemporary Western debate over population is frequently traced back to the work of Reverend Thomas Malthus, who published his most famous book, *An Essay on the Principle of Population*, in 1798. An Anglican Christian, Malthus worried most about food scarcity. As he saw it, human populations grow much more rapidly than food supplies, thus leading to inevitable poverty and human suffering.[16] The basis of his argument was the belief that human enterprise is inescapably constrained by nature's limits; when the land's limits are exceeded, "misery and vice" ensue among those who depend on that land for food. His pessimistic vision suggested that population growth could be limited in only two ways: through the "preventative check" of human discipline (at the time, this meant late marriage and sexual abstinence) or the "positive check" of food scarcity by which excess people would starve. Not surprisingly, he advocated for human beings to find moral ways to prevent population growth in order to avoid the unpleasant checks enforced by the natural world.[17]

Malthus wrote in response to contemporaries who believed that they could continually improve food production and distribution to feed ever more people. He believed that such work was in fact a futile and misdirected effort that went against God's plan. To overcome the limits of God's world "is, alas!, beyond the power of man." For Malthus, realizing this frees us for the more worthy work of understanding and aligning ourselves to God's will for humankind, living within the proper limits of the world created for us instead of trying to bend it to human will.[18]

In the centuries since his death, Malthus' name (if not his religious motivation) has come to represent anxiety about human population. In the late nineteenth and early twentieth centuries, England and the United States saw a proliferation of "Malthusian Leagues" dedicated to slowing population growth. Margaret Sanger, an early founder of Planned Parenthood, sought especially "to limit what she saw as the excess fertility of the poor."[19] Today, from the burgeoning movement of individuals who decline to have children for environmental reasons,[20] to efforts among some U.S. taxpayers to cut welfare benefits to families who have more children while receiving public assistance, countless modern enterprises are united by a basic Malthusian claim that having too many people leads to suffering. The number of children should not exceed available resources, and the human population must remain within the limits set by the natural world.

Meanwhile, libertarians who wish to discredit environmentalists worried about population have only to raise the specter of Malthus—who wrote at a time when there were fewer than one billion people on earth—to characterize such arguments as unfounded, alarmist fearmongering.[21] The "Green Revolution" of modern agriculture would seem to have proven Malthus incontrovertibly wrong.[22] With the help of fertilizers and technology, the earth has continued to feed incomprehensible numbers of people. It is worth at least considering, however, that history contains cautionary tales. Take, for example, Easter Island (Rapa Nui). Around the year 500 C.E., when the first Polynesians arrived, the sixty-four-square-mile island was covered with a subtropical forest, including palm trees that could be as wide as six feet around and eighty feet tall. At first the settlers thrived, with a population that grew to at least seven thousand people. However, there apparently came a time when the number of human beings were too numerous for the small island to support in the fashion to which they had grown accustomed, leading to an overharvesting of the trees, erosion of the soil, and widespread famine. When a Dutch explorer visited the island in 1722, he found its famous giant stone heads not surrounded by trees and thriving humans but on a grassy island with only about two thousand people, no other surviving mammals, and dwindling resources.[23] This would seem to offer proof of Malthus' thesis.

Stanford researchers and environmental activists Paul Ehrlich—who published *The Population Bomb* in 1968—and Anne Ehrlich use the story of Easter Island as a warning for the twenty-first century.[24] Drawing on their training in population biology, the Ehrlichs suggest that the basic lesson of Easter Island is about carrying capacity. Every habitat can support a limited number of lives, and every species has a carrying capacity within its habitat. A forest can support a certain number of deer; a pond can support a certain number of fish. If the deer or fish become too plentiful, they begin overconsuming, eating so much of the greenery or the fish lower on the food chain that they must begin competing for food. The only way to correct this situation in a limited habitat is for many of the deer or fish to die off in order for their population to be brought back into balance with their habitat.

Anne and Paul Ehrlich understand human beings as one species among many others. So, like Malthus, they believe humans live under the constraints of biological carrying capacity. While we have expanded our habitat to include most of the planet, the earth is essentially a larger version of the cautionary tale of Easter Island: people must either limit population or watch our civilizations and our resources dwindle through suffering and starvation. The front cover of *The Population Bomb* asserted: "While you are reading these words, three children are dying of starvation—and twenty-four more babies are being born."[25] Since then the Ehrlichs have shifted the focus of their fear from hunger to "resource wars"—conflicts that arise as too many people make claims on too few (or too heavily concentrated) resources, such as wars over oil or water.[26] Global hunger, species starvation and extinctions, and violent battles among humans all seem to be clear biological signs of overpopulation. For the Ehrlichs, the widespread environmental degradation of the planet is proof that we are already encountering the limits of the earth's ability to support human life.

While arguments about population can at times come across as misanthropic or antihuman, the Ehrlichs emphasize that they seek the good of humankind. But the good of humankind requires long-term thinking, not "cramming into the United States (or China, or Nigeria) as many people as possible in the next few decades until those nations self-destruct," instead promoting "permanently sustainable populations in those nations (and on the planet) for tens of thousands, perhaps millions, of years."[27] For the Ehrlichs, shrinking population is the best way to respond to contemporary problems like poverty and injustice. The nations with the most rapid population growth are also among the poorest and least developed, and their increasing numbers place increasing burdens on their already stretched governments and social institutions. Thus, the Ehrlichs argue, the best way to take care of people across the world and into the future is to ensure that there will not be too many of us.

Just as Malthus' vision of doom did not come to pass, a global "population bomb" has not materialized in the way Paul Ehrlich imagined in 1968. Instead, there seem to be localized "explosions" that harshly affect some groups of people, while others remain blissfully insulated from knowledge of the earth's limitations. The question of exactly how many people the earth could sustainably support is too complex a problem to be definitively solved; no one has enough data or enough time to evaluate every resource and its usage. More importantly, the answer depends on *how* human beings live and *how much* of earth's bounty we appropriate to ourselves.[28] There is a big difference between seven billion people living the most consumptive industrial lifestyle—with abundant animal-based diets, jetting from continent to continent, and identifying everything in sight as a resource for human use—and seven billion people subsisting on a more modest diet, a more localized life, and a more cooperative relationship to other species. The Ehrlichs critically label the United States "the Most Overpopulated Nation," suggesting that while our population is not growing as fast as those of others, our rate of consumption and technological expansion have a disproportionate environmental impact.[29] In other words, the earth's carrying capacity is not a given quantity but is relative; it is intimately dependent upon the type of "dominion" exercised by the creatures made uniquely in God's image. Human beings have already "taken over and transformed most of the planet's land surface to support themselves and increasingly have exploited the oceans as well, all at the expense of the rest of nature."[30] To expand this activity with no regard for the rest of the world or the fact that human well-being depends on the earth's health is presumptuously to ignore the realities of nature.

Ultimately, because the Ehrlichs doubt humans' willingness to make radical sacrifices in their consumption, their hope lies in shrinking the world's human population, preferably through fewer births rather than more deaths.[31] They seek to extend birth control and family planning services, calling on rich nations like the United States to fund extensive programs around the world. They also hope to expand opportunities for women, since women with access to education and employment have historically been known to bear fewer children. They do not fully support restrictive measures like China's one child policy, but they do assert that without such a policy, the environmental and social problems in that country would be far worse than they are today. They suggest that while democratic governments would never accept such centralized control of family planning, they should use their powers of taxation and education as means of persuading people to limit family size.[32]

Who Says Seven Billion Is Enough? Fear of Coercion

Not everyone finds the Ehrlichs' concern about overpopulation a healthy or appropriate fear. For example, some contemporary anthropologists have challenged the story the Ehrlichs tell about Easter Island. Mara Mulrooney argues that in fact the people of Rapa Nui intentionally cut down their forests in order to cultivate crops, and they had a very successful record of agriculture. "The new picture that emerges . . . is really one of sustainability and continuity rather than collapse, which sheds new light on what we can really learn from Rapa Nui." She suggests that "based on these new findings, perhaps Rapa Nui should be the poster-child of how human ingenuity can result in success, rather than failure."[33] According to this view, the collapse of the island's population was likely a result of European contact; the people were threatened not by natural limits but by the forces of human colonization.

Of course, there are limits to how many human beings the earth can support. But many environmentalists are far less concerned about reaching these limits than they are about the dangers of human coercion and oppression. For example, development economist and activist Betsy Hartmann argues that fear about population is essentially a fear of our own species. It turns human beings into statistics and then deems those statistics a problem. In her work, including the book *Reproductive Rights and Wrongs*, Hartmann celebrates human ingenuity and freedom, arguing that population fears lead in the wrong direction toward troubling policies and a denial of basic human rights.

Hartmann notes that Thomas Malthus' analysis of population was limited by a lack of social awareness. He did not inquire into the structures that made people poor but instead "confined the complexities of their lives, and the power relationships in which they were enmeshed, within the bounds of a simple and seemingly immutable mathematical law" about food production.[34] Along similar lines, she accuses the Ehrlichs of being more interested in the scientific concept of carrying capacity than in the complexity and richness of actual human lives. This, she says, is "the worst kind of biologism," using scientific studies of other species to make broad generalizations about human beings, ignoring cultural differences and historical contexts and the ingenuity of human beings to change their environments.[35] Hartmann insists that human beings are not mere slaves to our impulses and genetics, who passively respond to external stimuli with no choice, creativity, or freedom.[36]

Betsy Hartmann understands population as a *symptom* of environmental and economic problems rather than a cause. High birth rates are "a distress signal that people's survival is endangered"—they feel the need for lots of backup—so the best way to lower birth rates is to help populations to feel safer through social structures that support rather than limit their freedoms.[37] Her corresponding hope is for a world in which all people have inviolable, individual reproductive freedom as part of their basic human rights. Demographics work out when economic development is equitably distributed, raising standards of living across entire populations rather than merely for the wealthy.

Here Hartmann has hopes of a "demographic transition" by which societies that become more industrialized and more prosperous tend to have fewer children. As people live longer, their children are more likely to survive into adulthood; as they obtain regular access to birth control, they tend to choose smaller families. Thus, the vast majority of growth in population in the next decades will occur in the poorest parts of the world—for example, in rural areas of India, Indonesia, and some African countries.[38] The correlation between wealth and fewer births offers a reason to hope, because it could mean that the solution to overpopulation is economic growth. From this perspective, human beings do not need to work on limiting population growth; we need to work toward a world without poverty. As economic development expands, it brings with it the tools and motivations people need to slow their reproduction, so a wealthier human race will naturally have a more sustainably sized population.

Distrusting the fear of runaway population growth, Hartmann urges environmentalists to decry what she calls "degradation narratives," which insist that people, like locusts, inevitably destroy their environments. Such narratives nurture fear of looming collapse and close off options. Hartmann cautions: "Playing with fear is like playing with fire. You cannot be sure exactly where it will spread."[39]

Having said this, however, Hartmann also uses fear to motivate her readers. In her case, the legitimate fear is a fear of coercion. She cites cases of poor women in the developing world being forced or bribed into taking long-term contraceptives, or even being sterilized, by governmental and nonprofit activists seeking to respond to the population "problem."[40] Motivated to save the world from an expanding population, these activists frequently focus on widespread use of implanted and injected birth control methods, regardless of individual women's circumstances. Furthermore, despite the fact the United States is "the most overpopulated nation," the majority of population activists seem to focus elsewhere, on places where people are poorer and human numbers are expanding more rapidly. The outcome is both imperialistic and sexist: a "population establishment" ends up consisting of wealthy people telling the poor how to live and of men governing the bodies of women.[41]

Hartmann's concern recalls the worst-case scenarios of historical efforts to limit population. Such efforts have too often taken the form of one group of people abusing other peoples they consider inferior: think of Jews murdered in Nazi Germany or Native American women coerced into sterilization in the 1970s.[42] In more recent years, Christian ethicist Traci West has highlighted the rhetorical paradigm of "illegitimacy" as used by American politicians to characterize the children of poor black women. In this framework, African American "birthing—the spreading of life—is considered the spreading of pathology, of disease. And, it is a disease with catastrophic potential."[43] At its root, the thinking behind such efforts asserts that only *some* human lives (usually those most like "us") are worthy to be lived, while others should simply never be born.

To be clear, neither the Ehrlichs nor anyone else in the mainstream of the environmental movement advocates murder or forced sterilization. But Hartmann worries that fears about population represent a slippery slope toward such thinking, undermining an understanding of human rights for *all* people that is based on nothing more than their basic humanity.[44] By reducing people to problems, the fear of population dehumanizes them. Hartmann believes that self-determination is a basic human right: "No matter how perilous the population problem is," she insists, "the use of force or coercive incentives/disincentives to promote population control is an unjustifiable intrusion of government power into the lives of its citizenry."[45] Those who want contraception and those who want children should both have what they want. Hartmann is confident that the more control people have over themselves, the more responsible they will be about family sizes. The population problem is not that people have too much freedom but too little.

Betsy Hartmann agrees with Anne and Paul Ehrlich that there are limits to the natural world, but she strongly disagrees with their insistence that we have already reached this threshold. She also worries that their calls for government incentives and education of the public about the "population explosion" will be misused to force women and the poor to live according to someone else's choices, stifling freedom and therefore stifling the future of the human species. The best population policy, she insists, is "to concentrate on improving human welfare in all its many facets. . . . In fact, the great irony is that in most cases population growth comes down faster the less you focus on it as a policy priority, and the more you focus on women's rights and basic human needs."[46] Hartmann hopes for a world of equity and freedom, where people empowered to make their own choices will find ways to live together and with the earth, free to achieve their full potential.

Christian Hope and Human Population

If Christian hope is a virtue tempered by appropriate fears, what does this mean for Christian understandings of human fertility and global population growth? The Ehrlichs' approach to population is shaped importantly by fears that humankind is destroying the natural resources on which our own flourishing depends and causing both human and animal suffering in the process. The obvious response to this kind of fear is to have fewer children. An approach like Hartmann's, meanwhile, is predominantly shaped in response to fears of abusive authority; coercion, oppression, and even genocide are the almost inevitable results of attempts at population control. Responses to this kind of fear are to improve economic and social conditions so as to bring down numbers by increasing individual freedom and choice.

Neither side gives in to despair: both have hope that human civilizations can coexist with the rest of creation, and both understand the need for some kind of change that is within humankind's power to effect. Using Aquinas' words, both fears can be seen as "a gift from God," yet they represent two different cautions about the future ahead and therefore two different hopes for the world we want to help create.

However, each side would likely see the other as excessively presumptuous: the Ehrlichs would worry that Hartmann's trust in the demographic transition is too simplistically optimistic, counting on the population crisis to take care of itself rather than requiring genuine effort, organization, and work. Hartmann would worry that the Ehrlichs are being presumptuous by taking on too much responsibility, asking governments to make choices for others rather than trusting in human freedom. "There is presumption," says Aquinas, if a person "tends to a good as though it were possible to him, whereas it surpasses his powers."[47] A golden mean in human fertility calls us to walk the narrow path between abdicating the authority that is inherent to us as human beings and doing violence to other humans' dignity by taking on too much authority.

Christians must affirm, foremost, that God's creation is good and that humankind is an integral part of creation. Furthermore, we must affirm our hope that God intends good for humankind. God is, in short, *for* us, such that any fears we might have—whether about the nightmare of environmental degradation or the terrors of government coercion—are relativized by this affirmation. Christians are a hopeful people who lean on God's infinite power and understanding, which exist entirely beyond the narrow realm of our own experience. But Christians are also called to exercise the powers that are given to us as stewards of God's garden. As always, virtue is about balance. A hopeful Christian approach to the issue of population takes seriously the responsibility of human beings toward the rest of creation but does not forget the gifts of human life and human freedom.

Voices like Malthus' or the Ehrlichs' remind Christians that God created human beings to live in relationship with the earth and that our lives are utterly dependent on the land. The lesson that all creatures are subject to creation's limits is a vital one; human beings can flourish only in healthy ecosystems. The prophet Joel attests to this as clearly as any story from contemporary ecology. Written in the wake of a plague of locusts and a drought, Joel is an ancient story of environmental tragedy that emphasizes the intricate interdependence of human beings and land: "Is not the food cut off before our eyes, joy and gladness from the house of God? The seed shrivels . . . the storehouses are desolate; the granaries are ruined because the grain has failed" (Joel 1:16-17). Human beings can thrive only when their land and other creatures are healthy. Thus, the redemption God brings comes first to the land and animals: "Do not fear, O soil; be glad and rejoice, for the Lord has done great things! Do not fear, you animals of the field, for the pastures of the wilderness are green; the tree bears its fruit, the fig tree and vine give their full yield" (Joel 2:21-22).[48] The prophetic message of humankind's dependence on the earth's flourishing is vital to any Christian discussion of population.

But it is also vital to remember, as Hartmann has insisted, that discussions of population must treat human beings in all their complexity and richness. It is alarmingly easy to become so caught up in the overwhelming ideas of billions of people and global demographic trends that we forget the preciousness of each human being; we lose track of the fact that these are real people. Annie Dillard made this point with insightful irony when writing in 1999: "There are 1,198,500,000 people alive now in China. To get a feel for what this means, simply take yourself—in all your singularity, importance, complexity, and love—and multiply by 1,198,500,000. See? Nothing to it."[49] Christians must never dehumanize people as statistical data points or mouths to feed; we are called instead to recognize the humanity of each and every person. Every human being bears God's image. The poor woman with more children than she can support is a child of God. The rich man who consumes more than his share of the earth's resources is a child of God. The Chinese official who enforced her nation's one child policy is a child of God. The population debate is always about living, breathing human beings, beloved by God. In our decision making, we can never forget that we are talking about God's children to whom have been given the gifts of life and freedom.

When it comes to the earth's human population, Christians are called to lean upon the inherent wisdom of God's created order, and so we must recognize that the earth cannot support an unlimited number of people. Yet we are also called to recognize the ways in which that order depends not only upon God's preservation but also upon active human agency, so we must not simply accept an arbitrary limit as foreordained. Human fertility is not a simple matter of hopeless biological determinism; like every other gift given to humankind, it demands both gratitude and stewardship. A Christian attitude toward population is therefore a hopeful attitude, in that it recognizes both what is possible for God and what is possible for humans. Christians hope for a relationship between humans and creation that allows us both to live sustainably amid nonhuman creation and to protect the freedom God gave to humankind.

Learning Hope

Population is a global issue that concerns natural resources, the well-being of other species, economic development, poverty, and countless other complicated topics. However, it is also about the most intimate and personal of topics: having children. What distinguishes this debate from most environmental debates is that virtually everyone reading this book will take action on one side or the other. Though most of us are not oil magnates, politicians, or agricultural engineers, and while none of us is in complete control of our own fertility, most of us will eventually make decisions about whether, when, and how to be sexually active, to use birth control, or to try to become parents. If the virtue of hope truly sheds any light on the issue of population, if it is worth anything at all in the real world, then it should help Christians to consider such personal and pivotal decisions, asking what kind of family God is making possible for us and what we will do to reach toward that goal.

Many Christians feel called to be fruitful and to multiply. Perhaps the most famous advocate for this position is the hierarchy of the Catholic Church, which has forbidden the use of artificial birth control as a disruption of a natural process that God created specifically for the sake of procreation. This is often mistakenly understood to mean that Catholics should have lots and lots of offspring or have no discretion as to how many children they have (think *Monty Python's* catchy tune "Every Sperm Is Sacred"), but that misrepresents the Church's official teaching. Far from being careless or indiscriminate in their procreation, Catholics are called to "responsible parenthood." As such, even though they are forbidden to use chemical (e.g., the Pill) or barrier (e.g., condoms) methods of contraception, they are nevertheless allowed to control their fertility through methods of "natural family planning"—which, generally speaking, involves avoiding intercourse around the time of a woman's ovulation so as to minimize the chances of pregnancy. "With regard to physical, economic, psychological and social conditions," wrote Pope Paul VI in 1968, "responsible parenthood is exercised by those who prudently and generously decide to have more children, *and by those who, for serious reasons and with due respect to moral precepts, decide not to have additional children for either a certain or an indefinite period of time.*"[50] Christians in this view are not passive recipients of children but active participants in decisions about their own fertility.

However, the pope continues by asserting that global population growth is not sufficient reason to stop having children. He acknowledges that population is an issue but insists that it is not sufficient reason to do "violence to man's [*sic*] essential dignity" by proposing solutions based on an "utterly materialistic conception" of humankind.[51] He worries that those who choose not to have children for environmental reasons do violence *to themselves* by viewing their own existence, and that of their potential children, as burdens on the planet. Every child, every one of us, is made fully and uniquely in the image of God, and as such should not be reduced conceptually to "mouths to feed" or "mini-me's."

There are also Protestants who agree with the Catholic Church that children are first and foremost a blessing from God. One evangelical blogger, a father of five, explained that his decision to have a large family was motivated by Christian hope: "It is because we love children, which not everyone does. It is because we are optimistic about the future and believe it is a wonderful thing to come into a world, however fallen, that God is working to redeem. It is because we are willing to make the sacrifices that having a large family inevitably requires, living for others rather than ourselves. And it is because we believe that raising a godly family is a calling from God."[52] Out of thoughtfulness for those who may be unable to have as many children, he hastens to add that "this does not mean that big families glorify God more than small families do. Nowhere does the Bible dictate how many children a family ought to have. We need to be especially sensitive to the heartache that some couples experience in the area of childbirth. Many women lose children to miscarriages. In the providence of God, some couples do not give birth to children at all. We need to understand that a large family is not a sign of godliness." But the clear message here seems to be that couples who *can* have large families *should* have large families; only miscarriage and infertility are appropriate reasons not to. The implication is that those who *choose* to have few children probably do so for less-than-virtuous reasons: they do not love children, they are not optimistic, they are not willing to make sacrifices, or they embrace individualism and ambition. The decision to have many children is a decision to affirm God's goodness and a hope for God's world, to make sacrifices for the sake of others.

An opposing perspective comes from the environmentalist Bill McKibben, a Methodist who makes the case for limiting human fertility in his book *Maybe One*.[53] McKibben suggests that, given the fact that there are now billions of human beings populating the earth, Christians should look at the commandment to "be fruitful and multiply" and "check it off the list" in good conscience.[54] The world is in no danger of running out of people. But unlike some eugenics movements that focused their energies on limiting the fertility of the poor, or of populations in the developing world, McKibben targets the high-consuming citizens of the industrialized world. He argues that it is time for those in the United States and other wealthy countries, who hungrily consume a disproportionate amount of the earth's resources, to limit their fertility, perhaps to have no children or "maybe one." As the grateful father of one daughter, he affirms that having a child is indeed a blessing, an act of hopefulness, and a great joy. He then recounts the vasectomy he had to prevent her from having siblings.

McKibben's position is not widespread, but it certainly has precedent in the Christian tradition. While the Hebrew Bible emphasizes the importance of bloodlines and family ties, the New Testament and early Christianity shifted in the direction of spiritual families, linked not necessarily by biology but by faith. Jesus himself seems to have been single (*The Da Vinci Code* notwithstanding), and the apostle Paul followed his example, urging single Christians to remain lifelong virgins for the sake of having more time and energy to build up the church (1 Corinthians 7). Redemption in Christ means that anyone—even Gentiles—can become part of the body of Christ, regardless of genetic heritage; the Gospel can be spread through interaction and conversion rather than procreation.[55] Thus, it is possible to argue that Christians can, or even should, limit their fertility and focus instead on sharing and living out God's word by caring for others—including others' children.

Some people will decide to have children out of fear—fear of being alone, fear of being selfish, or fear of their mothers-in-law. Some will decide *not* to have children out of fear—fear of changing a relationship, fear of expense, or fear of environmental degradation. But Christians are called to hope rather than fear. "Do not be afraid," scripture says repeatedly. "Do not worry about your life," says Jesus; "Instead, strive for his kingdom, and these things will be given to you as well" (Luke 12:22, 31). While we have much to learn from a healthy respect for the material conditions of our lives on earth, our final and best decisions are made with hope: they take their shape not just from what we fear or what we want but from the truly good life that God makes possible.

Questions for Discussion

1. Hope can be seen as a golden mean between two extremes. What are the inherent costs and benefits of despair? Of presumption? Toward which end of the spectrum do you more often find yourself gravitating?

2. While China's one child policy is being phased out, it remains a quintessential political effort to manage population. Do you think such a policy could ever be justified? Could you imagine yourself ever advocating a rule like that in your own nation?

3. An extreme expression of population fears is the idea that human beings are a "cancer" or a "virus" on the earth. What are the dangers of such an idea? What are the dangers of not noticing the damage that humans can do (and have done) to the earth? What metaphor would you use to describe humanity's relationship to the rest of the planet?

4. Which do you think should take precedence in population policy for the common good: individual liberty (as Betsy Hartmann emphasizes) or environmental protection (as the Ehrlichs emphasize)?

5. Do you hope to have a child or children someday? If you already have a child/children, do you hope to have more? What are (or were) your primary considerations in coming to such an important decision? How are (or were) fear and hope part of the decision-making process?

8

LOVE
Between Public Protest and Personal Transformation

What Is Love?

In the middle of the first century, the apostle Paul authored the most famous words ever written on Christian love. In his Letter to the Corinthians, he addresses a particular church in a particular city with a particular problem. In our own time, however, it is such a popular reading at Christian weddings that it has become almost cliché and therefore hard to give our full attention. To wit: "Love is patient; love is kind; love is not envious or boastful or arrogant or rude. It does not insist on its own way; it is not irritable or resentful; it does not rejoice in wrongdoing, but rejoices in the truth. It bears all things, believes all things, hopes all things, endures all things. Love never ends. . . . And now faith, hope, and love abide, these three; and the greatest of these is love" (1 Corinthians 13:4-13). Christians who feel overly familiar with this well-worn passage might have to fight the urge to think, "Here we go again," when we see it; our eyes may glaze over, and our minds may begin to wander. It is difficult to read it with fresh eyes or listen to it with fresh ears.

Like Paul's famous and profound meditation on it, the word "love" is itself almost too common. It is used incessantly in movies and songs; many people use it multiple times in the course of their daily lives to refer to a snack, a couch, an Internet video. The danger of hearing and talking about love so often is that it can begin to lose its meaning and its complexity; it becomes easy to assume that this core virtue of the Christian life is a simple and straightforward one. When talking about love, it is a challenge for Christians to make the familiar seem strange again.

And "love," however familiar and natural it may seem, *is* a strange idea. One way to make it less familiar is to remind ourselves that this English word stands for four different Greek words: *agapé* or unconditional care, the subject of Paul's letter; *eros* or romantic or sexual attraction; *philia* or friendship, loyalty, and intellectual attachment; and *storgé* or affection, as for one's children. These multiple words call attention to one of the complexities of love: it differs depending on its object. To love one's spouse is different from loving one's child, which is different from loving one's hometown, which is different from loving a pizza topping. Other languages allow for even more nuance: ancient Sanskrit reportedly has almost a hundred words that translate into English as "love."[1]

In traditional Christian virtue ethics, the first of the Greek loves is the most important. *Agapé*, unconditional commitment to another, is the love modeled for us by God; it is love that does not depend on any action or quality in the beloved. God loves human beings without condition, even if we are unworthy of it; so human beings are called to cultivate the virtue of loving one another in the same way. "We love because God first loved us," scripture tells us (1 John 4:19), and God loved us "while we were yet sinners" (Romans 5:8). When Jesus teaches that we should love our neighbors and our enemies, he does not simply advocate a romantic, friendly, or affectionate relationship; rather, he calls us to care unconditionally, regardless of their qualities and characteristics. We may not like our neighbors, and by definition we most certainly do not like our enemies, but to be a Christian means to seek to love them all nevertheless. This is not the kind of love that comes naturally; it requires practice, right thinking, careful development, and commitment. It is this most difficult theological virtue that Paul called "the greatest" of them all, and Thomas Aquinas called "the mother of the other virtues."[2] When we truly love other people, we commit to dealing with them prudently, courageously, temperately, justly, faithfully, and hopefully. Love is therefore a fitting place to end this book's exploration of virtue.

A key task in thinking through the challenges of love is to avoid the platitudes that come quickly to mind. Thoughtful Christians must beware the temptation to believe that "all we need is love"—that the environment will be protected if we just love nature or other persons enough. In such formulations, love becomes its own fundamentalism, its own easy answer that cannot possibly match the complexity and difficulty of real environmental problems.[3] Love is always an appropriate and necessary motive for virtuous Christian action, but it is not a *sufficient* motive without understanding the specifics of each particular situation, the needs of each particular beloved.

Most importantly, love is not complete without the guidance of all the other virtues.[4] Christians are called to love unconditionally but not indiscriminately.

Catholic moral theologian Margaret Farley is an excellent guide through this distinction. Her book *Just Love* emphasizes that not all loves are created equal; there are "wise loves and foolish, good loves and bad, true loves and mistaken loves." The important question for people who seek to be virtuous is, therefore, "What *is* a right love, a good, just, and true love?"[5] Farley's own focus is on justice, and she explains that a "just love" is one that takes its object seriously: love is true and just, right and good, when it is focused on the well-being of the beloved at least as much as the lover. Love must be a response to the truth of the other's situation—her "concrete reality"—a genuine union between the one who loves and the one loved. One does not truly love that which one does not accurately see or perceive; love is false or mistaken when it projects something onto the beloved that is not really there or when it refuses to see the beloved in all her or his or its fullness. While Farley acknowledges that it is possible to "love someone beyond what we can know of him or her"—as human beings must do with God, for example—it is nevertheless the goal of true love to come ever closer truly to knowing the beloved as they *are* rather than merely as we imagine or want them to be.[6]

Love cannot demand that a child be an adult, for example, or that a neighbor agree with us on every political issue, or that a spouse surrender his individuality. A genuinely loving relationship is never one-sided but is rather a co-creation between and among lovers and those who are appropriately loved. Even when the beloved does not return the lover's love—as in the case of loving one's enemies—the Christian task is still to love the enemy precisely by coming to understand her in her "concrete reality," even if that reality involves hatred of, or desire to harm, the one doing the loving. In this case, Farley argues, "Even if we are not touched, awakened in love, by someone who according to some standard appears to be quite unlovable, the view of love that I am suggesting yields an obligation to try to discover the beauty of the other; and short of this, to *believe* that all persons are lovable (loved at least by God) even though we do not 'see' it, at least not at first."[7]

Margaret Farley's focus in *Just Love* is on sexual relationships in particular, but her lessons about love are informed by Christian scripture, tradition, and experience, and they are therefore also powerfully instructive for all who seek to love God, God's children, and God's creation. In order to respond lovingly to problems like climate change, population issues, or toxic waste, Christians must commit not only to loving those who suffer but first to understanding and developing a mutual relationship with them. Love means cultivating attention, consideration, and care for others, as if they were every bit as important to us as we are to ourselves. This is the challenging task to which virtuous Christians are called in a world of environmental degradation.

Whom to Love?

This chapter will bring love, the mother of all virtues, to bear on the mother of all environmental questions: How should we live given the current state of the world? The problems discussed in previous chapters—species loss, energy, food insecurity, injustice, climate change, and population—are all united by the challenge of figuring out how to take action. In each case, concerned persons are faced with the challenge of discerning how much to do, how much change to seek, and by what means. This gets even more complicated when all these problems are considered together, competing for our attention and asking us—people with inevitably limited time and energy—to move in multiple directions. As this book ends, this question remains for Christians who seek to be virtuous people: What should we do, and how should we do it?

In contemporary environmentalist discourse, this question is frequently asked under the heading of "sustainability." Environmentalists who seek to sustain a community or an economy or a civilization or an ecosystem must first articulate what the most important priorities are: "What, above all else, must be sustained?"[8] To answer this question requires a consideration of what harms are most urgent, what remedies are most promising, and what can be allowed to fall by the wayside. It requires careful consideration of what is making God's creation sick, how creation can be healthier, and how it might be possible to build a future in which human beings can live harmoniously on the earth. Almost any environmental issue is complex enough to warrant lifetimes of study and consideration, but they may become more approachable when viewed through the lens of virtuous love. Questions about saving ecosystems and communities, about sustainability, and about appropriate environmentalist methods are all essentially questions about love. For Christians, then, the most basic environmental question is not "what should we do?"; "what should we sustain?"; or even "how should we live?" It is instead: Who are we, and whom are we called to love?

Our tradition offers three straightforward answers that are relevant to this inquiry: love God, love the neighbor, and love creation. When a lawyer tested Jesus by asking him God's greatest commandment or what he must do to inherit eternal life, Jesus pointed him to this: "You shall love the Lord your God with all your heart, and with all your soul, and with all your mind. This is the greatest and first commandment. And a second is like it: You shall love your neighbor as yourself" (Matthew 22:37-39).[9] While there is no commandment to "love creation" quite so clearly articulated in scripture, there is an implicit love of all God's work that comes through scripture and Christian tradition.[10] But even for those who view creation in purely instrumental terms (i.e., it is there for the sole purpose of sustaining humankind), the fact remains that in a global ecosystem under conditions of environmental degradation, it is only possible to love God and the neighbor if we also care for the creation God has given us to live in, the creation upon which our neighbor's life depends. What follows is an exploration—without any simple instructions—of these three objects of Christian love.

Loving God

As Margaret Farley explains, to love someone requires perceiving the beloved rightly. To love God therefore means to see God rightly, and this is a supreme challenge given God's invisibility. Jesus assured his disciples that whoever had seen him had also seen God (John 14:9), but this may be little help to those of us not living in first-century Palestine who must rely on eyewitness accounts filtered through centuries of storytelling—without so much as a single selfie of Jesus for the record. To see God rightly, therefore, is to love God as a force that is mysteriously beyond human experience, transcending what we can know and understand and yet also mysteriously near. The God Christians are called to love cannot fit neatly into any category created by human beings, so true love of God forbids projecting qualities onto God that are not, in fact, God's qualities. None of us, for example, can speak reliably for God's political party affiliation or ideological perspective; God is beyond humanity and cannot be called with confidence to any side in any particular human debate. Neither can God be domesticated or captured, made small enough to serve human ends. To paraphrase Abraham Lincoln, Christians should be concerned not with whether God is on our side but rather with whether we are on God's side.

Alongside our Jewish sisters and brothers, Christians pledge fidelity to the God of Job, who mysteriously allows a faithful servant to suffer horrible losses and then asks from within a whirlwind: "Where were you when I laid the foundation of the earth? Tell me, if you have understanding. Who deter-mined its measurements—surely you know" (Job 38:4-5). To love this God is to be reminded that human beings do not know all the measurements of creation; we did not build it, and we cannot fully control the whirlwinds of this world, much less the God who made them. The love of this mysterious God is, therefore, a check on the kind of fundamentalism that this book seeks to avoid. It is to be loyal to something larger than our own certainties. Loving God is a risky and humbling business, but Christians are called to it with all of our hearts, our souls, and our minds.[11]

In a specifically environmental context, God's mystery is a reminder that human beings are not the masters, nor even the managers, of the universe. Even though ours is currently the dominant species on earth, this planet is an unimaginably tiny part of an unimaginably vast cosmic creation. Further-more, the facts of environmental degradation reveal that we have not always been wise managers of our homes, our land, or our earth. Human beings are not qualified to be God, and we are not meant to be God. "The world is not ours to save"; it is entirely God's.[12] We cannot truly love God until we see rightly, until we understand and accept that our relationship to God is one of complete and total dependence rather than rivalry or equality.

Loving Our Neighbors

The sometimes-frustrating incomprehensibility of God has often led Chris-tians to prioritize loving the neighbor as a finite embodiment of God's pres-ence in our midst. Jesus identified the close relationship between love of God and love of neighbor when he said that the second commandment, "Love your neighbor as yourself," is like the first, "Love the Lord your God." We cannot fully understand God's reality, so perhaps the best way to express our love of God is to care for our neighbors, whose concrete reality we can more readily comprehend. Jesus clarifies this idea in his parable of sheep and goats, explaining that when the Son of Man comes in his glory he will say to the sheep:

> I was hungry and you gave me food, I was thirsty and you gave me some-thing to drink, I was a stranger and you welcomed me, was naked and you gave me clothing, I was sick and you took care of me, I was in prison and you visited me . . . just as you did it to one of the least of these who are members of my family, you did it to me. (Matthew 25:35-46)

In other words, God does not punish us for not fully comprehending a God we cannot see; instead, God commands us to actively love those we *can* see (1 John 4:20).

The love of God leads us to love God through our neighbors. This is another inheritance from Christianity's Jewish roots. The Israelites understood their covenantal duty to be a demonstration of God's love for creation. God's generous and empowering covenant with Israel "demanded the same qualities of them. They were to be faithful to the Lord and not turn away to other gods; they were also to show covenantal love to one another (Lev. 19:18). The 'love with all their heart' they had toward God (Deut. 6:4) was manifested in their attitudes and actions toward other humans."[13] In explicitly Christian terms, the revelation of Jesus Christ is an affirmation that each and every one of our human neighbors bears the divine image, however tarnished. God became human as an expression of love, and so we are called to love humanity.

In an environmental context, loving our neighbors reminds us that we must pay careful attention to the human lives and human well-being at stake in every environmental decision. Preventing toxic waste from seeping into an aquifer is an expression of love both for neighbors who drink that water and for the God who created them. Preserving a pristine wilderness from destruction is an expression of love for the creatures who will enjoy that place for generations to come and for the God who called them good. Limiting the rising of the seas from climate change is an expression of love for poor and marginalized people who live on vulnerable coastlines and for the God who died to save them. To love our neighbors is to see each of them as fully human. Every person is capable of both happiness and suffering. Every person is equally dependent upon God's creation for survival. Every person deserves to be loved as we love ourselves.

Loving Creation

God is not only the redeemer of the world but also its creator. Thus, to love God changes our relationship to more than just our human neighbors. Indeed, it would be ridiculous to say that one loved God if one paid no attention to the variety, the majesty, and the wonder of God's handiwork. One of the most enduring paths to learning about the mystery of God has always been an exploration of God's artistry all around us. Even John Calvin, a famous theological stickler, conceded that "it can be said reverently, provided that it proceeds from a reverent mind, that nature is God"—namely, that the order of the world reflects God's own order.[14] Other theologians use the language of "sacrament" to describe nature, insisting that the entirety of creation is a path to and sign of God, just like the water of baptism and the bread and wine of communion.[15] The common theme is that we know more about God when we know God's material creation—that, as the psalmist declares, the heavens tell God's glory and the firmament proclaims God's handiwork (Psalm 19). God's creation is an indispensable means by which human beings can love God concretely and not merely in the abstract.

For some, the importance of creation is expressed with an assertion that the category of neighbor, whom Christians are called to love and to honor, includes not just human beings but all of "otherkind": all the creatures with whom we share the planet, all the ecosystems in which those creatures live, and even the earth itself.[16] Others reject such a close intermingling of humanity and the rest of nature, limiting the term *neighbor* to human beings, who alone are made in the image of God, rather than extending it to all creatures.[17] This touches on a disagreement about *how* Christians are to love creation, but it does not undermine the common ground—a foundational claim of Christian environmentalism—that Christians should live out the love of God by loving God's creation.

Loving the world is not exclusive to Christians; many environmentalists do the same and offer thoughtful justifications. For instance, biologist and prominent conservationist E. O. Wilson justifies his environmentalism partly with a sociobiological argument that human beings have evolved to care for other forms of life. He posits a "biophilia" (love of life) inherent in our social and genetic structures, a natural impulse to love creation to which we must listen carefully if we are to be true to ourselves, and to survive and thrive as a species.[18] Building on this hypothesis, other environmentalists have begun to speak of a modern ailment called "nature deficit disorder," which comes from a lack of exposure to natural settings.[19] Associated with problems such as stress, depression, attention deficit, and anxiety, nature deficit disorder is used to justify arguments to preserve undeveloped spaces (or to reclaim and restore spaces into natural parks) and to encourage closer and healthier human relationships to the nonhuman world. Christians have much to learn from these arguments, and we can go beyond them to offer deeper, theological justifications for conservation. Christian virtue calls people of faith to love creation: to understand its concrete reality, to know and honor its creator, and to care for all God's children who depend upon it.[20]

How to Love?

It is all well and good to talk about love in theory, but the difficult work of virtue is actually to live it out in practice. Thus, it is vital to consider what environmental love looks like on the ground when it is expressed in real lives. Christian environmentalists can express love in small private changes that shrink our environmental footprints and purify ourselves or in grand gestures like political activism, civil disobedience, "enviropreneurship," or "monkeywrenching." What follows are examples of six environmentalists who are all driven by love but who express that love in very different ways. These examples offer possibilities for Christians to consider when discerning how to engage the work of caring for God's world. Because each perspective emerges from a real life, there is no simple middle ground between them. Rather, Christians who seek to love God, the neighbor, and the creation must discern what can be learned from each.

Reimagining Love: Frances Moore Lappé and Hank Fischer

Environmentalists who love this earth and the people who depend upon it tend to start with small actions—recycling paper, cans, and bottles instead of throwing them away; choosing to consume less and to avoid excessive packaging; walking or biking to work instead of driving; cooking at home rather than eating fast food in our idling cars; installing low-flow showerheads in our bathrooms; or weatherizing our homes. These actions have concrete value, but as this book has made clear, environmental problems are complex enough that a few small consumer choices by a minority of individuals will not solve them.

Part of the problem, according to author and activist Frances Moore Lappé, is that concerned people do not yet have all the intellectual and conceptual tools we need. She encourages us to take a step back and reconsider our motivations, because she thinks environmentalism has traditionally relied too heavily on fear and guilt, pushing people to change their habits out of a sense of shame. This, she argues, can nurture a counterproductive sense of superiority over less enlightened people (like those who still use disposable coffee cups); or it can create a paralyzing sense that people are "naturally" voracious and greedy and therefore doomed to destroy the earth. Lappé argues that consumerism is ultimately a product not of ignorance or greed but of anxiety. "Buying things seems to be a common human strategy to ease feelings of insecurity and fear."[21] Rather than shame, then, environmentalism needs more imaginative strategies to help people feel safer, such as learning to love better, building stronger communities, and redefining luxury away from things and toward nonmaterial goods such as free time, beauty, and friendship.[22]

Lappé sees earth-friendly living as the path to true wealth, rather than as a sacrifice.[23] Environmentalists need to help others imagine a good life that goes beyond having lots of stuff, because it is ultimately "building on love," rather than "playing on guilt," that helps people adjust their habits: "Sustained change comes when we start to live differently from deep, positive emotions."[24] These positive emotions are made possible by imagining the world we want and working toward it.

Committed to what she calls "living democracy," Lappé celebrates small changes motivated by love because they can grow into courageous action and political change. She cites her own experience of becoming slowly politically aware, then politically active and thereby empowered: "Throughout my life, every time I've made a change that aligns with the world I want—whether it's nervously going door to door in a political campaign or choosing a plant-friendly diet—I feel a bit more convincing to myself. A bit more powerful. A bit more of a believer that we all can change."[25] Readers who lovingly take the time to recycle, for example, might soon make the time to lobby their elected leaders and so empower themselves to build a better community.

The living democracy Lappé imagines includes support for organizations that have already developed ways to work for environmental change. She points to Bill McKibben's 350.org, working to build a "global grassroots movement to solve the climate crisis" through "online campaigns, grassroots organizing, and mass public actions."[26] She calls students to join the Campus Climate Challenge in urging their university administrators to become climate neutral, divesting from fossil fuels in favor of renewable energies.[27] She calls landowners to join Wangari Maathai, winner of the 2004 Nobel Peace Prize and former member of Kenyan Parliament, in planting life-giving trees throughout the world.[28] She calls conscientious eaters to join with Food Democracy Now in online campaigns to pressure legislators to foster sustainable food systems that prioritize "people and our planet" over "profits."[29]

Lappé's primary expression of love is to imagine new ways of thinking about community. The idea that imagination matters should be familiar to Christians, who are called by St. Paul to the strange understanding of ourselves as "the body of Christ and individually members of it." We are "baptized into one body—Jews or Greeks, slaves or free—and we were all made to drink of one Spirit" (1 Corinthians 12:13). It is in this spirit that he goes on to make the famous declaration about love that began this chapter. Christians therefore have much to learn from Lappé and environmentalists like her about the transformation of the world through new ways of imagining the world community through education, legislation, and community building—and, we might add, Christian sacraments.

Others believe environmental problems can be more efficiently addressed through private channels than through public institutions. For example, the trend toward "enviropreneurship" highlights that self-interest and the profit motive can be harnessed to benefit the earth and our neighbors in it. Take, for example, Hank Fischer, a devotee of Yellowstone Park who wanted to bring back endangered gray wolf populations in order to keep the ecosystem in balance. He writes, "The large predators 'are the big things that run the world.' They create changes that ripple through the entire system, affecting everything from elk down to the smallest clump of bluebunch wheatgrass." But ranchers in the area were concerned about their livestock, wondering why they alone should have to pay the price for wolves to flourish. "Incentives are critical to wolf conservation," he realized, "The only solution was to pay these ranchers for their losses. I sent a fund-raising letter to several Defenders of Wildlife members in Montana, and I had the necessary funds within 48 hours."[30] By using his imagination to understand the ranchers' perspective, he was able to come up with an incentives-based solution that was a win-win for both the wolves and the ranchers.

Environmental entrepreneurship is still a fairly new concept, but Fischer is part of a growing movement of environmentalists who are imagining alternatives to regulation and legislation as ways of bringing about environmental change.[31] Others have established "benefit corporations"—hybrids between nonprofits and businesses that sell everything from solar energy to green roof plants—that "harness the power of private enterprise to create public benefit." The "declaration of interdependence" of one such entity does not include the word "love" but it might as well: it says that "all business ought to be conducted as if people and place mattered"; that "businesses should aspire to do no harm and to benefit all"; and that "we are each dependent upon another and thus responsible for each other and future generations."[32] Such creative and innovative thought on behalf of the environment is especially important when democratic processes do not respond quickly enough to solve urgent problems, and it reflects a commitment to make concrete change now, working within existing economic structures. "Systemic challenges require systemic solutions," and environmental entrepreneurs offer "a concrete, market-based and scalable solution" that does not require federal approval.[33]

Those who love God must creatively imagine new ways to act on behalf of creation and their neighbors. As Lappé points out, tired methods of making people feel guilty are not motivations but obstacles, squelching hope and dampening any spark of loving activism that might be trying to catch fire. Love can fuel this work, as it can fuel the entrepreneurial spirit that might save wolves in Yellowstone or create the next world-changing energy technology. Christians must be open to these lessons, as we must be open to all the ways love can change our lives and our communities.

Breaking the Law for Love: Tim DeChristopher and Sandra Steingraber

Few environmentalists would disagree that feeling personally empowered and expanding small actions into bigger ones are good and important steps, but not everyone has Lappé's patience for slow change or the entrepreneurial skill and willingness to work through traditional business channels. For some radical activists, more drastic action is needed. Take, for example, Tim DeChristopher, a young environmentalist who found himself bidding—with money he did not have—at a government oil and gas lease auction for land in southern Utah in 2008. He had originally intended simply to protest the auction, but he spontaneously changed his strategy and registered as a bidder in the auction. He reported afterward that part of what changed his mind was seeing a friend from church who was also at the auction weeping at the loss of beloved land. DeChristopher was spurred to action. He began bidding on the leases, driving up prices for many land parcels and placing the winning bids on a long series of them before he was discovered. The auction was declared invalid, and before it could be rescheduled a new presidential administration took power and canceled the sales of these lands.[34]

DeChristopher, meanwhile, was charged and convicted, earning two years in federal prison. When supporters began raising money to pay the Bureau of Land Management for his bids, DeChristopher urged them to stop. Rather than getting out of prison, he wanted to inspire acts of civil disobedience that would get more environmentalists thrown *into* prison. He sees such acts as they only way to deal with a broken system that has left behind the rule of law, helping to enrich corporations and government elites rather than benefiting the country or the human race: "The way the environmental movement has been is like a football game. And our team is getting slaughtered. The refs have been paid off, and then the other side is playing with dirty tricks. And so it's no longer acceptable for us to stay in the stands. It's time to rush the field. It's time to stop the game."[35]

DeChristopher, a Unitarian Universalist who enrolled in Divinity School after his release from prison, is very clear that his central motivation is love of human beings, pure and simple. "I would never go to jail to protect animals or plants or wilderness," he said in one interview. "For me, it's about the people. And even my value of wilderness is about what it brings to people. I have a very anthropocentric worldview." He goes on to say, "I'm for a humane world. A world that values humanity. I'm for a world where we meet our emotional needs not through the consumption of material goods, but through human relationships. A world where we measure our progress not through how much stuff we produce, but through our quality of life—whether or not we're actually promoting a higher quality of life for human beings. . . . I love people."[36] His is an environmental outlook that might appeal even to those Christians who prioritize human "dominion" over the earth.

For DeChristopher and many activists like him, the natural outgrowth of genuine love for people is a willingness to commit acts of civil disobedience on their behalf. Corrupt structures have left lovers of humanity feeling they have no way to live virtuously without getting in trouble. The system is rigged to force citizens to behave in unloving ways, such that any act of genuine love will come across as rebellion: "With countless lives on the line, *this* is what love looks like."[37] He has little patience for people who make excuses as to why they cannot do things that might land them in prison—for example, by claiming that they need financial stability in order to care for their families: "I think our current power structures only have power over us because of what they can take away from us. That's where their power comes from—their ability to take things away. And so if we have a lot that we're afraid of losing, or that we're not willing to lose, they have a lot of power over us."[38]

This is a radical stance, but it is not foreign to the Christian tradition. Consider the apostle Paul's advice to early Christians that they not get married precisely because it might prevent them from fully living out their faith: "The unmarried woman and the virgin are anxious about the affairs of the

Lord, so that they may be holy in body and spirit; but the married woman is anxious about the affairs of the world, how to please her husband" (1 Corinthians 7:34). Writing to a small sect of Christians in a world where they were vastly outnumbered and marginalized, Paul called for a rebellious love beyond exclusive attachment—which raised suspicions about early Christians in the Roman Empire. To live justly, really to love one's neighbors, is itself a rebellion against a broken system, likely to make one very unpopular with the powers that be. Tim DeChristopher suggests that the reality of climate change requires a similarly countercultural approach to love in our own time.

On the other hand, it is also possible that traditional attachments to family might be the very factor that motivates rebellious behavior. For biologist Sandra Steingraber, it was motherly love that compelled her illegally to block the driveway of a natural gas storage facility with her body. Seeking to protect the Finger Lakes near her home in New York State from the byproducts of hydraulic fracturing, Steingraber allowed herself to be arrested in order to draw attention, serving ten days in the Schuyler County jail before being released.[39]

Steingraber sees environmentalism as part of her responsibility as a mother: "The environmental crisis is a parenting crisis. It undermines my ability to carry out two fundamental duties: to protect my children from harm and to plan for their future. My responsibility as a mother thus extends beyond push mowers and clotheslines to the transformation of the nation's energy systems along renewable lines."[40] Writing from jail, she told the story of a Halloween when her son wanted to dress up as a polar bear. She made his costume knowing that he would likely outlive the last polar bear on earth: "The kinship that children feel for animals and their ongoing disappearance from us literally brought me to my knees that night." She goes on: "It was love that got me back up. It was love that brought me to this jail cell. My children need a world with pollinators and plankton stocks and a stable climate. They need lake shores that do not have explosive hydrocarbon gases buried underneath."[41]

Steingraber's crime was more carefully planned, was less disruptive, and earned significantly less jail time than DeChristopher's—perhaps partly because of her responsibility to her children. But like DeChristopher, she was willing publicly to break the law and serve her legal sentence in order to draw attention to the harms of fossil fuel extraction and climate change. Both appreciate the wonders of the natural world as a whole but were primarily motivated by a love for human beings. Both suggest that to love human beings requires a willingness to break the rules, to stand up and be counted as an advocate for a more sustainable future.

Fighting for Love: Dave Foreman and Edward Abbey

While they rebelled by breaking the law, both Steingraber and DeChristopher were civil in their disobedience, taking responsibility for their actions and fully cooperating with consequences meted out by existing authorities. For some environmentalists, such well-behaved resistance against the system is not enough. Ecological travesties call for more drastic measures. Dave Foreman offers one example. He spent the beginning of his career as a mainstream environmentalist, working with the Wilderness Society and the Nature Conservancy and lobbying in Washington, D.C. Eventually frustrated with this "professional" path, Foreman cofounded the radical organization Earth First! in the early 1980s so as to disrupt destructive systems less politely. His primary motivation, as he explained it, was love for the earth itself. The planet was here before human beings and will outlast us; it is the only "real world" that truly exists, and everything else humans make is deceptive and short lived. Foreman therefore argues for biocentrism (a primary focus on life) rather than anthropocentrism (a primary focus on humans). "We should be kind, compassionate, and caring with other people," he concedes, "but Earth comes first."[42]

Foreman emphasizes that human beings are merely one species among many. The earth does not exist for us in any special way; on the contrary, it exists for all species equally. Perhaps better, the earth exists for itself; we, like all other creatures, are part of it. "The oceans of the Earth course through my veins," he writes. "The winds of the sky fill my lungs, the very bedrock of the planet makes my bones. I am alive! I am not a machine, a mindless automaton, a cog in the industrial world, some New Age android." His self-identity informs his urgent activism: we should love the earth because we belong to it, and that love should help us to see the disastrous destruction around us: "When a chain saw slices into the heartwood of a two-thousand-year-old Coast Redwood, it's slicing into my guts. When a bulldozer rips through the Amazon rain forest, it's ripping into my side. When a Japanese whaler fires an exploding harpoon into a great whale, my heart is blown to smithereens. I am the land, the land is me."[43] Such close identification with the earth expresses his encompassing and empowering love.

According to environmental scholar Bron Taylor, radical environmental movements like Earth First! are motivated by three core ideas that justify drastic action: a moral claim that nonhuman life has value; an ecological claim that contemporary environmental degradation is an unprecedented crisis; and a political claim that presently existing democracy in the United States is unequal to the task of responding to this crisis.[44] Inspired by these ideas, Foreman characterizes his action as "non-violent defense of the wild," which includes disrupting and calling attention to development and greed, avoiding violence against people, but embracing the destruction of property as a self-defense mechanism against a system that destroys ecosystems.[45] Unlike civil disobedience, which aims to disrupt unjust political processes, Earth First!'s actions are directed specifically at "inanimate machines and tools that are destroying life," such as bulldozers and drills.[46] Foreman calls for such actions to be "safe, easy, fun," as well as "strategic" and "thoughtful," so that they may be "effective." His hope is that if enough eco-warriors defend the wild, they will make it prohibitively expensive and politically costly for corporations to cut down forests or blow off mountaintops. Corporations will give up and find other ways to make money, and the earth will endure. Against his critics, Foreman carefully distinguishes such acts of self-defense from "ecoterrorism" in that while he respects the concept of private property, "life—the biological diversity of this planet—is far more important."[47] The best interests of the earth always trump the interests of human beings. Earth always comes first.

One inspiration for Foreman's work was the iconoclastic anarchist Edward Abbey, a former national park ranger who became famous in the 1960s and 1970s for his fiction and nonfiction decrying the development of the American West. His most prominent book, *Desert Solitaire*, records his reflections from his time in Arches National Monument, celebrating the beauty of the landscape and reporting on his intimate knowledge of it. He is strongly critical of increasing tourist access and the growing development all around the park, both of which he understands as endangering the wilderness he loves. Abbey's revolutionary tendencies are clear in the preface, which laments that "most of what I write about in this book is already gone or going under fast. This is not a travel guide but an elegy." This lamentation for the disappearance of a beloved wilderness quickly moves into a call to action: "You're holding a tombstone in your hands. A bloody rock. Don't drop it on your foot—throw it at something big and glassy."[48]

Equally influential was Abbey's novel *The Monkey Wrench Gang*, which tells the story of four westerners who team up to engage in "monkeywrenching"

against development. On a rafting trip through the Grand Canyon, the protagonists discover a common love for the West and a deep frustration over the
forces of development changing its landscapes. They agree to work together
to disrupt that development by sabotaging construction sites. This begins a
trajectory of destruction that includes driving bulldozers off cliffs, cutting
pieces out of engines, removing surveying stakes, and dreaming about blow-
ing up dams and bridges. A clear rule is set early on that they damage only
things, not people, but they are indiscriminate in their willingness to destroy
machines and stop development. To emphasize the anarchism of their movement, two men agree that they will aggressively throw beer cans out their
windows as they drive: "Any road I wasn't consulted about that I don't like, I
litter. It's my religion."[49] The fictional account contains detailed descriptions
of how the protagonists sabotage machines and escape detection, which many
subsequent activists have used as guidelines for real-life monkeywrenching.

The sabotage and nonviolent earth defense of Abbey and Foreman is
clearly distinct from the civil disobedience of Steingraber and DeChristopher. While the latter two activists drew attention to their public activism,
the ideal in Earth First! is that "action speaks for itself," and practitioners are
never identified or caught.[50] The central goal is not to go to prison to push the
political system toward change but rather to disrupt the economic system—
not to speak for people who suffer from environmental degradation but to act
for the speechless earth itself.

Love in Action

The six approaches briefly profiled here offer very different expressions of
love: from the modest cultivation of new habits in community, to starting a
business, to dramatic public civil disobedience, to quiet sabotage. There is no
way for one Christian fully to embrace all of these approaches: from the perspective of a political activist, Lappé's transformation of the mind is too slow.
From the perspective of a radical environmentalist, the activism of Steingraber and DeChristopher is too patient, too trusting in the political system's
capacity to right itself. From the perspective of a mainstream environmentalist, the radical property destruction advocated by Abbey and Foreman is too
extreme, even violent, and alienates too many potential allies. Those who
love the creation, creatures, and their creator will have to choose among these
tactics and must be prepared to defend their choices.

Because Christian environmentalism beyond fundamentalism means
taking multiple perspectives seriously despite the fact that we may disagree

with them, it is crucial to acknowledge that all these environmentalists act from love: all love humanity and all love the earth, though they prioritize them differently. Love is a common ground, and so it can serve as a point of connection. Whatever approach Christians take to building a more sustainable world, we are called to love our neighbors who take other approaches. To love these different environmental activists means seeking to understand them on their own terms, to fully explore their motivations and their actions with caring attention.

The same common ground and caring attention should be extended to those who are not taking any environmentalist action at all. Christian environmentalists who seek to love may grow frustrated by those they see as working against the planet—refusing to recycle, join an organization, or protest, while insisting upon jobs in extractive industries or consumptive habits. But these people, too, are neighbors we are called to love. One way to love others is to ask what they themselves love. Many landowners in the American West, for example, love their ranches, hunting, and liberty. Many suburban parents love their children and want them to grow safely into adults who can fit in and support themselves in the world in which they live. Many oil and gas executives love the sense of accomplishment they get from accessing resources, satisfying consumers, pleasing shareholders, and creating jobs. Many loggers and farmers love being close to the land they work on and using their earnings to provide for their families. These loves are all real and worthy of respect.

It is vital to remember that God is bigger than our beliefs and our allegiances, so we can never be fundamentalist about a single approach. To cultivate love is to learn to understand people on their own terms even as we work to make the world better for them, for ourselves, and for all of God's creatures.

Learning Love

When Hurricane Katrina struck New Orleans and the Gulf Coast in 2005, most people knew the city as "The Big Easy," a popular convention and Spring Break destination and the site of a world-famous and famously intemperate Mardi Gras celebration. The racial politics of New Orleans were less widely known but are also vital to understanding the city: during the slave trade, it was a key port city in which human beings were bought and sold; but it was also a popular settling point for free blacks. In the twentieth century, racial politics continued to shape the city as whites fled to the suburbs, leaving behind an underfunded city with high rates of poverty that was 68 percent African American. New Orleans also has a fascinating environmental history: parts of the city lie as many as seventeen feet below sea level and so are particularly vulnerable to flooding. To deal with this, New Orleans has developed a complex system of levees, canals, and pumps to drain the city of frequent rains, which made building possible but also destroyed many of the wetlands surrounding the city that had historically absorbed rain and floodwaters.

These contextual details are essential to understanding what happened when Hurricane Katrina hit New Orleans on August 29, 2005. The most destructive hurricane in U.S. history, Katrina killed over 1,800 people and caused over $70 billion of insured damage. The worst flooding took place in the predominantly black and poor Lower Ninth Ward, which is considerably lower in elevation than other neighborhoods. While the majority of the city's residents followed evacuation orders and were safely away when the storm hit, a significant minority remained, most because they had no other option. Without cars, they were dependent on public transportation, which later investigations proved to be entirely inadequate. The city had only one quarter of the buses necessary for a full evacuation. Over sixty thousand people took refuge in the city's stadium and convention center, where conditions were profoundly unpleasant and, at times, dangerous. While Hurricane Katrina was a natural disaster, its impact was distributed by an imprudent and unjust social system that disproportionately affected the poor and people of color.[51]

In the years since Hurricane Katrina, Christians and others have sought to learn lessons from the disaster about what it means to love creation, our neighbors, and God. One lesson that some have drawn is that it is a mistake to have a major city so far below sea level, and that the most prudent way to prevent future disasters like Katrina would be to depopulate New Orleans, at least in low-lying areas that cannot be reliably protected by levees. Perhaps the centuries that engineers have spent courageously trying to keep the city dry have proven a failure; the responsible thing to do is accept that parts of New Orleans are simply uninhabitable, particularly in a world of increasingly strong and volatile hurricanes. Two years after Katrina, Joel Bourne of *National Geographic* wrote critically that "instead of rebuilding smarter or surrendering, New Orleans is doing what it has always done after such disasters: bumping up the levees just a little higher, rebuilding the same flood-prone houses back in the same low spots, and praying that the hurricanes hit elsewhere."[52] One can certainly imagine Earth First! activists lamenting these decisions and hoping to defend the wetlands of New Orleans from the encroachment of continued human life there. To truly love creation might mean accepting that a low-lying flood-prone coast is no place for people to live.

However, such a response to New Orleans' situation must be brought into conversation with the realities of race and class. Because the most endangered areas of the city are also among the poorest and the most highly African American, to begin closing or shrinking the endangered sections of New Orleans would mean disproportionately affecting those populations. Scholar and activist Robert Bullard observed shortly after Katrina that such efforts were already beginning, with cleanup efforts focused on wealthy neighborhoods rather than "emphasizing equitable rebuilding, uniform clean-up standards, equal protection, and environmental justice."[53] Hurricane Katrina was a human tragedy that particularly hit the poor and marginalized; to give up on low-lying neighborhoods of the city is to compound their suffering. Perhaps loving our neighbors requires a renewed commitment to all the neighborhoods and citizens of this historic city, a deeper hope that justice is possible.[54] One can easily imagine an enviropreneur seeing this as an opportunity, working to innovate safer ways for all citizens to live in New Orleans.

The continuing aftermath of Hurricane Katrina is a test of Christian love, as is the inevitability of more disasters like it in other parts of the world, perhaps even in New Orleans once again. Katrina revealed that human beings are living out of sync with the world's natural rhythms, that we have not been faithful, prudent, or just in the ways we have structured our societies. This revelation calls for new ways of imagining our communities and our roles within them. It may call for small acts of love, for civil disobedience, or for other forms of more radical protest. What is certain, however, is that love requires a response. The virtue of love, shockingly unfamiliar in a world that glorifies self-interest above all else, can only be cultivated through practice. To love God is to dwell in mystery, to lack clear answers; but this mystery calls for concrete acts of love in response to the concrete realities of our neighbors and the creation that sustains them.

Questions for Discussion

1. What do you love most? How does your answer connect to love of God, love of neighbor, and love of creation?

2. Aquinas refers to love as the "mother of the virtues." How would you identify the connections between love and the other six virtues in this book? Can you think of any situations in which love could be in tension with another virtue?

3. What does it mean to "love" creation? Should nonhuman species and ecosystems be loved as neighbors, or are neighbors exclusively human beings?

4. Compare and contrast the mainstream approaches of Lappé and the enviropreneurs; the civil disobedience of DeChristopher and Steinberger; and the monkeywrenching of Foreman and Abbey. Which of these seems to best embody the virtue of love? Do different situations call for different kinds of love?

5. What does Christian love require in response to a tragedy like Hurricane Katrina? What political and social structures need to change? Who should make decisions about where it is safe for people to live in a low-lying coastal city like New Orleans?

CONCLUSION
Practicing Virtue in a "World of Wounds"

Let us revisit that deceptively simple banana you had to think about in the introduction.

Having read about endangered species since then, you know that the land on which that banana was grown probably used to be a habitat for a diverse array of creatures, whose lives and livelihoods are intertwined with your own; you now have tools to reflect upon whether it is prudent to grow bananas on that land instead. Having read about energy, you are aware that the banana came to you with significant hidden costs in fossil fuels; you can access sufficient courage to think about how new technologies or legal regulations might change the availability of such fossil fuels and to consider whether you would have the fortitude to accept those costs as part of your own budget. Having read about temperance, you can reflect carefully on that banana as part of your diet as well as part of a global food system; you can consider how this snack affects your own life and the lives and well-being of other people and animals. Having read about justice, you realize that this banana has real-life effects for real people; you are prepared to think about the pesticides that might be on it and the exposure of the person who picked it for you, as well as the fact that your urban neighbors might not live near a store where they can buy a decent piece of fruit.

Having read about faith, you are aware that even something as ordinary as eating a banana expresses fidelity to something; you can contemplate the impact of this snack on your carbon footprint and how your eating habits can express commitment to God's created world in a time of climate change. Having read about hope, you might wonder how the world is going to keep feeding bananas to its population of seven billion (and counting) human beings; you can work to avoid both despair and presumption in considering this future. Finally, having read about love, you might receive this humble banana as a gracious gift, asking yourself how you—who bear the image of God—can lovingly turn the energy you gain from this food into environmental action that serves God, your neighbor, and the creation.

Buying a banana is a healthy choice: it is a whole food, mostly unpackaged, filled with vitamins, and your purchase supports jobs and good health through the production and sale of nutritious goods in your community and across the globe. However, buying a banana is also a choice that makes you complicit in environmental degradation: even if you eat only organic bananas, only on Sundays, and only when you are in the tropics, the tree, the peel, and your body will all eventually emit methane gases that contribute to atmospheric change.

You might be wishing you could go back to buying and eating a banana unthinkingly. You might not want every purchase to become a long discourse on the virtues, not least because this is likely to make you unpopular with friends and convenience store clerks alike. But every action we take shapes our character and our habits, and the world we live in is now so deeply interconnected that every purchase we make is an ineluctably environmental act with ethical implications.

Aldo Leopold, one of the foundational figures in the history of the American environmental movement, captured the challenge that comes with studying environmental issues in one of his journals: "One of the penalties of an ecological education is that one lives alone in a world of wounds."[1] To understand how serious environmental problems are, to know one's own complicity in the degradation of creation, and to feel responsible for helping to heal the world in the face of its deep sickness is indeed to live in a world of wounds. And to ponder these things while others seem to live a more carefree existence of simple enjoyment, happily distracted by technology or diverted by celebrity gossip, can indeed lead one to feel very much alone.

However, the virtue tradition discussed in this book offers some resources that might mitigate Leopold's gloomy observation. The approach of eco-virtue suggested in this book, by training us to see more of the world than just its wounds, can empower Christians to take positive action within our communities. The problems facing humanity are interconnected, as are the virtues that can help us respond to them. And the task of sustaining and building virtue is never the work of a lone individual but always undertaken in community.

The Unity of Environmental Challenges and Virtues

The Christian tradition teaches that the seven virtues are ultimately united and dependent upon one another. No virtue is truly virtuous unless it is accompanied by all the others. The same can be said about environmental problems, which are distinct and different in important ways but are always interconnected.

Endangered species and climate change, for example, are two distinct issues, but the two problems are also inextricably linked: changes in climate drive species from their habitats, while the shrinking of forest land increases the rate of climate change. Similarly, the issues of population, energy consumption, and toxic pollution cannot be fully understood without pondering their intersections; it is people who consume energy and create pollution, but it is precisely that polluting energy that has made it possible for more and more people to exist and live more comfortable lives. The question of what a virtuous person should eat in a world of environmental degradation is inseparable from the question of how a virtuous person should take political action; eating may seem like a private matter, but in reality it depends upon and fosters certain political and economic structures that encompass the entire globe. The challenges discussed in this book are thus not separate issues unto themselves; they form a complex web.

These problems are also connected to many others that have not been explored here in depth but are nevertheless vitally important. The chapters in this book have barely scratched the surface: the use of nuclear power, the disposal of waste in landfills, the acidification of oceans, the depletion of topsoil, the shortage of fresh water, urban sprawl, and countless other environmental problems deserve much more attention than they have received here. Meanwhile, new environmental problems are being identified all the time.

Adding more challenges to the seven discussed in this book runs the risk of overwhelming the reader because each one is so complex, involving contested facts, multiple possible solutions, and diverse voices. However, all of these problems are linked to the ones discussed here, and readers are encouraged to use this book as a beginner's tool kit to learn more. The virtues are applicable to the entire array of environmental problems; habits of loving God and our neighbors, of living out the Gospel in the midst of life's concrete perplexities, are always relevant. Indeed, responding wholeheartedly to the world's problems is possibly the most important way in which a Christian can practice and cultivate virtue.

To take environmental problems seriously is to feel deeply Leopold's observation that ours is a world of wounds, but Christian faith insists that the world has much more to offer than just its pain. It is also a world of beauty and goodness. Paying careful attention to the world means seeing opportunities for virtues such as prudence and faith and temperance at every turn.

The Community of Virtue

The virtues discussed in this book are part of a long tradition that began well before the time of Christ and has continued on in diverse Christian communities around the world for two millennia. While there is plenty of debate around the virtues and what they should look like when practiced on the ground, Christians generally agree that no one can be virtuous without both the guidance of a community and the grace of God. No individual invented the virtues, and no individual has final say or authority over them. Instead, this tradition is a conversation among good but imperfect people, a developing set of ideas across many times and places.

Virtue ethics is an important tool for engaging contemporary environmental issues because it emphasizes a process of community conversation. Environmentalism will thrive—indeed, humanity will thrive—only if environmentalists can learn to talk and cooperate across ideological, political, and personal differences, to allow the urgency and complexity of environmental problems to trump the bad habits and petty differences that divide us. The virtues teach us that it is more important to cultivate a good character than to be right, that it is more important to do good deeds than to seek purity and perfection. Character and goodness are learned and practiced in communities where human beings are challenged and tested by other viewpoints, habits, and opinions.

To be virtuous, moreover, requires that we honestly and critically consider our own viewpoints, habits, and opinions. There can be no virtue without self-awareness. We come into this world with particular tendencies in our DNA, and we are then formed in families and churches and communities that influence our ideas about everything from good food to fashion to environmental challenges. Some of us have been trained (or have a natural propensity) to emphasize values such as care and fairness when we think about ethics, while others have been trained (or have a natural propensity) to emphasize factors like authority, loyalty, and sanctity.[2] The better we know and understand our own assumptions and ideals, the better we can cultivate virtue. Just as importantly, understanding our own ideas and the communities from which they emerge allows us to understand others in a more open-minded and open-hearted way, listening carefully to their ideas and understanding that virtues shaped in different communities will likely be different but will nevertheless have something useful to teach us.

As this book has demonstrated, when we talk about the environment we can find much to disagree about: how radical our protest against environmental degradation should be; what is the most perilous environmental fear we face; whether technology or politics will provide a better path to addressing climate change; whether toxic pollution requires a revolution or a reform in industrial societies; whether food and energy production should become more or less industrial; or whether species will best be preserved by those who love them selflessly or own them self-interestedly. These vital disagreements must be considered in light of the facts about the world all people share, but they are also shaped importantly by our personalities, our upbringings, and our communities. We see facts differently depending on who we are and where we stand.

Knowing this about ourselves should enable us to turn our differences into the starting places of our conversations, rather than their downfalls. Anyone who has studied environmental issues can understand why Aldo Leopold called an ecological education lonely. But to bring environmental problems into conversation with the virtues is to enter into a conversational communion—friends over centuries and millennia, including a wide array of contemporary activists and thinkers across the globe, twenty or so of whom have been discussed in the chapters of this book. Each of us lives and acts in community at all times. When environmentalists commit to moving beyond fundamentalism, they develop a movement that is bigger than political debate, bigger than cultural difference, bigger than ethical taste or economic ideology. When Christians commit to serving the God who is beyond all human institutions, they become secure in the knowledge that they will never have all the answers. Eco-virtue entails faithful commitment to talking about and working across these differences, with fortitude, for as long as it takes.

Learning Virtue

This book began by acknowledging that both environmental problems and ethical conversations are very difficult. Nothing you have read since then changes that fact. The world is full of wounds, and Christians have been called by a suffering Messiah to pay attention to those wounds. This will not be an easy task.

Facing this task, Christians are invited to receive the gift of virtue. It is easy to let this word conjure up the worst possible images of cranky, self-righteous Christians we have known (or been) in our lives. If we are not careful, a focus on virtue can make us angry and bitter, counting up rights and wrongs joylessly, feeling constantly superior because we believe we are winning the virtue game or feeling insecure because we believe we are losing. But genuine virtue is a matter of grace. It is something we receive rather than just something we do. It is true, of course, that we can learn and must practice virtue. But it is a great gift to be able to develop virtue, performing our character and slowly developing the habits of living well in the world in conversation with a deep Christian tradition and a wide community of environmentalists, graced by the God who is beyond all human institutions.

The degradation of the natural environment encompasses many complex challenges that are difficult to understand fully, much less resolve. Christians are invited to respond prudently, with practical reason, seeking not absolute clarity but sensible steps forward, considering multiple perspectives and taking concrete action.

Another invitation comes from the potentially terrifying, complex web of climate change, dying species, and toxic pollution. Christians are invited to act courageously, facing our fears and using them to test our virtues, standing up for what is right and cultivating the fortitude we will need for the hard work ahead.

The overwhelming complexity of environmental challenges is also an invitation not to distract ourselves by overconsumption or obsessive self-purification but to enjoy God's world temperately, with responsibility and moderation.

The always-growing human influence over the earth is an ongoing invitation to justice; we have the chance to distribute resources and consequences justly, including all the members of God's community, rather than hoarding scarce resources for ourselves and letting others suffer more than their share of consequences.

The temptation to turn away from the world and ignore its travails is an invitation to faithfulness—a commitment to live fully in God's world rather than treating it as a station on the way to someplace better.

When the extent of environmental problems and heavy responsibilities pile up on our shoulders, the temptation to despair can become an invitation to hope. Christians may take careful action toward sustaining ourselves and a healthy earth without going to the opposite extreme of optimistic presumption.

Finally, with so much to do and so many problems to solve, it is difficult to know where to start. Our confusion is an invitation to participate in God's love despite the fact that we lack God's omniscience and omnipotence. Christian eco-virtue cultivates the habit of taking immediate steps, however small, to love creation and our neighbors, recognizing our own limits while nevertheless committing ourselves wholeheartedly to serving the others with whom we share the amazing grace of creation.

Virtue is hard work. And it is worth it.

NOTES

Introduction

1 Martin Luther, "Defense and Explanation of All the Articles," in *Luther's Works*, ed. Christopher Boyd Brown (St. Louis: Concordia, 2009), 32:99.

2 See Frances Moore Lappé, *EcoMind: Changing the Way We Think, to Create the World We Want* (New York: Nation Books, 2011).

3 This book questions fundamentalism but takes Christian traditions and environmental goals as givens. Whitney Bauman has undertaken a more radical project, arguing that a committed "planetary" life requires questioning all basic assumptions, challenging received ideas about religion, identity, selfhood, sexuality, education, and ethics. See Whitney A. Bauman, *Religion and Ecology: Developing a Planetary Ethic* (New York: Columbia University Press, 2014).

4 Matthew 22:37-39; in this passage Jesus is loosely quoting Deuteronomy 6:5. All biblical quotations in this book are taken from the New Revised Standard Version (NRSV), and further quotations will be cited parenthetically.

5 The first quotation is from theologian Paul Tillich, *Dynamics of Faith* (New York: Harper & Row, 1957), 5; the second is from William James, *Varieties of Religious Experience: A Study in Human Nature* (New York: Routledge, 2002), 155.

6 A few of these arguments include Larry L. Rasmussen, *Earth Community, Earth Ethics* (Maryknoll, N.Y.: Orbis Books, 1996); Sallie McFague, *Super, Natural Christians: How We Should Love Nature* (Minneapolis: Fortress, 1997); Steven Bouma-Prediger, *For the Beauty of the Earth: A Christian Vision for Creation Care* (Grand Rapids: Baker Academic, 2010); Michael S. Northcott, *The Environment and Christian Ethics* (New York: Cambridge University Press, 1996); Tobias Winright, ed., *Green Discipleship: Catholic Theological Ethics and the Environment* (Winona, Minn.: Anselm Academic, 2011); Tri Robinson and Jason Chatraw, *Saving God's Green Earth: Rediscovering the Church's Responsibility to Environmental Stewardship* (Boise, Idaho: Ampelon, 2006); Karen Baker-Fletcher, *Sisters of Dust, Sisters of Spirit: Womanist Wordings on God and Creation* (Minneapolis: Fortress, 1998); John Chryssavgis, "The Earth as Sacrament: Insights from Orthodox Christian Theology and Spirituality," in *The Oxford Handbook of Religion and Ecology*, ed. Roger S. Gottlieb (New York: Oxford University Press, 2006).

7   This point is made well by J. Matthew Sleeth, *Serve God, Save the Planet: A Christian Call to Action* (White River Junction, Vt.: Chelsea Green, 2006), 31–32.

8   See, e.g., Katharine Hayhoe and Andrew Farley, *A Climate for Change: Global Warming Facts for Faith-Based Decisions* (New York: FaithWords, 2009); Bill McKibben, *Eaarth: Making a Life on a Tough New Planet* (New York: Time Books, 2010).

9   Frances Westley, Michael Quinn Patton, and Brenda Zimmerman, *Getting to Maybe: How the World Is Changed* (Toronto: Vintage Canada, 2007), 6–11.

Chapter 1

1   Aristotle, *Nicomachean Ethics* (New York: Macmillan, 1962), 35 (bk. II, chap. 1).

2   This idea has been popularized in recent years by Stanley Hauerwas, who is probably the best-known contemporary Christian virtue ethicist. See, e.g., Stanley Hauerwas, *The Peaceable Kingdom: A Primer in Christian Ethics* (Notre Dame, Ind.: University of Notre Dame Press, 1983).

3   Bouma-Prediger, *For the Beauty of the Earth*, chap. 6.

4   Louke van Wensveen, *Dirty Virtues: The Emergence of Ecological Virtue Ethics* (Amherst, N.Y.: Humanity Books, 2000).

5   Philip Cafaro, "Thoreau, Leopold, and Carson: Toward an Environmental Virtue Ethics," *Environmental Ethics* 22, no. 1 (2001).

6   James A. Nash, *Loving Nature: Ecological Integrity and Christian Responsibility* (Nashville: Abingdon, 1991), chap. 2.

7   In philosophical terms, our approach is what Ronald Sandler calls "extentionist": we take preexisting virtues and assume that they can extend to an environmental age. For extensive analysis of environmental virtue ethics, see Philip Cafaro and Ronald D. Sandler, *Environmental Virtue Ethics* (Lanham, Md.: Rowman & Littlefield, 2004); Ronald L. Sandler, *Character and Environment: A Virtue-Oriented Approach to Environmental Ethics* (New York: Columbia University Press, 2009); Philip Cafaro, ed., "Environmental Virtue Ethics," special issue, *Journal of Agricultural and Environmental Ethics* 23, nos. 1–2 (2010).

8   Thomas Aquinas, *Summa Theologica* (New York: Blackfriars, 1964), I.II, Q. 55–67.

9   Aristotle, *Nicomachean Ethics*, 43–44 (bk. II, chap. 6). As an introduction to environmental ethics, the present book is not strictly Aristotelian or Thomist in its approach; subsequent chapters will not be consistently precise about the use of the mean in comparing natural extremes. Readers seeking more rigorous Christian interpretations of Aristotle are encouraged to look to other scholarly explorations, such as Stanley Hauerwas and Charles Pinches, *Christians among the Virtues* (Notre Dame, Ind.: University of Notre Dame Press, 1999); Michael G. Lawler and Todd A. Salzman, "Virtue Ethics: Natural and Christian," *Theological Studies* 74, no. 2 (2013); Elizabeth Agnew Cochran, "Jesus Christ and the Cardinal Virtues: A Response to Monica Hellwig," *Theology Today* 65, no. 1 (2008); Robert Kruschwitz, "Christian Virtues and the Doctrine of the Mean," *Faith and Philosophy* 3, no. 4 (1986); and of course the works of Aquinas.

10   Aquinas, *Summa*, I.II, 64.4.

11   "Resisting the Green Dragon: A Biblical Response to One of the Greatest Deceptions of Our Day," Cornwall Alliance, accessed July 16, 2012, http://www.resistingthegreen dragon.com. Robert Nelson makes a related argument about the theology that underlies

environmentalism, suggesting that it is essentially a secular form of American Calvinism. Robert H. Nelson, *The New Holy Wars: Economic Religion vs. Environmental Religion in Contemporary America* (University Park: Pennsylvania State University Press, 2010).

12 Patrick Curry, *Ecological Ethics: An Introduction* (Malden, Mass.: Polity, 2011), 66–68.

13 As the Southern Baptist environmentalist Jonathan Merritt puts it: "Forcing environmentalism into a left-right dichotomy harms us all. If you consider yourself a conservative, you can remain a solid supporter of biblical values like the sanctity of life, but you should expand your political interests to include historically progressive issues like global poverty, human rights, and aggressive care for God's creation. If you consider yourself more progressive, you can continue to support the political goals you find important while working with conservatives of mutual goodwill on issues like this one." Jonathan Merritt, *Green Like God: Unlocking the Divine Plan for Our Planet* (New York: FaithWords, 2010), 85–86.

14 Deirdre N. McCloskey, *The Bourgeois Virtues: Ethics for an Age of Commerce* (Chicago: University of Chicago Press, 2006), 1.

15 Most environmental economists agree with McCloskey that communism is much more environmentally destructive than capitalism. "The absence of property rights brought the ecological endangerment." McCloskey, *The Bourgeois Virtues*, 32.

16 McCloskey, *The Bourgeois Virtues*, 23, 30.

17 Theologian Eugene McCarraher excoriates McCloskey's "attempts at theologizing" as being "clumsy and haphazard," steeped in calculating utilitarianism and willful blindness to capitalism's harms rather than genuine virtue. He argues, instead, that capitalism is Christianity's most insidious contemporary competitor, "the theology of a new religion of economics." He understands the church as being not a partner with idolatrous market systems but rather an antidote or alternative to them. Eugene McCarraher, "Break on through to the Other Side," *Books and Culture: A Christian Review* (2007), http://www.booksandculture.com/articles/2007/novdec/15.37.html?paging=off.

18 Hauerwas, *The Peaceable Kingdom*, 60.

19 Hauerwas, *The Peaceable Kingdom*, 101.

20 Martin Luther King Jr., "Conversation with Martin Luther King Jr.," in *A Testament of Hope: The Essential Writings of Martin Luther King, Jr.*, ed. James Melvin Washington (San Francisco: HarperCollins, 1986), 661.

21 Aquinas, *Summa*, I.II, 59.5.

Chapter 2

1 Some material in this chapter is adapted from Kathryn Blanchard and Kevin O'Brien, "Prophets Meet Profits: What Christian Ecological Ethics Can Learn From Free Market Environmentalism," *The Journal of the Society of Christian Ethics* 34, no. 1 (2014): 103–23.

2 Camilo Mora et al., "How Many Species Are There on Earth and in the Ocean?" *PLoS Biology* 9, no. 8 (2011); Carl Zimmer, "How Many Species? A Study Says 8.7 Million, but It's Tricky," *New York Times*, August 23, 2011.

3 Dr. Seuss, *The Lorax* (New York: Random House, 1999), 1.

4 Dr. Seuss, *The Lorax*, 12, 16.

5 Dr. Seuss, *The Lorax*, 21–24.

6   Dr. Seuss, *The Lorax*, 56.

7   Dr. Seuss, *The Lorax*, 58.

8   A recent film version of *The Lorax* doubles down on the antibusiness stance of the book. After the Lorax tells him it is bad to cut down the trees, the Once-ler responds with a song in the explicit spirit of social Darwinism and Ayn Rand: "How bad can I be? / I'm just doing what comes naturally / There's a principle of nature / Called survival of the fittest/ The animal that wins got to scratch and bite and claw and fight and punch / And the animal that doesn't . . . winds up someone else's lunch." The Once-ler continues establishing himself as a caricature of right-wing politics by arguing that money makes the world go around, that "biggering" is the only path to business success, and that even though this will inevitably end in total environmental destruction, he is not concerned with such problems, only with his own individual interests: "Me, I'll take care of mine, mine, mine, mine, mine." *The Lorax*, directed by Kyle Balda and Chris Renault (Santa Monica, Calif.: Illumination Entertainment, 2012), DVD.

9   The executive director of the Sierra Club writes that they lead wilderness excursions precisely to inspire people to conservation, because "words and images are powerful tools for persuading people to advocate for wild places, but nothing touches someone more deeply than personal experience." Michael Brune, "Why We Explore," *Sierra*, May/June 2012.

10   Philosopher Michael Sandel develops this argument carefully in his book *What Money Can't Buy*, cautioning that "putting a price on the good things in life can corrupt them," because market values tend to be so overpowering that they colonize other kinds of values. In regard to issues like species protection, Sandel worries that economic logic "entrenches an instrumental attitude toward nature, and it undermines the spirit of shared sacrifice that may be necessary to create a global environmental ethic." Michael J. Sandel, *What Money Can't Buy: The Moral Limits of Markets* (New York: Farrar, Straus & Giroux, 2012), 9, 75.

11   Wendell Berry, *Sex, Economy, Freedom, & Community* (New York: Pantheon Books, 1992), 100, 115.

12   Terry L. Anderson, "Postscript: Who Owns the Environment?" in *The Political Economy of Environmental Justice*, ed. H. Spencer Banzhaf (Stanford, Calif.: Stanford University Press, 2012), 267.

13   See Terry Lee Anderson and Donald Leal, *Free Market Environmentalism* (New York: Palgrave, 2001), 12; Garrett Hardin, "The Tragedy of the Commons," *Science* 162 (1968).

14   Elizabeth Brubaker, "Unnatural Disaster: How Politics Destroyed Canada's Atlantic Groundfisheries," in *Political Environmentalism: Going behind the Green Curtain*, ed. Terry Lee Anderson (Stanford, Calif.: Hoover Institution, 2000), 202.

15   Economist Stephen Horwitz asserts that clear-cutting of forests happens only on land that no one owns, "because the property rights of the owner are tenuous, substantially reducing the expectation of future profits and making it more rational to extract all the value now." He goes on to explain, "This normally happens when governments threaten to nationalize resources or where the property claims are uncertain and one party wishes to grab all the value before another party enters the competition." Stephen Horwitz, "The Economics of the Lorax," 2012, accessed December 3, 2012, http://www.fee.org/the_freeman/detail/the-economics-of-the-lorax/#axzz2Dz0AxLi5.

16   Terry Lee Anderson and Laura E. Huggins, *Greener than Thou: Are You Really an Environmentalist?* (Stanford, Calif.: Hoover Institution, 2008), 98. Anderson and Leal cite

evidence that elephant populations actually increased in Botswana and Zimbabwe where the ivory trade is legal, as opposed to other African nations where it is illegal (Anderson and Leal, *Free Market Environmentalism*, 64–66).

17 Anderson and Leal, *Free Market Environmentalism*, 4. One can of course imagine a situation in which a very rich landowner would be shortsighted or senile or would simply have an irrational hatred of elephants or Truffula Trees; if pressed, proponents of FME will admit that the extinction of species in such a case is indeed a risk, but it is a risk that they prefer over those risks associated with governmental usurpation of individuals' private property.

18 See the Nature Conservancy's website for information on conservation easements: http:// www.nature.org/about-us/private-lands-conservation/conservation-easements/all-about -conservation-easements.xml.

19 Clement of Alexandria, "Who Is the Rich Man That Shall Be Saved?" in *Ante-Nicene Fathers* (Grand Rapids: Eerdmans, 1979), 2:595.

20 Pope Leo XIII, "Rerum Novarum," in *Catholic Social Thought: The Documentary Heritage*, ed. David J. O'Brien and Thomas A. Shannon (Maryknoll, N.Y.: Orbis Books, 1992), 17, §7.

21 As noted in the first chapter, the idea of a "mean" is used here to create a dialogue between differing environmental philosophies. Free market environmentalism and traditional conservation do not, strictly speaking, represent natural opposites; nevertheless, placing them in contrast this way illustrates the ways prudence takes different forms in different schools of thought.

22 Meredith Kile, "U.S. Scientists Work to Save the Bee Population and America's Food," *Al Jazeera America*, September 29, 2013, http://america.aljazeera.com/watch/shows/ techknow/blog/2013/9/29/u-s-scientists-worktosavethebeepopulationandamericasfood. html. The supply of honeybees has been rapidly decreasing in recent decades due to the mysterious phenomenon of "colony collapse disorder," probably caused in large part by pesticides used widely in the farming industry.

23 For a discussion of the various economic and social values of other species, see Edward O. Wilson, *The Future of Life* (New York: Vintage Books, 2002), chap. 5.

24 For more on this "sacramental" value of other species, see Kevin J. O'Brien, *An Ethics of Biodiversity: Christianity, Ecology, and the Variety of Life* (Washington, D.C.: Georgetown University Press, 2010), chap. 3.

25 Anderson and Leal, *Free Market Environmentalism*, 10.

26 Adam Smith, *The Theory of Moral Sentiments* (Oxford: Clarendon, 1976). For a fuller treatment of the importance of sympathy as a check on economic self-interest, not only in Smith's thought but also in Christian thinking about capitalism, see Kathryn D'Arcy Blanchard, *The Protestant Ethic or the Spirit of Capitalism: Christians, Freedom, and Free Markets* (Eugene, Ore.: Cascade, 2010), chap. 3.

27 Pope Francis, "Evangelii Gaudium" [the Joy of the Gospel], November 24, 2013, §215, accessed January 18, 2014, http://www.vatican.va/holy_father/francesco/apost _exhortations/documents/papa-francesco_esortazione-ap_20131124_evangelii -gaudium_en.html.

28 Natural News, "Anti-cancer Fungus Found to Naturally Eat Away Plastic Waste," *International Business Times*, February 28, 2012.

29 The fund's website, which contains extensive information, is at http://mptf.undp.org/ yasuni (accessed February 9, 2013).

30 See, e.g., Felix Salmon, "Why Ecuador Isn't Drilling in Yasuni," *Reuters*, January 2, 2012.
31 Felicity Le Quesne, "Conservation v Oil: Ecuador's Yasuni-ITT Initiative," *International*, September 6, 2013, http://www.theinternational.org/articles/461-conservation-v-oil-ecuadors-yasuni-it.

Chapter 3

1 Melissa Jackson's book on women in the Hebrew Bible includes a chapter on courageous—and comical—actions of the women of Moses' infancy. Melissa A. Jackson, *Comedy and Feminist Interpretation of the Bible: A Subversive Collaboration* (Oxford: Oxford University Press, 2012), 67ff.
2 Daniel Erlander, *Manna and Mercy: A Brief History of God's Unfolding Promise to Mend the Entire Universe* (Mercer Island, Wash.: Order of Saints Martin and Teresa, 1992), 7–9.
3 Aristotle, *Nicomachean Ethics*, 12–14, 1115b.
4 C. S. Lewis, *The Screwtape Letters* (New York: Macmillan, 1944), 148–49. Emphasis added.
5 Charles C. Mann, "What if We Never Run Out of Oil?" *Atlantic*, April 24, 2013, http://www.theatlantic.com/magazine/archive/2013/05/what-if-we-never-run-out-of-oil/309294/?single_page=true.
6 A good starting point for information on the process and potential dangers of mountaintop removal and hydraulic fracturing is the U.S. Environmental Protection Agency. See "Natural Gas Extraction: Hydraulic Fracturing," http://www2.epa.gov/hydraulicfracturing, accessed March 22, 2014.
7 Bruce E. Johansen, "The Inuit's Struggle with Dioxins and Other Organic Pollutants," *American Indian Quarterly* 26, no. 3 (2002).
8 With few notable exceptions (such as Norway), evidence suggests that nations with oil are more likely to have authoritarian governments and severe economic inequality, a phenomenon known as the "resource curse." See Macartan Humphreys, Jeffrey Sachs, and Joseph E. Stiglitz, eds., *Escaping the Resource Curse* (New York: Columbia University Press, 2007).
9 The term comes from former president George W. Bush. See Elisabeth Bumiller and Adam Nagourney, "Bush: America Is Addicted to Oil," *New York Times*, February 1, 2006, http://www.nytimes.com/2006/02/01/world/americas/01iht-state.html?pagewanted=all&_r=0.
10 "How Much of the World's Energy Does the United States Use?" U.S. Energy Information Administration, last modified April 30, 2013, http://www.eia.gov/tools/faqs/faq.cfm?id=87&t=1.
11 While a few right-wing politicians continue to insist that all regulation of corporations is bad, the corporations themselves have begun to make plans for what they see as the inevitable arrival of governmental restrictions (most particularly carbon taxes) designed to protect the air and the climate. Coral Davenport, "Large Companies Prepared to Pay Price on Carbon," *New York Times*, December 5, 2013, http://www.nytimes.com/2013/12/05/business/energy-environment/large-companies-prepared-to-pay-price-on-carbon.html.
12 "Exactly How Much Green Can You Combine with Growth?" asks Lucy Williamson, "South Korea's Drive for Renewable Energy," *BBC News*, December 1, 2011.
13 As of May 2013, about 60 percent of the oil used in the United States is from domestic sources and about 40 percent comes from overseas. Of that imported oil, about half

comes from the Western Hemisphere, with Canada supplying about a third. About 13 percent of America's oil imports come from Saudi Arabia. See "How Dependent Are We on Foreign Oil?" U.S. Energy Information Administration, last modified May 10, 2013, http://www.eia.gov/energy_in_brief/article/foreign_oil_dependence.cfm.

14 T. Boone Pickens, *The First Billion Is the Hardest: How Believing It's Still Early in the Game Can Lead to Life's Greatest Comebacks* (New York: Crown, 2008), 238, 131.

15 Pickens, *The First Billion Is the Hardest*, 239. Pickens spent years developing a giant wind farm in Texas as part of his investment in the Pickens Plan, but in December of 2010 he determined that the price of natural gas was so low and the cost of building new transmission lines so high that it was not economically feasible to invest in wind. Nathanael Baker, "T. Boone Pickens Drops Wind Power from His Energy Plan," *Energy Collective*, last modified December 15, 2010, http://theenergycollective.com/nathanaelbaker/48644/t-boone-pickens-drops-wind-power-his-energy-plan.

16 Pickens, *The First Billion Is the Hardest*, 146–47.

17 "Annual Energy Review," U.S. Energy Information Administration, last modified September 27, 2012, http://www.eia.gov/totalenergy/data/annual/pecss_diagram.cfm.

18 Three hundred and fifty refers to the CO_2 parts per million ("ppm") in the earth's atmosphere recommended by some climate scientists and activists to stave off climate disaster. See http://www.350.org.

19 The term "represents the idea that we have entered a new epoch in Earth's geological history, one characterized by the arrival of the human species as a geological force. The biologist Eugene F. Stoermer and the Nobel-Prize-winning chemist Paul Crutzen advanced the term in 2000, and it has steadily gained acceptance as evidence has increasingly mounted that the changes wrought by global warming will affect not just the world's climate and biological diversity, but its very geology—and not just for a few centuries, but for millenniums." Roy Scranton, "Learning to Die in the Anthropocene," *New York Times*, November 10, 2013, http://opinionator.blogs.nytimes.com/2013/11/10/learning-how-to-die-in-the-anthropocene/.

20 Bill McKibben, "The Fossil Fuel Resistance," *Rolling Stone*, April 11, 2013.

21 Bill McKibben, "Global Warming's Terrifying New Math," *Rolling Stone*, August 2, 2012.

22 Because of the relative novelty of fracking, experts remain divided on the environmental harm caused by that method of extracting natural gas. Two authors on *Salon* demonstrate the controversy well. One writes, "I am not trying to imply that fracking is safe, but that its danger depends upon local geology, the competence of the drillers themselves, and—above all—effective regulation." Lisa Margonelli, "Is the Environmental Defense Fund Ruining Environmentalism?" *Salon*, May 25, 2013. Almost as if in response, the other writes, "Illinois is now standing in violation of state law for failing to provide enough coal mining inspectors. How can we imagine fracking oversight will be any different?" Jeff Biggers, "Illinois' Fracking and Coal Rush Is a National Crisis," *Salon*, May 25, 2013.

23 Bill McKibben, "Why Not Frack?" *New York Review of Books*, March 8, 2012; Bill McKibben, "The Methane beneath Our Feet," *New York Review of Books*, April 1, 2013.

24 McKibben, *Eaarth*, 52.

25 McKibben, *Eaarth*, 148, 128.

26 Furthermore, the materials and technologies currently used to make green power are often much less clean—both environmentally and ethically—than the power itself, requiring mining and energy-intensive manufacturing. Aaron Robbins, "Out of Africa:

Where Electric-Vehicle Batteries Come From, Part II," *Car and Driver*, November 2010, http://www.caranddriver.com/columns/aaron-robinson-out-of-africa-where-electric -vehicle-batteries-come-from-part-ii; Jennifer Grayson, "Eco-Etiquette: How Green Are Solar Panels?" *Huffington Post*, April 28, 2010, http://www.huffingtonpost.com/ jennifer-grayson/eco-etiquette-how-green-a_b_554717.html.

27 Lester R. Brown, *Plan B 4.0: Mobilizing to Save Civilization* (New York: W. W. Norton, 2009), 118.

28 McKibben, *Eaarth*, 206.

29 "Amory Lovins on Energy," Principal Voices, *CNN*, last modified October 16, 2008, http://edition.cnn.com/2008/WORLD/americas/10/10/amory.lovins/.

30 Erlander, *Manna and Mercy*, 13.

31 Laura M. Hartman, *The Christian Consumer: Living Faithfully in a Fragile World* (New York: Oxford University Press, 2011), 152.

32 Brayton Shanley, *The Many Sides of Peace: Christian Nonviolence, the Contemplative Life, and Sustainable Living* (Eugene, Ore.: Resource Publications, 2013), 87.

33 Shanley, *The Many Sides of Peace*, 93, 149.

34 Shanley, *The Many Sides of Peace*, 158–59.

35 Shanley, *The Many Sides of Peace*, 159.

36 David Owen reports: Google's "server farms, along with the rest of the Internet, use a huge and rapidly growing amount of electricity. Google has revealed very little about its energy consumption, but the total is known to be immense. Searching, accessing, and storing an ever-increasing volume of Web pages [etc.] . . . requires energy, and most of that energy is currently generated by burning fossil fuels. The Internet's energy and carbon footprints almost certainly now exceed those of air travel . . . and they are growing faster than those of almost all other human activities." David Owen, *The Conundrum: How Scientific Innovation, Increased Efficiency, and Good Intentions Can Make Our Energy and Climate Problems Worse* (New York: Riverhead Books, 2012), 211–12.

37 For more information on how fracking works, see the Michigan Watershed Council's website. "Oil and Gas Development Using High Volume Hydraulic Fracturing," Tip of the Mitt Watershed Council, accessed December 14, 2013, http://www.watershedcoun-cil.org/learn/hydraulic-fracturing. Opponents of fracking worry not only about the process itself but about the fact that politicians and corporate business leaders are too "cozy" to ensure sufficient oversight: "Fracking is inherently unsafe and we cannot rely on regulation to protect communities' water, air and public health." "Fracking," Food & Water Watch, accessed December 14, 2013, http://www.foodandwaterwatch.org/water/frack-ing/. Regulations vary widely, however, state by state: Kate Galbraith, "California Plans Tighter Control of Fracking, but Not Enough for Some," *New York Times*, December 13, 2013, http://www.nytimes.com/2013/12/14/business/energy-environment/california -plans-tighter-control-of-fracking-but-not-enough-for-some.html.

38 Earth Ministry website, http://www.earthministry.org.

39 The authors thank LeeAnne Beres and Jessie Dye for extensive conversations about their experience, from which this account is drawn.

40 LeeAnne Beres and Jessie Dye, "From Church Sanctuaries to the Steps of the Capitol: Faithful Advocacy for a Coal-Free Washington," in *Sacred Acts: How Churches Are Working to Protect Earth's Climate*, ed. Mallory McDuff (Gabriola Island, B.C.: New Society, 2012), 129–30.

Chapter 4

1 *Babette's Feast*, directed by Gabriel Axel (Copenhagen, Denmark: Nordisk Film, 1987), DVD.

2 He wrote, "If we consider for what end [God] created food, we shall find that he consulted not only for our necessity, but also for our enjoyment and delight. . . . Have done, then, with that inhuman philosophy which, in allowing no use of the creatures but for necessity, not only maliciously deprives us of the lawful fruit of the divine beneficence, but cannot be realised without depriving man of all his senses, and reducing him to a block." John Calvin, *Institutes of the Christian Religion* (Philadelphia: Westminster, 1960); III.10.2-3.

3 Aquinas, *Summa*, II.II, Q. 141, A.3.

4 Aquinas, *Summa*, II.II, Q. 141, A.4.

5 Aquinas, *Summa*, II.II, Q. 142, A.2.

6 Aquinas, *Summa*, II.II, Q. 142, A.4.

7 Aquinas, *Summa*, II.II, Q. 142, A.1.

8 He further writes, "We consider such needs regarding both the fitness of body and the fitness of external things—namely, riches and responsibilities—and, much more, the fitness of honorable character . . . [as] regards both the needs of this life and the person's responsibilities." Aquinas, *Summa*, II.II, Q. 142, A.6.

9 Francine Prose, *Gluttony* (Oxford: Oxford University Press, 2006), 79.

10 For a more comprehensive account of the global food system that includes more discussion of the various costs to human beings and the political institutions creating food policy in the United States, see Jennifer R. Ayres, *Good Food: Grounded Practical Theology* (Waco, Tex.: Baylor University Press, 2013), chaps. 1–2.

11 Wendell Berry, *Bringing It to the Table: On Farming and Food* (Berkeley, Calif.: Counterpoint, 2009), 228.

12 The World Bank and International Finance Corporation estimates that meat accounts for 51 percent of greenhouse gases, over against a 2006 estimate putting "Livestock's Long Shadow" at 18 percent. Robert Goodland, "FAO Yields to Meat Industry Pressure on Climate Change," *New York Times*, July 11, 2012, http://bittman.blogs.nytimes.com/2012/07/11/fao-yields-to-meat-industry-pressure-on-climate-change/. See also Michelle Maisto, "Eating Less Meat Is World's Best Chance for Timely Climate Change, Say Experts," *Forbes*, April 28, 2012, http://www.forbes.com/sites/michellemaisto/2012/04/28/eating-less-meat-is-worlds-best-chance-for-timely-climate-change-say-experts/.

13 Lester R. Brown, "Agriculture Industry's Oil Addiction Threatens Food Security," *Inside Climate News*, July 16, 2009, http://insideclimatenews.org/news/20090716/agriculture-industrys-oil-addiction-threatens-food-security.

14 The authors thank Ashton Ritchie, an agronomist and resident lawn and garden expert at the Scotts Miracle-Gro Company, for sharing his thoughts on fertilizer and food in June of 2013. He places great hope for the future in teaching kids about how to grow their own food—e.g., Ashton Ritchie, "Texas Master Gardeners Blew Me Away," *Tips from Ashton Ritchie* (blog), May 6, 2012, http://tipsfromashton.wordpress.com/2012/05/06/texas-master-gardeners-blew-me-away/.

15 Matthew Scully, *Dominion: The Power of Man, the Suffering of Animals, and the Call to Mercy* (New York: St. Martin's, 2002), 249, 270, 289.

16 David Grumett and Rachel Muers, *Theology on the Menu: Asceticism, Meat and Christian Diet* (New York: Routledge, 2010), x.

17 One pacifist Christian blogger insists that his fellow pacifist Christians must give up meat if they are serious about peace: "Practice nonviolence in a tangible manner. Stop feeding on other bodies to satiate your own taste-buds, then, maybe . . . just maybe, all of your inane rhetoric about nonviolence will have some merit." The Amish Jihadist, "The Defecation That Is, Often, Christian Nonviolence," *Other Journal* (blog), July 15, 2013, http://theotherjournal.com/amishjihadi/2013/07/15/the -defecation-that-is-often-christian-nonviolence/.

18 "Hunger Statistics," United Nations World Food Programme, accessed June 10, 2013, http://www.wfp.org/hunger/stats.

19 Alisha Coleman-Jensen, Mark Nord, Margaret Andrews, and Steven Carlson, *Household Food Security in the United States in 2011: Statistical Supplement* (Washington, D.C.: United States Department of Agriculture Economic Research Service, 2012), 6, http://www.ers.usda.gov/publications/ap-administrative-publication/ap-058.aspx #.UtrrKHmtsog.

20 Institution of Mechanical Engineers, *Global Food: Waste Not, Want Not; Feeding the 9 Billion; The Tragedy of Waste* (London: Institution of Mechanical Engineers, 2012), http:// www.imeche.org/knowledge/themes/environment/global-food.

21 Dana Gunders, "Wasted: How America Is Losing Up to 40 Percent of Its Food from Farm to Fork to Landfill," NRDC Issue Papers, August 2012, 4, http://www.nrdc.org/food/ wasted-food.asp. She then holds out hope: "This means there was once a time when we wasted far less, and we can get back there again."

22 "Produce may not be harvested because of damage caused by pests, disease, and weather. In other cases, it is due to economics. If market prices are too low at the time of harvest, growers may leave some crops in the field because they will not cover their costs after accounting for the costs of labor and transport. In addition, growers may plant more crops than there is demand for in the market in order to hedge against weather and pest pressure or speculate on high prices. This further lowers prices in bumper crop years, leading to more crops not warranting the cost of harvest. . . . Even fields that are harvested may have significant amounts of food left behind. Workers are trained to selectively harvest, leaving any produce that will not pass minimum quality standards in terms of shape, size, color, and time to ripeness." Gunders, "Wasted," 8.

23 *Food, Inc.*, directed by Robert Kenner (Los Angeles: Participant Media, 2009), DVD; *Fast Food Nation*, directed by Richard Linklater (Los Angeles: Participant Media, 2006), DVD; Eric Schlosser, *Fast Food Nation: The Dark Side of the All-American Meal* (New York: Houghton Mifflin, 2001).

24 Eric Schlosser, "The Most Dangerous Job in America," *Mother Jones*, July/August 2001.

25 Some workers under such dehumanizing conditions begin to take out their frustrations on the animals. Nancy Perry and Peter Brandt, "A Case Study on Cruelty to Farm Animals: Lessons Learned from the Hallmark Meat Packing Case," *Michigan Law Review* 106, no. 117 (2008); Paul Solotaroff, "In the Belly of the Beast," *Rolling Stone*, December 10, 2013.

26 See chapter 7 for further discussion of Malthus and the debate about population that continues today.

27 Pierre Desrochers and Hiroko Shimizu, *The Locavore's Dilemma: In Praise of the 10,000-Mile Diet* (New York: Public Affairs, 2012), xxiii. There are many who share a radical disdain for what they see as the inexcusably naïve idea of traditional, local diets; as one farmer, Blake Hurst, writes in the foreword of *The Locavore's Dilemma*, "Desrochers and Shimizu take the idea of local food to the back of the barn and beat the holy livin' tar out of it. The idea of food miles will never again rear its ugly head in polite company, nor should we have to hear about how far farmers are from their consumers" (xiii).

28 Even "organic" food, according to the U.S. Government Printing Office (mission: "Keeping America Informed"), can contain an overwhelming list of substances. "Electronic Code of Federal Regulations," U.S. Government Printing Office, last modified February 27, 2014, http://www.ecfr.gov/cgi-bin/text-idx?c=ecfr&SID=9874504b6f1025eb0e6b6 7cadf9d3b40&rgn=div6&view=text&node=7:3.1.1.9.32.7&idno=7.

29 "Statistics FAQs," The Fertilizer Institute, accessed July 7, 2013, http://www.tfi.org /statistics/statistics-faqs. Statistics are for 2008. This includes not only the nutrients but also the other chemicals required to stabilize and deliver fertilizer, which make up over half the weight; 21.5 tons were actual nutrients—nitrogen, phosphate, and potash.

30 Dan Charles, "Fertilized World," *National Geographic*, May 2013. He writes, "Giant factories capture inert nitrogen gas from the vast stores in our atmosphere and force it into a chemical union with the hydrogen in natural gas, creating the reactive compounds that plants crave. That nitrogen fertilizer—more than a hundred million tons applied worldwide every year—fuels bountiful harvests. . . . In fact, almost half of the nitrogen found in our bodies' muscle and organ tissue started out in a fertilizer factory."

31 Center for Veterinary Medicine, *Summary Report on Antimicrobials Sold or Distributed for Use in Food-Producing Animals*, last modified 2011, http://www.fda.gov/downloads/ ForIndustry/UserFees/AnimalDrugUserFeeActADUFA/UCM338170.pdf; Arthur Grabe et al., *Pesticide Industry Sales and Usage: 2006 and 2007 Market Estimates*, last modified February 2011, http://www.epa.gov/opp00001/pestsales/07pestsales/market_est mates2007.pdf.

32 Michael Pollan, "Farmer in Chief," *New York Times Magazine*, October 9, 2008.

33 Michael Pollan, "Power Steer," *New York Times Magazine*, March 31, 2002. Pollan does not argue against treating sick animals, but he notes that the vast majority of antibiotics are given preventively to animals that are not yet sick but are stored so close together and in such unnatural conditions that they can only stay healthy with the help of drugs. Regarding animal parts in animal feed, see "They Eat What?" Union of Concerned Scientists, last modified August 8, 2006, http://www.ucsusa.org/food_and_agriculture/our-failing-food-system/industrial-agriculture/they-eat-what-the-reality-of.html.

34 Michael Pollan, *In Defense of Food: An Eater's Manifesto* (New York: Penguin, 2008).

35 Blake Hurst, "The Omnivore's Delusion: Against the Agri-intellectuals," *American*, July 30, 2009.

36 David H. Freedman, "How Junk Food Can End Obesity," *Atlantic*, July 2013. Many other examples of technological efforts to create more ethical food could be cited. Perhaps the most intriguing is the attempt to engineer beef in laboratories in response to the world's growing demand for meat, in hopes that "full-scale production of cultured meat could greatly reduce water, land and energy use, and emissions of methane and other greenhouse gases" compared to conventional meat production while ending the need for

factory farming of cows; see Henry Fountain, "Building a $325,000 Burger," *New York Times*, May 14, 2013, D1. Emphasis in the original.

37   Charles, "Fertilized World."

38   Dan Merica, "Christie Reveals Weight Loss Surgery," *Political Ticker* (blog), *CNN*, May 7, 2013, http://politicalticker.blogs.cnn.com/2013/05/07/christie-reveals-weight -loss-surgery/?hpt=hp_c2.

39   Amanda Blum, "It's Official: Chris Christie Was Fat Shamed into Weight Loss Sur- gery," *Issues* (blog), *xoJane*, May 7, 2013, http://www.xojane.com/issues/chris-christie -lapband-surgery. Later that year, *Time* magazine put Christie's picture on its cover with the caption, "The Elephant in the Room," garnering criticism; e.g., Laura E. Davis, "*Time* Magazine Cover: Chris Christie, 'Elephant'—Clever or Cruel?" *Los Angeles Times*, November 8, 2013, http://articles.latimes.com/2013/nov/08/news/ la-sh-time-magazine-cover-chris-christie-elephant-20131108.

40   Kate Harding, "Fat, Yes. Ashamed, No," *Guardian*, August 1, 2010, http://www.guard- ian.co.uk/commentisfree/2010/aug/01/fat-shame-obesity-doctors.

41   It is vital to understand that anorexia nervosa and bulimia are not simple matters of food preference or "choice" but are serious illnesses in need of medical treatment. Indeed, overeating can also sometimes fit under the category of "addiction" and may need to be addressed medically. In using these examples the authors simply mean to point out the overly simplified ways that "too much" and "too little" eating, as well as popular under- standings of temperance or moderation, are often addressed in public media.

42   The editors at *Scientific American* argue that federal support for farmers, which started during the Great Depression, made sense at a specific time when so many Americans were food insecure; food was seen as a public good, and the government wanted to make sure farmers did not stop producing. "Nearly eight decades later," however, "the benefits flow primarily to large commodity producers of corn and soy, which are as profitable as ever." Subsidies have created "perverse incentives" rewarding commodity crops and unhealthy foods that keep for a long time and can be widely distributed. In other words, farm subsidies have made it sensible for everyone to eat huge quantities of corn, soy, and livestock fed on corn and soy. Meanwhile, fresh, unprocessed fruits and vegetables are seen as "specialty crops" for the affluent, undeserving of government assistance. (Edi- tors, "For a Healthier Country, Overhaul Farm Subsidies," *Scientific American*, April 19, 2012, http://www.scientificamerican.com/article.cfm?id=fresh-fruit-hold-the-insu- lin.) Apologists, on the other hand, argue that everyone—not just farmers and corpora- tions—benefits from subsidies. "Without these subsidies," they warn, "many corn farmers may simply not find it economically viable to keep producing crops for public consump- tion," leading to food shortages. Moreover, they argue, "it keeps the prices of food," includ- ing meat, "affordable for the masses." ("Why We Need Corn Subsidies," Corn Subsidies, last modified June 12, 2011, http://cornsubsidies.com/why-we-need-corn-subsidies.)

43   Michael Moss, "(Salt + Fat² / Satisfying Crunch) × Pleasing Mouth Feel = a Food Designed to Addict," *New York Times Magazine*, February 24, 2013, 46. He writes, "Dis- cover what consumers want to buy and give it to them with both barrels. Sell more, keep your job! How do marketers often translate these 'rules' into action on food? Our limbic brains love sugar, fat, salt. . . . So formulate products to deliver these. Perhaps add low- cost ingredients to boost profit margins. Then 'supersize' to sell more. . . . And advertise/ promote to lock in 'heavy users.' Plenty of guilt to go around here!"

44 Evagrius Ponticus, *The Praktikos & Chapters on Prayer* (Kalamazoo, Mich.: Cistercian, 1981), 21.

45 Grumett and Muers, *Theology on the Menu*, 11.

46 Of course, Evagrius did not seek to deny or abandon the world; his influence during his own time, and the fact that he remains an important voice in Christian spirituality and theology, demonstrates that he continued to engage the wider world. However, his authority came from a kind of purity that required separation. See Julia Konstantinovsky, "Evagrius Ponticus on Being Good in God and Christ," *Studies in Christian Ethics* 26, no. 3 (2013).

47 Mary Clare Jalonick, "Frozen Berry Mix Sold to Costco Linked to Hepatitis A," *Mercury News*, June 4, 2013, http://www.mercurynews.com/health/ci_23384692/frozen-berry-mix-sold-costco-linked-hepatitis; "Export Summary—Japan Buys Wheat, China Buys Indian Corn," *Reuters*, March 14, 2013, http://www.reuters.com/article/2013/03/14/grain-exportsummary-idUSL1N0C5HBW20130314; Ethan Huff, "Organic Groups, Farmers File Preemptive Lawsuit against Monsanto to Protect Themselves from Inevitable Destruction by GMOs," *Natural News*, last modified April 1, 2011, http://www.natural news.com/031922_Monsanto_lawsuit.html#ixzz2VGqEFS76; http://www.pubpat.org/assets/files/seed/OSGATA-v-Monsanto-Complaint.pdf.

48 Ayres, *Good Food*, 4.

49 Ayres, *Good Food*, 95. Emphasis in the original.

50 Ayres, *Good Food*, chap. 7.

51 Ayres, *Good Food*, chap. 6.

52 Indeed, even the concept of "hunger" can itself be problematic in that it may place too much emphasis on "helpers" and donors who step in during emergencies while undermining political will to create long-term food security, argues Laura B. DeLind, in "Celebrating Hunger in Michigan: A Critique of an Emergency Food Program and an Alternative for the Future," *Agriculture and Human Values* 11, no. 4 (1994). For further complexity, see Paul Roderick Gregory, "Even Matt Damon and Beyoncé Could Not Sell the True Child Hunger Statistic (One in a Thousand)," *Forbes*, June 2, 2013, http://www.forbes.com/sites/paulroderickgregory/2013/06/02/even-matt-damon-and-beyonce-could-not-sell-the-true-child-hunger-statistic/.

53 "Walmart Produce: Our Commitment to You," Walmart, accessed March 30, 2014, http://instoresnow.walmart.com/article.aspx?Center=Food&top=87508&id=44214. International food aid is another important area of food distribution in need of temperance, but it is beyond the scope of this chapter. American Jewish World Service and Oxfam recommend that, instead of distributing American food to people overseas (which benefits American farmers more than hungry people), the United States should instead buy food from food growers closer to the hunger or just offer financial aid. Needless to say, this would also save a great deal of energy in transportation and storage, though farmers elsewhere may be less temperate in their use of fertilizers. See Oxfam America and American Jewish World Service, "Reverse Hunger," http://ajws.org/reversehunger/docs/0312_saving_money_and_lives.pdf; "Learn about SNAP Benefits at Farmers' Markets," USDA Food and Nutrition Service, accessed March 30, 2014, http://www.fns.usda.gov/snap/ebt/fm.htm.

54 Aoife Boothroyd, "GM Golden Rice to Be Launched in the Philippines," *Food Magazine*, November 2013, http://www.foodmag.com.au/news/gm-golden-rice-to-be

-launched-in-the-philippines. See also http://www.goldenrice.org; and Bjørn Lomborg, "The Deadly Opposition to Genetically Modified Food," *Slate*, February 2013, http://www.slate.com/articles/health_and_science/project_syndicate0/2013/02/gm_food_golden_rice_will_save_millions_of_people_from_vitamin_a_deficiency.html.

55 "Vitamin A Deficiency," World Health Organization, accessed March 30, 2014, http://www.who.int/nutrition/topics/vad/en/.

56 See Vandana Shiva, *Monocultures of the Mind: Perspectives on Biodiversity and Biotechnology* (London: Zed Books, 1993); Vandana Shiva, "The 'Golden Rice' Hoax—When Public Relations Replaces Science," Norfolk Genetic Information Network, October 26, 2000, accessed March 30, 2014, http://ngin.tripod.com/11.htm.

Chapter 5

1 Utah American Indian Digital Archive, http://www.utahindians.org/archives/goshute.html. See also Confederate Tribes of the Goshute Indian Reservation website, http://goshutetribe.com/ (accessed November 17, 2013).

2 Jim Woolf, "Tribe Digs into Mystery of Sheep that Died near Dugway in 1968," *Salt Lake Tribune*, December 14, 1997; Jim Woolf, "Army: Nerve Agent near Dead Utah Sheep in '68," *Salt Lake Tribune*, January 1, 1998.

3 See David Rich Lewis, "Skull Valley Goshutes and the Politics of Nuclear Waste: Environment, Identity and Sovereignty," in *Native Americans and the Environment: Perspectives on the Ecological Indian*, ed. Michael Eugene Harkin and David Rich Lewis (Lincoln: University of Nebraska Press, 2007); James B. Martin-Schramm and Robert L. Stivers, *Christian Environmental Ethics: A Case Method Approach* (Maryknoll, N.Y.: Orbis Books, 2003), chap. 10; Valerie L. Kuletz, *The Tainted Desert: Environmental Ruin in the American West* (New York: Routledge, 1998), 109–11; Winona LaDuke, *All Our Relations: Native Struggles for Land and Life* (Cambridge, Mass.: South End, 1999), 104–6; Goldhawk Productions, *Radioactive Reservations,* VHS (New York: Filmakers Library, 1995).

4 See Jim Woolf, "Utah's Not Aglow over Goshute Deal to Store N-Waste," *Salt Lake Tribune*, December 25, 1996; Brent Israelsen, "Tribe Keeps Pro N-Waste Chairman," *Salt Lake Tribune*, November 28, 2000.

5 Judy Fahys, "Utah N-Waste Site Backers Call It Quits," *Salt Lake Tribune*, December 21, 2012.

6 Their website says, "A nuclear electrical power plant on the Confederated Tribes of the Goshute Reservation would be very attractive. The Reservation has adequate land, water resources, low population, and ready access to major electrical power transmission lines. . . . The successful establishment of such a major electrical energy supplier would be very beneficial to the Tribe for more than 50 years. . . . The income and work opportunities from such a major development would provide the Goshute with an annual income of about $350 million. Income from the electricity plant would provide for full development of schools including a college, improved and expanded roads, a Reservation hospital, an airport, numerous local industries, Tribal government support, and other essential facilities. Goshute children would have employment and career opportunities on the Reservation. The Tribe would become economically independent and have the financial resources to develop the Reservation as the Tribe elected." Confederate Tribes of the Goshute Indian Reservation, accessed November 17, 2013, http://goshutetribe.com/ADN/energy/nuclear/.

7   For an introduction to the environmental issues raised by nuclear energy and waste, see Jonathan B. King, "Learning to Solve the Right Problems: The Case of Nuclear Power in America," *Journal of Business Ethics* 12, no. 2 (1993); Harold A. Feiveson, "A Skeptic's View of Nuclear Energy," *Daedalus* 138, no. 4 (2009).

8   Jace Weaver, ed., *Defending Mother Earth: Native American Perspectives on Environmental Justice* (Maryknoll, N.Y.: Orbis Books, 1996).

9   Beverly Wright, "Living and Dying in Louisiana's 'Cancer Alley,'" in *The Quest for Environmental Justice: Human Rights and the Politics of Pollution*, ed. Robert D. Bullard (San Francisco: Sierra Club Books, 2005), 87–107.

10 Vandana Shiva, *Earth Democracy: Justice, Sustainability, and Peace* (Cambridge, Mass.: South End, 2005).

11 Typhoon Haiyan, which devastated the Philippines in late 2013, highlighted the rift over climate change between rich and poor nations. See Stephan Richter, "Climate Change as Terrorism against the People," *Globalist*, November 17, 2013, http://www.the globalist.com/haiyan-climate-change-as-terrorism-against-the-people/; Steven Lee Myers and Nicholas Kulish, "Growing Clamor about Inequities of Climate Crisis," *New York Times*, November 16, 2013, http://www.nytimes.com/2013/11/17/world/growing -clamor-about-inequities-of-climate-crisis.html?_r=0.

12 James H. Cone, "Whose Earth Is It, Anyway?" in *Earth Habitat: Eco-injustice and the Church's Response*, ed. Dieter T. Hessel and Larry L. Rasmussen (Minneapolis: Fortress, 2001), 23, 32. See also Larry L. Rasmussen, "Environmental Racism and Environmental Justice: Moral Theory in the Making?" *Journal of the Society of Christian Ethics* 24, no. 1 (2004); Larry L. Rasmussen, *Earth-Honoring Faith: Religious Ethics in a New Key* (New York: Oxford University Press, 2013), chaps. 7 and 11.

13 By focusing on environmental justice, this chapter explicitly calls attention to the human beings threatened by environmental degradation. A broader term, ecojustice, emphasizes that all of creation—including other species, ecosystems, and places alongside human beings—deserve just treatment, which would call for different examples. For more on the distinction, see Whitney Bauman, Richard Bohannon, and Kevin J. O'Brien, *Grounding Religion: A Field Guide to the Study of Religion and Ecology* (New York: Routledge, 2010), chap. 12.

14 Recognizing the place of justice in King's thinking is vital for recognizing how challenging his witness continues to be in the twenty-first century. Along these lines, James Cone argues that King's emphasis on love developed later in his thinking, while justice was a central theme from the beginning: James H. Cone, *Martin & Malcolm & America: A Dream or a Nightmare* (Maryknoll, N.Y.: Orbis Books, 1991), 63. Vincent Harding emphasizes that King is an "inconvenient hero" because his legacy continues to reveal contemporary injustices: Vincent Harding, *Martin Luther King, the Inconvenient Hero* (Maryknoll, N.Y.: Orbis Books, 1996).

15 See Brian Koenig, "Controversial 'Drum Major' Paraphrase Removed from MLK Memorial," *Political Ticker* (blog), *CNN*, August 1, 2013, http://politicalticker.blogs.cnn. com/2013/08/01/controversial-drum-major-paraphrase-removed-from-mlk-memorial/.

16 King, "The American Dream," in *Testament of Hope*, 208.

17 For King, this led to questions about the assumptions of capitalism. Pondering the fact that forty million people lived in poverty in the United States in 1967, he wrote: "We've got to begin to ask questions about the whole society. We are called upon to help the

discouraged beggars in life's marketplace. But one day we must come to see that an edifice that produces beggars needs restructuring. It means the questions must be raised. You see, my friends, when you deal with this, you begin to ask the question, 'Who owns the oil?' You begin to ask the question, 'Who owns the iron ore?' You begin to ask the question, 'Why is it that people have to pay water bills in a world that is two-thirds water?'" King, "Where Do We Go from Here?" in *Testament of Hope*, 250.

18   King, "I Have a Dream," in *Testament of Hope*, 218.

19   King, "A Testament of Hope," in *Testament of Hope*, 317.

20   Martin Luther King Jr., "Letter from Birmingham Jail," in *Why We Can't Wait* (New York: Penguin, 1964), 77. Along similar lines, in a 1967 television interview, he insisted: "Justice is indivisible. Injustice anywhere is a threat to justice everywhere. And wherever I see injustice, I'm going to take a stand against it whether it's in Mississippi or whether it's in Vietnam" (King, *Testament of Hope*, 408).

21   On this, see especially Martin Luther King Jr., *"In a Single Garment of Destiny": A Global Vision of Justice*, ed. Lewis V. Baldwin (Boston: Beacon, 2012); Hak Joon Lee, *The Great World House: Martin Luther King, Jr., and Global Ethics* (Cleveland, Ohio: Pilgrim, 2011).

22   King, "Where Do We Go from Here?" in *Testament of Hope*, 252.

23   Robert D. Bullard, "Environmental Justice in the Twenty-First Century," in Bullard, *Quest for Environmental Justice*, 19.

24   United Church of Christ Commission for Racial Justice, *Toxic Wastes and Race in the United States: A National Report on the Racial and Socioeconomic Characteristics of Communities with Hazardous Waste Sites* (New York: Public Data Access, 1987); Robert D. Bullard et al., *Toxic Wastes and Race at Twenty: 1987–2007* (Cleveland, Ohio: United Church of Christ Justice & Witness Ministries, 2007), http://www.ucc.org/assets/pdfs/toxic20.pdf.

25   Swati Prakash, *Breathe at Your Own Risk: Dirty Diesels, Environmental Health & Justice* (Washington, D.C.: Summit II National Office, 2002), http://www.ejrc.cau.edu/summit2/AtYourOwnRisk.pdf.

26   Marianne Lavelle and Marcia Coyle, "Unequal Protection: The Racial Divide in Environmental Law," *National Law Journal* 15, no. 3 (1992): S2.

27   See, e.g., Andrea Azuma, *Food Access in Central and South Los Angeles: Mapping Injustice, Agenda for Action* (Los Angeles: Urban and Environmental Policy Institute, 2007), http://scholar.oxy.edu/uep_faculty/346/.

28   See Robert D. Bullard, "Anatomy of Environmental Racism and the Environmental Justice Movement," in *Confronting Environmental Racism: Voices from the Grassroots*, ed. Robert D. Bullard (Boston: South End, 1993).

29   See Bill Lawson, "Living for the City: Urban United States and Environmental Justice," in *Faces of Environmental Racism: Confronting Issues of Global Justice*, ed. Laura Westra and Peter S. Wenz (London: Rowman & Littlefield, 1995), 41–55. The World Health Organization's Global Health Observatory says that, as of 2010, more than half the world's population lived in cities; by 2050 it will be closer to 70 percent: http://www.who.int/gho/urban_health/situation_trends/urban_population_growth_text/en/ (accessed November 12, 2013).

30   See Robert D. Bullard, *Dumping in Dixie: Race, Class, and Environmental Quality* (Boulder, Colo.: Westview, 1994).

31   Luke W. Cole and Sheila R. Foster, *From the Ground Up: Environmental Racism and the Rise of the Environmental Justice Movement* (New York: New York University Press, 2001), chap. 2; Mark Wallace, *Finding God in the Singing River: Christianity, Spirit, Nature* (Minneapolis: Fortress, 2005), chap. 3.

32   Chester Environmental Partnership website, http://www.chesterenvironmentalpartnership.org (accessed December 15, 2013).

33   *Laid to Waste: A Chester Neighborhood Fights for Its Future*, directed by Robert Bahar and George McCollogh (Berkeley, Calif.: Berkeley Media, 1996), DVD.

34   Philabundance website: http://www.philabundance.org/programs-2/chesterfoodaccess/ (accessed March 31, 2014).

35   Mark I. Wallace, *Green Christianity: Five Ways to a Sustainable Future* (Minneapolis: Fortress, 2010), 93–97.

36   Quoted in Laura Pulido, *Environmentalism and Economic Justice: Two Chicano Struggles in the Southwest* (Tucson: University of Arizona Press, 1996), 110–11.

37   Marion Moses, "Farmworkers and Pesticides," in Bullard, *Confronting Environmental Racism*.

38   Grabe et al., *Pesticide Industry Sales and Usage*.

39   For an extensive review of how pesticides harm farm workers in the United States, see Moses, "Farmworkers and Pesticides," in Bullard, *Confronting Environmental Racism*, 161–78. For a report focused on farm workers in California, see Margaret Reeves, Anne Katten, and Martha Guzmán, *Fields of Poison 2002* (Oakland, Calif.: Californians for Pesticide Reform, 2002), http://www.ufw.org/white_papers/report.pdf. For a program regarding the particular problems faced by female farm workers, including their daughters, see Lowell Bergman and Andres Cediel, *FRONTLINE: Rape in the Fields* (Boston: WGBH, 2013), DVD.

40   *Illnesses and Injuries in California Associated with Pesticide Residue in Agricultural Fields, 1982–2010* (Sacramento, Calif.: California Department of Pesticide Regulation, 2010), http://www.cdpr.ca.gov/docs/whs/pisp/2010/2010fld_residue_year.pdf.

41   Reeves, Katten, and Guzmán, *Fields of Poison*, 19.

42   César Chávez and Ilan Stavans, *An Organizer's Tale: Speeches* (New York: Penguin, 2008), 185.

43   César Chávez, Richard J. Jensen, and John C. Hammerback, *The Words of César Chávez* (College Station: Texas A&M University Press, 2002), 142.

44   Chávez, Jensen, and Hammerback, *Words of César Chávez*, 168–69. For a discussion of what Chávez can add to understandings of environmental justice broadly, see Robert Melchior Figueroa, "Other Faces: Latinos and Environmental Justice," in *Faces of Environmental Racism: Confronting Issues of Global Justice*, ed. Laura Westra and Bill E. Lawson (New York: Rowman & Littlefield, 2001). For a more extended discussion of what Chávez can teach Christian environmentalists, see Kevin J. O'Brien, "*La Causa* and Environmental Justice: César Chávez as a Resource for Christian Ecological Ethics," *Journal of the Society of Christian Ethics* 32, no. 1 (2012).

45   M. Reeves and K. S. Schafer, "Greater Risks, Fewer Rights: U.S. Farmworkers and Pesticides," *International Journal of Occupational and Environmental Health* 9, no. 1 (2003). See also Farmworker Justice website, http://harvestingjustice.org/content/pesticide-safety (accessed November 17, 2013).

46 See Devon G. Peña, *Environmental Justice and Sustainable Agriculture: Linking Ecological and Social Sides of Sustainability* (Washington, D.C.: Summit II National Office, 2002), http://www.ejrc.cau.edu/summit2/SustainableAg.pdf; Devon G. Peña, "Structural Violence, Historical Trauma, and Public Health: The Environmental Justice Critique of Contemporary Risk Science and Practice," in *Communities, Neighborhoods, and Health: Expanding the Boundaries of Place*, ed. Linda M. Burton et al. (New York: Springer, 2011).

47 "The Principles of Environmental Justice," First National People of Color Environmental Leadership Summit, last modified April 6, 1996, http://www.ejnet.org/ej/principles.html.

48 "Principles of Environmental Justice."

49 Daniel Faber, *Capitalizing on Environmental Injustice: The Polluter-Industrial Complex in the Age of Globalization* (Lanham, Md.: Rowman & Littlefield, 2008).

50 Peña, "Structural Violence, Historical Trauma, and Public Health."

51 Chávez and Stavans, *An Organizer's Tale*, 14.

52 H. Spencer Banzhaf and Eleanor McCormick, "Moving beyond Cleanup: Identifying the Crucibles of Environmental Gentrification," in *The Political Economy of Environmental Justice*, ed. Spencer Banzhaf (Stanford, Calif.: Stanford University Press, 2012), 23–51.

53 For more on such free market environmentalism, look back to chap. 2.

54 King, "Where Do We Go from Here?" in *Testament of Hope*, 252.

55 For an extended argument that Native Americans have long traditions of private property rights and could thrive if such rights were respected today, see Terry L. Anderson, *Sovereign Nations or Reservations? An Economic History of American Indians* (San Francisco: Pacific Research Institute for Public Policy, 1995).

56 See Robert J. Miller, "Creating Economic Development on Indian Reservations: Why Fostering Local Business Matters," *PERC Report* 30, no. 3 (2012).

57 Terry L. Anderson and Shawn Regan, "Unlocking the Wealth of Indian Nations," PERC (blog), September 27, 2013, http://perc.org/articles/unlocking-wealth-indian-nations. See also Terry L. Anderson, "How the Government Keeps Indians in Poverty," *PERC* (blog), November 22, 1995, http://perc.org/articles/how-government-keeps-indians-poverty.

58 See Ward Churchill, *A Little Matter of Genocide: Holocaust and Denial in the Americas, 1492 to the Present* (San Francisco: City Lights, 1997).

59 George Tinker, "An American Indian Theological Response to Ecojustice," in Weaver, *Defending Mother Earth*, 171.

60 See Corbin Harney, *The Way It Is: One Water—One Air—One Mother Earth* (Nevada City, Calif.: Blue Dolphin, 1995); LaDuke, *All Our Relations*; Goldhawk Productions, *Radioactive Reservations*; Vincent Schilling, *Native Defenders of the Environment* (Summertown, Tenn.: 7th Generation/Native Voices, 2011); Tinker, "An American Indian Theological Response to Ecojustice," in Weaver, *Defending Mother Earth*, 171.

61 For more on the theme of clean energy, see the section on Bill McKibben in chap. 3 on courage.

Chapter 6

1 Dietrich Bonhoeffer, *Letters and Papers from Prison* (New York: Touchstone, 1997), 369–70. Emphasis added.

2   Bonhoeffer has a great deal to offer Christian environmentalists. For the most complete account of how his insight applies to contemporary struggles to develop "an earth faith and ethic," see Rasmussen, *Earth Community, Earth Ethics*, 295–316.

3   Tim Donovan, "We Are Deluding Ourselves: The Apocalypse Is Coming—and Technology Can't Save Us," *Salon*, December 9, 2013, http://www.salon.com/2013/12/09/we_are_deluding_ourselves_the_apocalypse_is_coming_and_technology_cant_save_us/.

4   Andrew Simms, "Apocalypse? No. But Unless We Change Tack, the Planet Is Running Out of Time," *Guardian*, March 1, 2013, http://www.theguardian.com/environment/2013/mar/01/100-months-apocalypse-warnings.

5   *Hearing before the Subcommittee on Energy and Environment: Preparing for Climate Change; Adaptation Policies and Programs*, 111th Cong. 9 (2009) (statement of Representative John Shimkus).

6   U. Cubasch et al., "Introduction," in *Climate Change 2013: The Physical Science Basis: Contribution of Working Group I to the Fifth Assessment Report of the Intergovernmental Panel on Climate Change*, ed. T. F. Stocker et al. (New York: Cambridge University Press, 2013), 121.

7   Christopher Field et al., *Climate Change 2014: Impacts, Adaptation, and Vulnerability— Summary for Policymakers*, accessed April 1, 2014, http://ipcc-wg2.gov/AR5/images/uploads/IPCC_WG2AR5_SPM_Approved.pdf. For the most updated reports from the Intergovernmental Panel on Climate Change, see http://www.ipcc.ch.

8   Brian Kahn, "Superstorm Sandy and Sea Level Rise," Climate.gov, November 4, 2012, http://www.climate.gov/news-features/features/superstorm-sandy-and-sea-level-rise.

9   McKibben, *Eaarth*, 16.

10 Colin Beavan, *No Impact Man: The Adventures of a Guilty Liberal Who Attempts to Save the Planet, and the Discoveries He Makes about Himself and Our Way of Life in the Process* (New York: Farrar, Straus & Giroux, 2009), 8.

11 Beavan, *No Impact Man*, 6, 13.

12 Beavan, *No Impact Man*, 73–74.

13 Beavan, *No Impact Man*, 215. Hunter S. Thompson (1937–2005) was a countercultural journalist and author, known for his risky behaviors (including abuse of alcohol and illegal drugs), who finally committed suicide when his health took a turn for the worse. Partying "like it's 1999" comes from the 1982 hit song by Prince. That year has come and gone, but the question underlying it retains its relevance.

14 Beavan, *No Impact Man*, 218.

15 Naomi Klein, "Capitalism vs. the Climate," *Nation*, November 9, 2011, http://www.thenation.com/article/164497/capitalism-vs-climate#.

16 Pope Francis makes a related point: "The thirst for power and possessions knows no limits. In this system, which tends to devour everything which stands in the way of increased profits, whatever is fragile, like the environment, is defenseless before the interests of a deified market, which become the only rule." Pope Francis, "Evangelii Gaudium," §56.

17 Klein, "Capitalism vs. the Climate."

18 Along these lines, a recent study found evidence that about two-thirds of the world's climate-changing emissions had come from just ninety companies. The study looked at "50 leading investor-owned, 31 state-owned, and 9 nation-state producers of oil, natural gas, coal, and cement," and found that more than half of their emissions had happened

since 1986. Richard Heede, "Tracing Anthropogenic Carbon Dioxide and Methane Emissions to Fossil Fuel and Cement Producers, 1854–2010," *Climatic Change* 122, nos. 1–2 (2014): 229,

19   Klein, "Capitalism vs. the Climate."

20   A United Nations "universal climate agreement" centered on deforestation is set to go into effect in 2015. The 2013 meeting in Warsaw also saw commitments made by rich countries to pay damages to poor countries for the effects of climate change. "UN Climate Change Conference in Warsaw Keeps Governments on a Track towards 2015 Climate Agreement," United Nations Framework Convention on Climate Change (UNFCCC), Bonn, Germany, November 23, 2013, http://unfccc.int/files/press/news_room/pres s_releases_and_advisories/application/pdf/131123_pr_closing_cop19.pdf   (accessed March 31, 2014).

21   See the websites for 350.org (http://350.org); the United States Conference of Mayors, and specifically the U.S. Conference of Mayors Climate Protection Agreement (http:// www.usmayors.org/climateprotection/agreement.htm); and the Association for the Advancement of Sustainability in Higher Education (http://www.aashe.org).

22   Bjørn Lomborg, *Cool It: The Skeptical Environmentalist's Guide to Global Warming* (New York: Vintage Books, 2008), ix.

23   Bjørn Lomborg, conclusion to *Smart Solutions to Climate Change: Comparing Costs and Benefits* (New York: Cambridge University Press, 2010), 395.

24   Lomborg, *Cool It*, 159. Bill McKibben meanwhile saw the Copenhagen conference (a follow-up on the Kyoto conference) as "a fiasco of the first order" and a "debacle" that accomplished nothing. *Eaarth*, 18–19.

25   Bjørn Lomborg, *The Skeptical Environmentalist: Measuring the Real State of the World* (New York: Cambridge University Press, 2001), 351.

26   Lomborg, *Smart Solutions*.

27   Alan Robock, "20 Reasons Why Geoengineering May Be a Bad Idea," *Bulletin of the Atomic Scientists* 64, no. 2 (2008); *The British Royal Society, Geoengineering the Climate: Science, Governance, and Uncertainty* (London: Royal Society Reports, 2009).

28   This is the subject of Dietrich Bonhoeffer and John W. Doberstein, *Life Together* (San Francisco: HarperSanFrancisco, 1993).

29   Along these lines, South African theologian Ernst Conradie argues that the global community can learn from the way Christians in his nation responded to the failings of apartheid—communally facing, lamenting, and redressing past wrongs. Climate change, he argues, calls for communal penance of the type demonstrated by the Truth and Reconciliation Commission. See Ernst M. Conradie, *The Church and Climate Change* (Pietermaitzburg, South Africa: Cluster Publications, 2008).

30   Ecumenical Patriarch Bartholomew, "Saving Souls and the Planet Go Together," *CNN*, October 19, 2010, http://edition.cnn.com/2010/OPINION/10/19/bartholomew.souls. planet/index.html.

31   Bartholomew, "Saving Souls."

32   Forrest Clingerman, "Between Babel and Pelagius: Religion, Theology, and Geoengineering," in *Engineering the Climate: The Ethics of Solar Radiation Management*, ed. Christopher J. Preston (New York: Lexington Books, 2012).

33   This is the argument of David Owen in *The Conundrum: How Scientific Innovation,*

Increased Efficiency, and Good Intentions Can Make Our Energy and Climate Problems Worse. Owen summarizes the book in a short video: http://www.youtube.com/watch?v=2S1mPOWRsSc.

34   Dietrich Bonhoeffer, *A Testament to Freedom: The Essential Writings of Dietrich Bonhoeffer,* ed. Geffrey B. Kelly and F. Burton Nelson (San Francisco: Harper & Row, 1990), 109. Emphasis in the original.

35   Bonhoeffer, *A Testament to Freedom,* 108.

36   See "Dover Friends Meeting Epistle on Divestment" and "Speaking Out about Divestment," in *Befriending Creation* 26, no. 6 (2013), http://www.quakerearthcare.org/sites/quakerearthcare.org/files/bfc/bfc2606_lowres.pdf.

37   "Dover Friends Meeting" and "Speaking Out about Divestment," in *Befriending Creation.*

38   See http://gofossilfree.org.

39   Naomi Klein, "Time for Big Green to Go Fossil Free," *Nation,* May 20, 2013.

Chapter 7

1   *The Matrix,* directed by Andy Wachowski and Larry Wachowski (Burbank, Calif.: Warner Brothers Pictures, 1999), DVD.

2   Louise Gray, "David Attenborough—Humans Are Plague on Earth," *Telegraph* January 22, 2013, http://www.telegraph.co.uk/earth/earthnews/9815862/Humans-are-plague-on-Earth-Attenborough.html.

3   Lisa Hymas, "I Decided Not to Have Children for Environmental Reasons," *Guardian,* September 27, 2011, http://www.theguardian.com/environment/2011/sep/27/not-have-children-environmental-reasons.

4   Jonathan V. Last, "America's Baby Bust," *Wall Street Journal,* February 12, 2013, http://online.wsj.com/article/SB10001424127887323375204578270053387770718.html. While many reports tend to link declining birth rates narrowly to the economic downturn that began in 2008, environmental concerns—especially the costs of land and natural resources—are always part and parcel of economic growth or recession.

5   A 2014 film turned this biblical question about God's apparent ambivalence toward humankind into a major plot point; see *Noah,* directed by Darron Aronofsky (Paramount Pictures, 2014).

6   For an ongoing estimate of the world's human population, see the constantly running "population clock" on the U.S. Census' page: http://www.census.gov/popclock/.

7   "400 Million Births Prevented by One-Child Policy," *People's Daily Online,* October 28, 2011, http://english.people.com.cn/90882/7629166.html.

8   Peter Ford, "As China's One-Child Policy Fades, New Challenges Lie Ahead," *Christian Science Monitor,* November 27, 2013, http://www.csmonitor.com/World/Asia-Pacific/2013/1127/As-China-s-one-child-policy-fades-new-challenges-lie-ahead. See also Edward Wong, "Reports of Forced Abortions Fuel Push to End Chinese Law," *New York Times,* July 22, 2012; *Associated Press,* "China Think Tank Urges End of One-Child Policy," *Guardian,* October 31, 2012.

9   Aquinas, *Summa,* II.II, Q. 17, A.1.

10   Aquinas, *Summa,* II.II, Q. 17, A.2.

11   Aquinas, *Summa,* II.II, Q. 20, A.3.

12 Hauerwas and Pinches, *Christians among the Virtues*, xii.

13 Aquinas, *Summa*, II.II, Q. 19, A.9.

14 "When happiness is no longer future, but present, it is incompatible with the virtue of hope. Consequently hope, like faith, is voided in heaven, and neither of them can be in the blessed." Aquinas, *Summa*, II.II, Q. 18, A.2.

15 Aquinas, *Summa*, II.II, Q. 17, A.4.

16 Thomas Malthus, *An Essay on the Principle of Population and a Summary View of the Principle of Population* (New York: Penguin, 1985).

17 Malthus, *Essay on the Principle of Population*, 89.

18 Malthus, *Essay on the Principle of Population*, 202, 89, 102.

19 Germaine Greer, *Sex and Destiny* (London: Picador, 1984), 303. Sanger herself wrote of "the wickedness of creating large families," and argued: "The most immoral practice of the day is breeding too many children. . . . The immorality of large families lies not only in the injury to the members of those families but in their injury to society." Margaret Sanger, *Woman and the New Race* (New York: Brentano's, 1920), 57.

20 Lisa Hymas, "The GINK Manifesto: Say It Loud—I'm Childfree and I'm Proud," *Grist* (blog), March 31, 2010, http://grist.org/article/2010-03-30-gink-manifesto-say -it-loud-im-childfree-and-im-proud/.

21 Laura Huggins, "Halloween Fright, Population Fear Are Both Fantasy," *Washington Times*, October 27, 2011, http://perc.org/articles/halloween-fright-population-fear-are -both-fantasy.

22 See, e.g., this article about Norman Borlaug: Gregg Easterbrook, "The Man Who Defused the 'Population Bomb,'" *Wall Street Journal*, September 16, 2009, http://online.wsj.com/ article/SB10001424052970203917304574411382676924044.html.

23 This argument has been recently popularized by Jared M. Diamond, *Collapse: How Societies Choose to Fail or Succeed* (New York: Penguin, 2005).

24 Paul R. Ehrlich and Anne H. Ehrlich, *Betrayal of Science and Reason: How Antienvironmental Rhetoric Threatens Our Future* (Washington, D.C.: Island, 1996), 84–89.

25 Paul R. Ehrlich, *The Population Bomb* (Rivercity, Mass.: Rivercity, 1975).

26 Paul R. Ehrlich and Anne H. Ehrlich, *The Dominant Animal: Human Evolution and the Environment* (Washington, D.C.: Island, 2008), 352–54.

27 Ehrlich and Ehrlich, *Betrayal of Science and Reason*, 73.

28 The Ehrlichs introduce a formula for environmental impact (I) as the product of population (P), affluence (A), and technology (T): I = PAT. Carrying capacity depends not only upon P, how many people there are, but also on A and T, the amount that a population consumes and the waste produced and energy used in the course of that consumption. Paul R. Ehrlich and Anne H. Ehrlich, *One with Nineveh: Politics, Consumption, and the Human Future* (Washington, D.C.: Island, 2004), 12.

29 Paul Ehrlich and Anne H. Ehrlich, *The Most Overpopulated Nation* (Teaneck, N.J.: Negative Population Growth, 1996). Part of the danger of the U.S. overconsumption, they argue, is the example it sets: "We are the archetype of a gigantic, overpopulated, overconsuming rich nation, one that many ill-informed decision makers in poor nations would like to emulate. Unless we demonstrate by example that we understand the horrible mistakes made on our way to overdevelopment, and that we are intent on reversing them, we see little hope for the persistence of civilization."

30 Ehrlich and Ehrlich, *Dominant Animal*, 219, 148.

31   Ehrlich and Ehrlich, *Betrayal of Science and Reason*, 77.

32   Ehrlich and Ehrlich, *One with Nineveh*, 185–95.

33   Mara Ann Mulrooney, "Continuity or Collapse? Diachronic Settlement and Land Use in Hanga Ho'onu, Rapa Nui (Easter Island)," dissertation, University of Auckland, 2012. See also Terry Hunt and Carl Lipo, *The Statues That Walked: Unraveling the Mystery of Easter Island* (New York: Free Press, 2011).

34   Betsy Hartmann, "The Parable of the Herdsman and Other Tall Tales," keynote address given at the Conference on Rethinking Climate Change, Conflict and Security, University of Sussex, U.K., October 18, 2012, 1.

35   She notes that the Ehrlichs "refer to babies born in Bangladesh and the Philippines as 'mouths'—a common Malthusian slur," and that they reductionistically see all humans as "takers from, rather than enhancers of, the natural environment." Betsy Hartmann, *Reproductive Rights and Wrongs: The Global Politics of Population Control* (Boston: South End, 1995), 22, 24.

36   In this, she echoes Karl Marx's mid-nineteenth-century critique of Malthus. While Marx's theories have become associated with authoritarian governments in the contemporary world, he himself wrote passionately about the importance of human freedom, particularly in hopes of liberating the poor from the oppression of unjust systems. Marx saw discussions of a "population problem" as a perfect example of how the rich oppress the poor, suggesting that "even the existence of men [*sic*] is a pure luxury;" if human life is only for those who can afford it, the poor must then see their very existence as somehow illicit, as a burden on the world. Karl Marx, "Economic and Philosophic Manuscripts of 1844," in *The Marx-Engels Reader*, ed. Robert C. Tucker (New York: W. W. Norton, 1978), 97. Marx believed that Malthus "stupidly" assumed that there was a limit to what human beings could get from the earth's resources, ignoring human ingenuity. For more of Marx's frequently colorful critiques of Malthus, see Karl Marx and Friedrich Engels, *Marx and Engels on the Population Bomb: Selections from the Writings of Marx and Engels Dealing with the Theories of Thomas Robert Malthus*, trans. Ronald L. Meek (Berkeley, Calif.: Ramparts, 1971).

37   Hartmann, *Reproductive Rights and Wrongs*, 39.

38   "World Population Projected to Reach 9.6 Billion by 2050 with Most Growth in Developing Regions, Especially Africa—Says UN," UN Population Division, last modified June 13, 2013, http://esa.un.org/unpd/wpp/Documentation/pdf/WPP2012_Press_Release.pdf.

39   Betsy Hartmann, "Rethinking Climate Refugees and Climate Conflict: Rhetoric, Reality and the Politics of Policy Discourse," *Journal of International Development* 22 (2010): 234, 239. See also Betsy Hartmann, Banu Subramaniam, and Charles Zerner, *Making Threats: Biofears and Environmental Anxieties* (Lanham, Md.: Rowman & Littlefield, 2005); Betsy Hartmann, "Rethinking the Role of Population in Human Security," in *Global Environmental Change and Human Security*, ed. Richard A. Matthew et al. (Cambridge, Mass.: MIT Press, 2010).

40   Hartmann, *Reproductive Rights and Wrongs*, 65–67.

41   Betsy Hartmann, "Will World Population Day Open the Gates to Coercive Contraception?" *Common Dreams* (blog), July 9, 2012, https://www.commondreams.org/view/2012/07/09-4.

42   The same kind of double standard is evident in recent U.S. history. See Andrea Smith,

"Malthusian Orthodoxy and the Myth of ZPG: Population Control as Racism," in Weaver, *Defending Mother Earth*, 122–43.

43 Traci West, "The Policing of Poor Black Women's Sexual Reproduction," in *God Forbid: Religion and Sex in American Public Life*, ed. Kathleen M. Sands (New York: Oxford University Press, 2000).

44 She cites one UN official who says that people have the right to determine family size, but "what is a human right in one country may not be a right in another." Hartmann, *Reproductive Rights and Wrongs*, 170.

45 Hartmann, "Rethinking Climate Refugees," xviii.

46 Hartmann, *Reproductive Rights and Wrongs*, 303.

47 Aquinas, *Summa*, II.II, Q. 21, A.1.

48 For a more complete analysis of the environmental lessons of the prophet Joel, see Jose Pepz M. Cunanan, "The Prophet of Environment and Development," in *Ecotheology: Voices from South and North*, ed. David G. Hallman (Maryknoll, N.Y.: Orbis Books, 1994).

49 Annie Dillard, *For the Time Being* (New York: Knopf, 1999), 47.

50 Pope Paul VI, "Humanae Vitae," 1968, §10, http://www.vatican.va/holy_father/paul_vi/encyclicals/documents/hf_p-vi_enc_25071968_humanae-vitae_en.html. Emphasis added.

51 Pope Paul VI, "Humanae Vitae," §23.

52 Phil Ryken, "Call Me a Natalist," *Reformation 21* (blog), June 2006, http://www.reformation21.org/counterpoints/post-36.php.

53 Bill McKibben, *Maybe One: A Case for Smaller Families* (New York: Simon & Schuster, 1998). While articles written by Christians in support of large families are plentiful, it is much more difficult to find explicitly Christian articles encouraging small families (or not having children at all). Perhaps this is because smaller families have generally become the norm in the industrialized world (and increasingly even in the developing world), such that Christians do not feel the need to defend them.

54 The situation for Jews may be quite different. While Christians make up roughly one-third of the world's population, Jews today number only in the millions. For many reasons, Orthodox Jews tend to have large families and may not feel comfortable "checking off the list" the command to be fruitful and multiply in the same way Christians might.

55 Karl Barth emphasizes that this is a key distinction between Christianity and Judaism, explaining: "Parenthood may be a consequence of marriage which is both joyful and rich in duties, but from a Christian point of view . . . children may be at least a serious threat to what man and wife [*sic*] should together mean in marriage for the surrounding world. From this point of view, childlessness can be a release and therefore a chance which those concerned ought to seize and exploit." Barth, *The Doctrine of Creation: Church Dogmatics, Volume III, 4* (Edinburgh: T&T Clark, 1961), 54.2 (Parents and Children), 269. For an extended look at Protestant teachings about fertility and contraception, see Kathryn D'Arcy Blanchard, "The Gift of Contraception," *Journal of the Society of Christian Ethics* 27, no. 1 (2007).

Chapter 8

1 See, e.g., the online Sanskrit dictionary, Spokensanskrit.de: http://www.spokensanskrit.de/index.php?page=1.

2   Aquinas, *Summa*, II.II, Q. 23, A.8.

3   As Steve Wilkens puts it, "Love is not enough by itself. Even when we know that we ought to love in all situations, we still need to know the details of the situation before we give an ethical answer." Wilkens, *Beyond Bumper Sticker Ethics* (Downers Grove, Ill.: InterVarsity, 1995), 139.

4   In her memoir, economist Deirdre N. McCloskey tells a story of when her sister had her committed to a mental hospital, not because she was ill but because she was a man who wanted to be a woman. "You know Donny, I'm doing this for love," his sister said. "Yes, dear," McCloskey replied. "And Hitler loved Germany." McCloskey, *Crossing: A Memoir* (Chicago: University of Chicago Press, 2009), 103.

5   Margaret Farley, *Just Love* (London: Continuum, 2006), 197. Emphasis original.

6   Farley, *Just Love*, 203.

7   Farley, *Just Love*, 204n52. Emphasis in the original.

8   Willis Jenkins articulates this helpful question at the heart of any effort toward sustainability. See Willis Jenkins, *The Future of Ethics: Sustainability, Social Justice, and Religious Creativity* (Washington, D.C.: Georgetown University Press, 2013).

9   Luke 10:27 offers a similar formulation as the path to eternal life. Both texts make implicit reference to Deuteronomy 6:4-5: "Hear, O Israel: The LORD is our God, the LORD alone. You shall love the LORD your God with all your heart, and with all your soul, and with all your might."

10 For the classic account of Christian environmentalism grounded in love for creation, see Nash, *Loving Nature*.

11 For a reflection on the environmental lessons taught by the book of Job, see Carol A. Newsom, "The Moral Sense of Nature: Ethics in Light of God's Speech to Job," *Princeton Seminary Bulletin* 15, no. 1 (1994).

12 Tyler Wigg-Stevenson, *The World Is Not Ours to Save: Finding the Freedom to Do Good* (Downers Grove, Ill.: InterVarsity, 2013).

13 Luke Timothy Johnson, *The Writings of the New Testament: An Interpretation* (Philadelphia: Fortress, 1986), 42.

14 Calvin, *Institutes of the Christian Religion*, I.v.5. Calvin then quickly urges his readers to be very cautious with such a potentially dangerous verbal formulation.

15 See O'Brien, *Ethics of Biodiversity*, chap. 3.

16 E.g., Larry Rasmussen cites a British legal definition of "neighbor" as "anyone or anything that we think may reasonably be affected by our actions," and notes that this includes all beings: "Those affected by my actions are thus almost infinite in extent, with no preordained boundaries, given the complex supracommunity of the ecosphere." Rasmussen, *Earth-Honoring Faith*, 221–22.

17 For instance, the influential evangelical theologian Francis A. Schaeffer argued that human beings can only fully understand our relationship to God—and thereby care for God's creation—if we understand our uniqueness: "I am separated from [nature] because I am made in the image of God; my integration point is upward not downward; it is not turned back on creation. Yet at the same time I am united to it because nature and man [*sic*] are both created by God." Schaeffer, *Pollution and the Death of Man* (Wheaton, Ill.: Crossway Books, 1970), 52.

18 Edward O. Wilson, *Biophilia* (Cambridge, Mass.: Harvard University Press, 1984).

19 Richard Louv, *Last Child in the Woods* (Chapel Hill, N.C.: Algonquin Books, 2008).

20 Recognizing this, Edward O. Wilson wrote an entire book reaching out to Christians and requesting a theological argument to bolster his biological perspectives because "religion and science are the two most powerful forces in the world today, including especially the United States. If religion and science could be united on the common ground of biological conservation, the problem would soon be solved." Wilson, *The Creation: An Appeal to Save Life on Earth* (New York: W. W. Norton, 2006), 5.

21 Lappé, *EcoMind*, 47.

22 Lappé, *EcoMind*, 54.

23 In this way, she has a great deal in common with Colin Beavan (*No Impact Man*), discussed in chapter 3.

24 Lappé, *EcoMind*, 57. Famous for a 1971 book that made one of the first sustained arguments for environmentally motivated vegetarianism, Lappé has since expanded her attention more broadly to help build communities that nurture healthy lives—healthy foods, healthy relationships, healthy ecosystems. See Frances Moore Lappé, *Diet for a Small Planet* (New York: Ballantine Books, 1971).

25 Lappé, *EcoMind*, 190.

26 350.org, "Our Mission," http://350.org/mission.

27 Campus Climate Challenge, http://climatechallenge.org/.

28 "The Billion Tree Campaign," United Nations Environmental Programme website: http://www.plant-for-the-planet-billiontreecampaign.org/.

29 Food Democracy Now, http://www.fooddemocracynow.org/about/.

30 Hank Fischer, "Who Pays for Wolves?" *PERC Report* 19, no. 4 (2001); Hank Fischer, *Wolf Wars: The Remarkable Inside Story of the Restoration of Wolves to Yellowstone* (Helena, Mont.: Falcon, 1995).

31 For a fuller explanation of enviropreneurship, see Michael Lenox and Jeffrey G. York, "Environmental Entrepeneurship," in *The Oxford Handbook of Business and the Natural Environment*, ed. Pratima Bansal and Andrew J. Hoffman (New York: Oxford University Press, 2013).

32 B Corporation (B Lab) website, "The B Corp Declaration," http://www.bcorporation.net/what-are-b-corps/the-b-corp-declaration (accessed March 31, 2014).

33 B Corporation website, "Why B Corps Matter," http://www.bcorporation.net/what-are-b-corps/why-b-corps-matter (accessed March 31, 2014). As of 2013, nineteen U.S. states and the District of Columbia had approved legislation for the formation of certified benefit corporations.

34 See Kirk Johnson, "Federal Jury in Utah Convicts Environmentalist," *New York Times*, March 3, 2011; and "Tim's Story," Peaceful Uprising website, http://www.peacefuluprising.org/tim-dechristopher/tims-story (accessed December 17, 2013).

35 Tim DeChristopher, in *Bidder 70*, directed by George Gage and Beth Gage (New York: First Run Features, 2012), DVD.

36 Terry Tempest Williams, "What Love Looks Like: A Conversation with Tim DeChristopher," *Orion*, January/February 2012.

37 Tim DeChristopher, "I Do Not Want Mercy, I Want You to Join Me," *Common Dreams* (blog), July 27, 2011, http://www.commondreams.org/view/2011/07/26-13. Emphasis added.

38   DeChristopher, "I Do Not Want Mercy."

39   Bill McKibben, "Tale of Two Earth Day Heroes," *Grist* (blog), April 21, 2013, http://grist.org/climate-energy/a-tale-of-two-earth-day-heroes/.

40   Sandra Steingraber, *Raising Elijah: Protecting Our Children in an Age of Environmental Crisis* (Philadelphia: Da Capo, 2011), 281.

41   Sandra Steingraber's Facebook page, "Letter from Chemung County Jail, Part 2," last modi -fied April 19, 2013, https://www.facebook.com/notes/raising-elijah-by-sandra-stein graber/sandra-steingraber-letter-from-chemung-county-jail-part-2/572156746138145.

42   Dave Foreman, *Confessions of an Eco-warrior* (New York: Clown Trade, 1991), 26.

43   Foreman, *Confessions of an Eco-warrior*, 4–5.

44   Bron Raymond Taylor, "Earth First! and Global Narratives of Popular Ecological Resis-tance," in *Ecological Resistance Movements: The Global Emergence of Radical and Popular Environmentalism*, ed. Bron Taylor (Albany: State University of New York Press, 1995), 15–17.

45   Foreman, *Confessions of an Eco-warrior*, 115.

46   Foreman, *Confessions of an Eco-warrior*, 113.

47   Foreman, *Confessions of an Eco-warrior*, 121.

48   Edward Abbey, *Desert Solitaire: A Season in the Wilderness* (New York: Simon & Schuster, 1990), xiv.

49   Edward Abbey, *The Monkey Wrench Gang* (Philadelphia: Lippincott, 1975), 67.

50   See David Rothenberg, "Have a Friend for Lunch: Norwegian Radical Ecology versus Tradition," in Taylor, *Ecological Resistance Movements*, 201–18. Rothenberg points out that Abbey's sequel to *The Monkey Wrench Gang* even contains a critique of Earth First! along these grounds: "The Earth First! activists cause a lot of fracas and get media cover-age, but they are unable to stop the giant Goliath earth moving machine. Only the covert Monkey Wrench Gang can get the job done. And no one ever sees them, no one knows who they are. Their actions speak for themselves, actions which were done for their own sakes, not for glory or results of any kind" (217).

51   These paragraphs are based on Anna Duke, Brenda Llewellyn Ihssen, and Kevin J. O'Brien, "Natural Disasters as Moral Lessons: Nazianzus and New Orleans," *Journal for the Study of Religion, Nature, and Culture* 6, no. 1 (2012). That essay includes more extensive reflections on religious responses to Katrina and other natural disasters. See also Robert D. Bullard, "Differential Vulnerabilities: Environmental and Economic Inequal-ity and Government Response to Unnatural Disasters," *Social Research* 75 (2009); Robert D. Bullard and Beverly Wright, *Race, Place, and Environmental Justice after Hurricane Katrina: Struggles to Reclaim, Rebuild, and Revitalize New Orleans and the Gulf Coast* (Boulder, Colo.: Westview, 2009); Craig Colten, "Vulnerability and Place: Flat Land and Uneven Risk in New Orleans," *American Anthropologist* 108, no. 4 (2006).

52   Joel K. Bourne Jr., "New Orleans: A Perilous Future," *National Geographic*, August 2007.

53   Robert D. Bullard, "Katrina and the Second Disaster: A Twenty-Point Plan to Destroy Black New Orleans," *San Francisco Bayview*, February 1, 2006, http://news.newamerica media.org/news/view_article.html?article_id=ad54cb41686743ebb33ed2eb16647b16.

54   See Cheryl A. Kirk-Duggan, ed., *The Sky Is Crying: Race, Class, and Natural Disaster* (Nashville: Abingdon, 2006).

Conclusion

1   Aldo Leopold and Luna B. Leopold, *Round River* (Minocqua, Wis.: NorthWord, 1991), 165.

2   In *The Righteous Mind*, social psychologist Jonathan Haidt identifies the former values as traditionally "liberal" and the latter as "conservative." He posits that these ethical or moral "tastes" evolved into the human species as means of creating cohesive communities. Each taste developed as a response to a certain kind of antisocial behavior: care vs. harm; fairness vs. cheating; authority vs. subversion; sanctity vs. degradation. Interestingly, he notes that both sides of the political spectrum tend to value liberty, a response to antisocial oppression. Jonathan Haidt, *The Righteous Mind: Why Good People Are Divided by Politics and Religion* (New York: Vintage Books, 2012).

BIBLIOGRAPHY

Abbey, Edward. *Desert Solitaire: A Season in the Wilderness*. New York: Simon & Schuster, 1990.

———. *The Monkey Wrench Gang*. Philadelphia: Lippincott, 1975.

Anderson, Terry Lee, ed. *Political Environmentalism: Going behind the Green Curtain*. Stanford, Calif.: Hoover Institution, 2000.

———. *Sovereign Nations or Reservations? An Economic History of American Indians*. San Francisco: Pacific Research Institute for Public Policy, 1995.

Anderson, Terry Lee, and Donald Leal. *Free Market Environmentalism*. New York: Palgrave, 2001.

Anderson, Terry Lee, and Laura E. Huggins. *Greener than Thou: Are You Really an Environmentalist?* Stanford, Calif.: Hoover Institution, 2008.

Aristotle. *Nicomachean Ethics*. New York: Macmillan, 1962.

Ayres, Jennifer R. *Good Food: Grounded Practical Theology*. Waco, Tex.: Baylor University Press, 2013.

Azuma, Andrea. *Food Access in Central and South Los Angeles: Mapping Injustice, Agenda for Action*. Los Angeles: Urban and Environmental Policy Institute, 2007. http://scholar.oxy.edu/uep_faculty/346/.

Babette's Feast. Directed by Gabriel Axel. Copenhagen, Denmark: Nordisk Film, 1987. DVD.

Baker-Fletcher, Karen. *Sisters of Dust, Sisters of Spirit: Womanist Wordings on God and Creation*. Minneapolis: Fortress, 1998.

Banzhaf, H. Spencer, ed. *The Political Economy of Environmental Justice*. Stanford, Calif.: Stanford University Press, 2012.

Barth, Karl. *The Doctrine of Creation: Church Dogmatics, Volume III, 4*. Edinburgh: T&T Clark, 1961.

Bauman, Whitney A. *Religion and Ecology: Developing a Planetary Ethic*. New York: Columbia University Press, 2014.

Bauman, Whitney, Richard Bohannon, and Kevin J. O'Brien. *Grounding Religion: A Field Guide to the Study of Religion and Ecology*. New York: Routledge, 2010.

Beavan, Colin. *No Impact Man: The Adventures of a Guilty Liberal Who Attempts to Save the Planet, and the Discoveries He Makes about Himself and Our Way of Life in the Process*. New York: Farrar, Straus & Giroux, 2009.

Beres, LeeAnne, and Jessie Dye. "From Church Sanctuaries to the Steps of the Capitol: Faithful Advocacy for a Coal-Free Washington." In *Sacred Acts: How Churches Are Working to Protect Earth's Climate*, edited by Mallory McDuff, 117–33. Gabriola Island, B.C.: New Society, 2012.

Bergman, Lowell, and Andres Cediel. *FRONTLINE: Rape in the Fields*. Boston: WGBH, 2013. DVD.

Berry, Wendell. *Bringing It to the Table: On Farming and Food*. Berkeley, Calif.: Counterpoint, 2009.

———. *Sex, Economy, Freedom, & Community*. New York: Pantheon Books, 1992.

Bidder 70. Directed by George Gage and Beth Gage. New York: First Run Features, 2012. DVD.

Blanchard, Kathryn D'Arcy. "The Gift of Contraception." *Journal of the Society of Christian Ethics* 27, no. 1 (2007): 225–49.

———. *The Protestant Ethic or the Spirit of Capitalism: Christians, Freedom, and Free Markets*. Eugene, Ore.: Cascade, 2010.

Blanchard, Kathryn, and Kevin O'Brien. "Prophets Meet Profits: What Christian Ecological Ethics Can Learn From Free Market Environmentalism." *Journal of the Society of Christian Ethics* 34, no. 1 (2014): 103–23.

Bonhoeffer, Dietrich. *Letters and Papers from Prison*. New York: Touchstone, 1997.

———. *A Testament to Freedom: The Essential Writings of Dietrich Bonhoeffer*. Edited by Geffrey B. Kelly and F. Burton Nelson. San Francisco: Harper & Row, 1990.

Bonhoeffer, Dietrich, and John W. Doberstein. *Life Together*. San Francisco: Harper-SanFrancisco, 1993.

Bouma-Prediger, Steven. *For the Beauty of the Earth: A Christian Vision for Creation Care*. Grand Rapids: Baker Academic, 2010.

The British Royal Society. *Geoengineering the Climate: Science, Governance, and Uncertainty*. London: Royal Society Reports, 2009.

Brown, Lester R. *Plan B 4.0: Mobilizing to Save Civilization*. New York: W. W. Norton, 2009.

Bullard, Robert D., ed. *Confronting Environmental Racism: Voices from the Grassroots*. Boston: South End, 1993.

———. "Differential Vulnerabilities: Environmental and Economic Inequality and Government Response to Unnatural Disasters." *Social Research* 75 (2009): 753–84.

————. *Dumping in Dixie: Race, Class, and Environmental Quality*. Boulder, Colo.: Westview, 1994.

————, ed. *The Quest for Environmental Justice: Human Rights and the Politics of Pollution*. San Francisco: Sierra Club Books, 2005.

Bullard, Robert D., and Beverly Wright. *Race, Place, and Environmental Justice after Hurricane Katrina: Struggles to Reclaim, Rebuild, and Revitalize New Orleans and the Gulf Coast*. Boulder, Colo.: Westview, 2009.

Bullard, Robert D., Paul Mohai, Robin Saha, and Beverly Wright. *Toxic Wastes and Race at Twenty: 1987–2007*. Cleveland, Ohio: United Church of Christ Justice & Witness Ministries, 2007. Accessed October 27, 2013. http://www.ucc.org/assets/pdfs/toxic20.pdf.

Cafaro, Philip, ed. "Environmental Virtue Ethics." Special issue, *Journal of Agricultural and Environmental Ethics* 23, nos. 1–2 (2010).

————. "Thoreau, Leopold, and Carson: Toward an Environmental Virtue Ethics." *Environmental Ethics* 22, no. 1 (2001): 3–17.

Cafaro, Philip, ed.

Cafaro, Philip, and Ronald D. Sandler. *Environmental Virtue Ethics*. Lanham, Md.: Rowman & Littlefield, 2004.

Calvin, John. *Institutes of the Christian Religion*. Philadelphia: Westminster, 1960.

Center for Veterinary Medicine. *Summary Report on Antimicrobials Sold or Distributed for Use in Food-Producing Animals*. 2011. http://www.fda.gov/downloads/ForIndustry/UserFees/AnimalDrugUserFeeActADUFA/UCM338170.pdf.

Chávez, César, and Ilan Stavans. *An Organizer's Tale: Speeches*. New York: Penguin, 2008.

Chávez, César, Richard J. Jensen, and John C. Hammerback. *The Words of César Chávez*. College Station: Texas A&M University Press, 2002.

Chryssavgis, John. "The Earth as Sacrament: Insights from Orthodox Christian Theology and Spirituality." In *The Oxford Handbook of Religion and Ecology*, edited by Roger S. Gottlieb, 92–114. New York: Oxford University Press, 2006.

Churchill, Ward. *A Little Matter of Genocide: Holocaust and Denial in the Americas, 1492 to the Present*. San Francisco: City Lights, 1997.

Clement of Alexandria. "Who Is the Rich Man That Shall Be Saved?" In *Ante-Nicene Fathers*. Vol. 2. Grand Rapids: Eerdmans, 1979.

Clingerman, Forrest. "Between Babel and Pelagius: Religion, Theology, and Geoengineering." In *Engineering the Climate: The Ethics of Solar Radiation Management*, edited by Christopher J. Preston, 201–19. New York: Lexington Books, 2012.

Cochran, Elizabeth Agnew. "Jesus Christ and the Cardinal Virtues: A Response to Monica Hellwig." *Theology Today* 65, no. 1 (2008): 81–94.

Cole, Luke W., and Sheila R. Foster. *From the Ground Up: Environmental Racism and the Rise of the Environmental Justice Movement.* New York: New York University Press, 2001.

Coleman-Jensen, Alisha, Mark Nord, Margaret Andrews, and Steven Carlson. *Household Food Security in the United States in 2011: Statistical Supplement.* Washington, D.C.: United States Department of Agriculture Economic Research Service, 2012. http://www.ers.usda.gov/publications/ap-administrative-publication/ap-058.aspx#.UtrrKHmtsog.

Colten, Craig. "Vulnerability and Place: Flat Land and Uneven Risk in New Orleans." *American Anthropologist* 108, no. 4 (2006): 731–34.

Cone, James H. *Martin & Malcolm & America: A Dream or a Nightmare.* Maryknoll, N.Y.: Orbis Books, 1991.

———. "Whose Earth Is It, Anyway?" In *Earth Habitat: Eco-injustice and the Church's Response*, edited by Dieter T. Hessel and Larry L. Rasmussen, 23–32. Minneapolis: Fortress, 2001.

Conradie, Ernst M. *The Church and Climate Change.* Pietermaitzburg, South Africa: Cluster Publications, 2008.

Cubasch, U., D. Wuebbles, D. Chen, M. C. Facchini, D. Frame, N. Mahowald, and J.-G. Winther. "Introduction." In *Climate Change 2013: The Physical Science Basis; Contribution of Working Group I to the Fifth Assessment Report of the Intergovernmental Panel on Climate Change*, edited by T. F. Stocker, D. Qin, G.-K. Plattner, M. Tignor, S. K. Allen, J. Boschung, A. Nauels, Y. Xia, V. Bex, and P. M. Midgley, 119–58. New York: Cambridge University Press, 2013.

Cunanan, Jose Pepz M. "The Prophet of Environment and Development." In *Ecotheology: Voices from South and North*, edited by David G. Hallman, 13–27. Maryknoll, N.Y.: Orbis Books, 1994.

Curry, Patrick. *Ecological Ethics: An Introduction.* Malden, Mass.: Polity, 2011.

DeLind, Laura B. "Celebrating Hunger in Michigan: A Critique of an Emergency Food Program and an Alternative for the Future." *Agriculture and Human Values* 11, no. 4 (1994): 58–68.

Desrochers, Pierre, and Hiroko Shimizu. *The Locavore's Dilemma: In Praise of the 10,000-Mile Diet.* New York: Public Affairs, 2012.

Diamond, Jared M. *Collapse: How Societies Choose to Fail or Succeed.* New York: Penguin, 2005.

Dillard, Annie. *For the Time Being.* New York: Knopf, 1999.

Dr. Seuss. *The Lorax.* New York: Random House, 1999.

Duke, Anna, Brenda Llewellyn Ihssen, and Kevin J. O'Brien. "Natural Disasters as Moral Lessons: Nazianzus and New Orleans." *Journal for the Study of Religion, Nature, and Culture* 6, no. 1 (2012): 56–70.

Ehrlich, Paul R. *The Population Bomb.* Rivercity, Mass.: Rivercity, 1975.

Ehrlich, Paul R., and Anne H. Ehrlich. *Betrayal of Science and Reason: How Anti-environmental Rhetoric Threatens Our Future*. Washington, D.C.: Island, 1996.

———. *The Dominant Animal: Human Evolution and the Environment*. Washington, D.C.: Island, 2008.

———. *The Most Overpopulated Nation*. Teaneck, N.J.: Negative Population Growth, 1996.

———. *One with Nineveh: Politics, Consumption, and the Human Future*. Washington, D.C.: Island, 2004.

Erlander, Daniel. *Manna and Mercy: A Brief History of God's Unfolding Promise to Mend the Entire Universe*. Mercer Island, Wash.: Order of Saints Martin and Teresa, 1992.

Faber, Daniel. *Capitalizing on Environmental Injustice: The Polluter-Industrial Complex in the Age of Globalization*. Lanham, Md.: Rowman & Littlefield, 2008.

Farley, Margaret. *Just Love*. London: Continuum, 2006.

Fast Food Nation. Directed by Richard Linklater. Los Angeles: Participant Media, 2006. DVD.

Feiveson, Harold A. "A Skeptic's View of Nuclear Energy." *Daedalus* 138, no. 4 (2009): 60–70.

Field, Christopher, et al. *Climate Change 2014: Impacts, Adaptation, and Vulnerability—Summary for Policymakers*. Accessed April 1, 2014. http://ipcc-wg2.gov/AR5/images/uploads/IPCC_WG2AR5_SPM_Approved.pdf.

Figueroa, Robert Melchior. "Other Faces: Latinos and Environmental Justice." In *Faces of Environmental Racism: Confronting Issues of Global Justice*, edited by Laura Westra and Bill E. Lawson, 167–85. New York: Rowman & Littlefield, 2001.

Fischer, Hank. "Who Pays for Wolves?" *PERC Report* 19, no. 4 (2001).

———. *Wolf Wars: The Remarkable Inside Story of the Restoration of Wolves to Yellowstone*. Helena, Mont.: Falcon, 1995.

Food, Inc. Directed by Robert Kenner. Los Angeles: Participant Media, 2009. DVD.

Foreman, Dave. *Confessions of an Eco-warrior*. New York: Clown Trade, 1991.

Grabe, Arthur, David Donaldson, Timothy Kiely, and La Wu. *Pesticide Industry Sales and Usage: 2006 and 2007 Market Estimates*. Accessed April 1, 2014. http://www.epa.gov/opp00001/pestsales/07pestsales/market_estimates2007.pdf.

Greer, Germaine. *Sex and Destiny*. London: Picador, 1984.

Grumett, David, and Rachel Muers. *Theology on the Menu: Asceticism, Meat and Christian Diet*. New York: Routledge, 2010.

Gunders, Dana. "Wasted: How America Is Losing Up to 40 Percent of Its Food from Farm to Fork to Landfill." *NRDC Issue Papers*, August 2012. http://www.nrdc.org/food/wasted-food.asp.

Haidt, Jonathan. *The Righteous Mind: Why Good People Are Divided by Politics and Religion*. New York: Vintage, 2012.

Hardin, Garrett. "The Tragedy of the Commons." *Science* 162 (1968): 1243–48.

Harding, Vincent. *Martin Luther King, the Inconvenient Hero*. Maryknoll, N.Y.: Orbis Books, 1996.

Harney, Corbin. *The Way It Is: One Water—One Air—One Mother Earth*. Nevada City, Calif.: Blue Dolphin, 1995.

Hartman, Laura M. *The Christian Consumer: Living Faithfully in a Fragile World*. New York: Oxford University Press, 2011.

Hartmann, Betsy. "The Parable of the Herdsman and Other Tall Tales." Keynote address given at the Conference on Rethinking Climate Change, Conflict and Security, University of Sussex, U.K., October 18, 2012.

———. *Reproductive Rights and Wrongs: The Global Politics of Population Control*. Boston: South End, 1995.9

———. "Rethinking Climate Refugees and Climate Conflict: Rhetoric, Reality and the Politics of Policy Discourse." *Journal of International Development* 22 (2010): 233–46.

———. "Rethinking the Role of Population in Human Security." In *Global Environmental Change and Human Security*, edited by Richard A. Matthew, Jon Barnett, Bryan McDonald, and Karen L. O'Brien, 193–214. Cambridge, Mass.: MIT Press, 2010.

Hartmann, Betsy, Banu Subramaniam, and Charles Zerner. *Making Threats: Biofears and Environmental Anxieties*. Lanham, Md.: Rowman & Littlefield, 2005.

Hauerwas, Stanley. *The Peaceable Kingdom: A Primer in Christian Ethics*. Notre Dame, Ind.: University of Notre Dame Press, 1983.

Hauerwas, Stanley, and Charles Pinches. *Christians among the Virtues*. Notre Dame, Ind.: Notre Dame University Press, 1999.

Hayhoe, Katharine, and Andrew Farley. *A Climate for Change: Global Warming Facts for Faith-Based Decisions*. New York: FaithWords, 2009.

Hearing before the Subcommittee on Energy and Environment: Preparing for Climate Change; Adaptation Policies and Programs. 111th Congress. 2009.

Heede, Richard. "Tracing Anthropogenic Carbon Dioxide and Methane Emissions to Fossil Fuel and Cement Producers, 1854–2010." *Climatic Change* 122, nos. 1–2 (2014): 229–241.

Humphreys, Macartan, Jeffrey Sachs, and Joseph E. Stiglitz, eds. *Escaping the Resource Curse*. New York: Columbia University Press, 2007.

Hunt, Terry, and Carl Lipo. *The Statues That Walked: Unraveling the Mystery of Easter Island*. New York: Free Press, 2011.

Illnesses and Injuries in California Associated with Pesticide Residue in Agricultural

Fields, 1982–2010. Sacramento, Calif.: California Department of Pesticide Regulation, 2010. Accessed October 26, 2013. http://www.cdpr.ca.gov/docs/whs/pisp/2010/2010fld_residue_year.pdf.

Jackson, Melissa A. *Comedy and Feminist Interpretation of the Bible: A Subversive Collaboration*. Oxford: Oxford University Press, 2012.

James, William. *Varieties of Religious Experience: A Study in Human Nature*. New York: Routledge, 2002. Originally published in 1902.

Jenkins, Willis. *The Future of Ethics: Sustainability, Social Justice, and Religious Creativity*. Washington, D.C.: Georgetown University Press, 2013.

Johansen, Bruce E. "The Inuit's Struggle with Dioxins and Other Organic Pollutants." *American Indian Quarterly* 26, no. 3 (2002): 479–90.

Johnson, Luke Timothy. *The Writings of the New Testament: An Interpretation*. Philadelphia: Fortress, 1986.

King, Jonathan B. "Learning to Solve the Right Problems: The Case of Nuclear Power in America." *Journal of Business Ethics* 12, no. 2 (1993): 105–16.

King, Martin Luther, Jr. *"In a Single Garment of Destiny": A Global Vision of Justice*. Edited by Lewis V. Baldwin. Boston: Beacon, 2012.

———. *A Testament of Hope: The Essential Writings of Martin Luther King, Jr*. Edited by James Melvin Washington. San Francisco: HarperCollins, 1986.

———. *Why We Can't Wait*. New York: Penguin, 1964.

Kirk-Duggan, Cheryl A., ed. *The Sky Is Crying: Race, Class, and Natural Disaster*. Nashville: Abingdon, 2006.

Konstantinovsky, Julia. "Evagrius Ponticus on Being Good in God and Christ." *Studies in Christian Ethics* 26, no. 3 (2013): 317–32.

Kruschwitz, Robert. "Christian Virtues and the Doctrine of the Mean." *Faith and Philosophy* 3, no. 4 (1986): 416–28.

Kuletz, Valerie L. *The Tainted Desert: Environmental Ruin in the American West*. New York: Routledge, 1998.

LaDuke, Winona. *All Our Relations: Native Struggles for Land and Life*. Cambridge, Mass.: South End, 1999.

Laid to Waste: A Chester Neighborhood Fights for Its Future. Directed by Robert Bahar and George McCollogh. Berkeley, Calif.: Berkeley Media, 1996. DVD.

Lappé, Frances Moore. *Diet for a Small Planet*. New York: Ballantine Books, 1971.

———. *EcoMind: Changing the Way We Think, to Create the World We Want*. New York: Nation Books, 2011.

Lavelle, Marianne, and Marcia Coyle. "Unequal Protection: The Racial Divide in Environmental Law." *National Law Journal* 15, no. 3 (1992): S1–S12.

Lawler, Michael G., and Todd A. Salzman. "Virtue Ethics: Natural and Christian." *Theological Studies* 74, no. 2 (2013): 442–73.

Lee, Hak Joon. *The Great World House: Martin Luther King, Jr., and Global Ethics.* Cleveland, Ohio: Pilgrim, 2011.

Lenox, Michael, and Jeffrey G. York. "Environmental Entrepreneurship." In *The Oxford Handbook of Business and the Natural Environment,* edited by Pratima Bansal and Andrew J. Hoffman, 70–82. New York: Oxford University Press, 2013.

Leopold, Aldo, and Luna B. Leopold. *Round River.* Minocqua, Wis.: NorthWord, 1991.

Lewis, C. S. *The Screwtape Letters.* New York: Macmillan, 1944.

Lewis, David Rich. "Skull Valley Goshutes and the Politics of Nuclear Waste: Environment, Identity and Sovereignty." In *Native Americans and the Environment: Perspectives on the Ecological Indian,* edited by Michael Eugene Harkin and David Rich Lewis, 304–42. Lincoln: University of Nebraska Press, 2007.

Lomborg, Bjørn. *Cool It: The Skeptical Environmentalist's Guide to Global Warming.* New York: Vintage, 2008.

———. *The Skeptical Environmentalist: Measuring the Real State of the World.* New York: Cambridge University Press, 2001.

———, ed. *Smart Solutions to Climate Change: Comparing Costs and Benefits.* New York: Cambridge University Press, 2010.

The Lorax. Directed by Kyle Balda and Chris Renault. Santa Monica, Calif.: Illumination Entertainment, 2012. DVD.

Louv, Richard. *Last Child in the Woods.* Chapel Hill, N.C.: Algonquin Books, 2008.

Luther, Martin. *Luther's Works,* vol. 32. Edited by Christopher Boyd Brown. St. Louis: Concordia, 2009.

Malthus, Thomas. *An Essay on the Principle of Population and a Summary View of the Principle of Population.* New York: Penguin, 1985. Originally published in 1798.

Martin-Schramm, James B., and Robert L. Stivers. *Christian Environmental Ethics: A Case Method Approach.* Maryknoll, N.Y.: Orbis Books, 2003.

Marx, Karl, and Friedrich Engels. *Marx and Engels on the Population Bomb: Selections from the Writings of Marx and Engels Dealing with the Theories of Thomas Robert Malthus.* Translated by Ronald L. Meek. Berkeley, Calif.: Ramparts, 1971.

The Matrix. Directed by Andy Wachowski and Larry Wachowski. Burbank, Calif.: Warner Brothers Pictures, 1999. DVD.

McCloskey, Deirdre N. *The Bourgeois Virtues: Ethics for an Age of Commerce.* Chicago: University of Chicago Press, 2006.

———. *Crossing: A Memoir.* Chicago: University of Chicago Press, 2009.

McFague, Sallie. *Super, Natural Christians: How We Should Love Nature.* Minneapolis: Fortress, 1997.

McKibben, Bill. *Eaarth: Making a Life on a Tough New Planet.* New York: Time Books, 2010.

————. *Maybe One: A Case for Smaller Families.* New York: Simon & Schuster, 1998.

Merritt, Jonathan. *Green like God: Unlocking the Divine Plan for Our Planet.* New York: FaithWords, 2010.

Miller, Robert J. "Creating Economic Development on Indian Reservations: Why Fostering Local Business Matters." *PERC Report* 30, no. 3 (2012).

Mora, Camilo, Derek P. Tittensor, Sina Adl, Alastair G. B. Simpson, and Boris Worm. "How Many Species Are There on Earth and in the Ocean?" *PLoS Biology* 9, no. 8 (2011). Online only: e1001127 DOI: 10.1371/journal.pbio.1001127.

Moses, Marion. "Farmworkers and Pesticides." In *Confronting Environmental Racism: Voices from the Grassroots,* edited by Robert D. Bullard, 161–78. Boston: South End, 1993.

Mulrooney, Mara Ann. "Continuity or Collapse? Diachronic Settlement and Land Use in Hanga Ho'onu, Rapa Nui (Easter Island)." Dissertation, University of Auckland, 2012.

Nash, James A. *Loving Nature: Ecological Integrity and Christian Responsibility.* Nashville: Abingdon, 1991.

Nelson, Robert H. *The New Holy Wars: Economic Religion vs. Environmental Religion in Contemporary America.* University Park: Pennsylvania State University Press, 2010.

Newsom, Carol A. "The Moral Sense of Nature: Ethics in Light of God's Speech to Job." *Princeton Seminary Bulletin* 15, no. 1 (1994): 9–27.

Northcott, Michael S. *The Environment and Christian Ethics.* New York: Cambridge University Press, 1996.

O'Brien, David J., and Thomas A. Shannon, eds. *Catholic Social Thought: The Documentary Heritage.* Maryknoll, N.Y.: Orbis Books, 1992.

O'Brien, Kevin J. *An Ethics of Biodiversity: Christianity, Ecology, and the Variety of Life.* Washington, D.C.: Georgetown University Press, 2010.

————. "*La Causa* and Environmental Justice: César Chávez as a Resource for Christian Ecological Ethics." *Journal of the Society of Christian Ethics* 32, no. 1 (2012): 151–68.

Owen, David. *The Conundrum: How Scientific Innovation, Increased Efficiency, and Good Intentions Can Make Our Energy and Climate Problems Worse.* New York: Riverhead Books, 2012.

Peña, Devon G. *Environmental Justice and Sustainable Agriculture: Linking Ecological and Social Sides of Sustainability.* Washington, D.C.: Summit II National Office, 2002. Accessed October 26, 2013. http://www.ejrc.cau.edu/summit2/SustainableAg.pdf.

————. "Structural Violence, Historical Trauma, and Public Health: The Environmental Justice Critique of Contemporary Risk Science and Practice." In

Communities, Neighborhoods, and Health: Expanding the Boundaries of Place, edited by Linda M. Burton, Susan P. Kemp, ManChei Leung, Stephen A. Matthews, and David T. Takeuchi, 203–18. New York: Springer, 2011.

Perry, Nancy, and Peter Brandt. "A Case Study on Cruelty to Farm Animals: Lessons Learned from the Hallmark Meat Packing Case." *Michigan Law Review* 106 (2008): 117–22.

Pickens, T. Boone. *The First Billion Is the Hardest: How Believing It's Still Early in the Game Can Lead to Life's Greatest Comebacks*. New York: Crown, 2008.

Pollan, Michael. *In Defense of Food: An Eater's Manifesto*. New York: Penguin, 2008.

Ponticus, Evagrius. *The Praktikos & Chapters on Prayer*. Kalamazoo, Mich.: Cistercian Publications, 1981.

Pope Francis. "Evangelii Gaudium." November 24, 2013. Accessed January 18, 2014. http://www.vatican.va/holy_father/francesco/apost_exhortations/documents/papa-francesco_esortazione-ap_20131124_evangelii-gaudium_en.html.

Pope Paul VI. "Humanae Vitae." 1968. Accessed January 18, 2014. http://www.vatican.va/holy_father/paul_vi/encyclicals/documents/hf_p-vi_enc_2507 1968_humanae-vitae_en.html.

Prakash, Swati. *Breathe at Your Own Risk: Dirty Diesels, Environmental Health & Justice*. Washington, D.C.: Summit II National Office, 2002. Accessed October 27, 2013. http://www.ejrc.cau.edu/summit2/AtYourOwnRisk.pdf.

Prose, Francine. *Gluttony*. Oxford: Oxford University Press, 2006.

Pulido, Laura. *Environmentalism and Economic Justice: Two Chicano Struggles in the Southwest*. Tucson: University of Arizona Press, 1996.

Radioactive Reservations. Goldhawk Productions. New York: Filmakers Library, 1995.

Rasmussen, Larry L. *Earth Community, Earth Ethics*. Maryknoll, N.Y.: Orbis Books, 1996.

———. *Earth-Honoring Faith: Religious Ethics in a New Key*. New York: Oxford University Press, 2013.

———. "Environmental Racism and Environmental Justice: Moral Theory in the Making?" *Journal of the Society of Christian Ethics* 24, no. 1 (2004): 3–28.

Reeves, M., and K. S. Schafer. "Greater Risks, Fewer Rights: US Farmworkers and Pesticides." *International Journal of Occupational and Environmental Health* 9, no. 1 (2003): 30–39.

Reeves, Margaret, Anne Katten, and Martha Guzmán. *Fields of Poison 2002*. Oakland, Calif.: Californians for Pesticide Reform, 2002. Accessed October 26, 2013. http://www.ufw.org/white_papers/report.pdf.

Robinson, Tri, and Jason Chatraw. *Saving God's Green Earth: Rediscovering the Church's Responsibility to Environmental Stewardship*. Boise, Idaho: Ampelon, 2006.

Robock, Alan. "20 Reasons Why Geoengineering May Be a Bad Idea." *Bulletin of the Atomic Scientists* 64, no. 2 (2008): 14–18.

Sandel, Michael J. *What Money Can't Buy: The Moral Limits of Markets.* New York: Farrar, Straus & Giroux, 2012.

Sandler, Ronald L. *Character and Environment: A Virtue-Oriented Approach to Environmental Ethics.* New York: Columbia University Press, 2009.

Sands, Kathleen M., ed. *God Forbid: Religion and Sex in American Public Life.* New York: Oxford University Press, 2000.

Sanger, Margaret. *Woman and the New Race.* New York: Brentano's, 1920.

Schaeffer, Francis A. *Pollution and the Death of Man.* Wheaton, Ill.: Crossway Books, 1970.

Schilling, Vincent. *Native Defenders of the Environment.* Summertown, Tenn.: 7th Generation/Native Voices, 2011.

Schlosser, Eric. *Fast Food Nation: The Dark Side of the All-American Meal.* New York: Houghton Mifflin, 2001.

Scully, Matthew. *Dominion: The Power of Man, the Suffering of Animals, and the Call to Mercy.* New York: St. Martin's, 2002.

Shanley, Brayton. *The Many Sides of Peace: Christian Nonviolence, the Contemplative Life, and Sustainable Living.* Eugene, Ore.: Resource Publications, 2013.

Shiva, Vandana. *Earth Democracy: Justice, Sustainability, and Peace.* Cambridge, Mass.: South End, 2005.

———. *Monocultures of the Mind: Perspectives on Biodiversity and Biotechnology.* London: Zed Books, 1993.

Sleeth, J. Matthew. *Serve God, Save the Planet: A Christian Call to Action.* White River Junction, Vt.: Chelsea Green, 2006.

Smith, Adam. *The Theory of Moral Sentiments.* Oxford: Clarendon, 1976.

Steingraber, Sandra. *Raising Elijah: Protecting Our Children in an Age of Environmental Crisis.* Philadelphia: Da Capo, 2011.

Taylor, Bron Raymond, ed. *Ecological Resistance Movements: The Global Emergence of Radical and Popular Environmentalism.* Albany: State University of New York Press, 1995.

Thomas Aquinas. *Summa Theologica.* New York: Blackfriars, 1964.

Tillich, Paul. *Dynamics of Faith.* New York: Harper & Row, 1957.

Tucker, Robert C., ed. *The Marx-Engels Reader.* New York: W. W. Norton, 1978.

United Church of Christ Commission for Racial Justice. *Toxic Wastes and Race in the United States: A National Report on the Racial and Socioeconomic Characteristics of Communities with Hazardous Waste Sites.* New York: Public Data Access, 1987.

Wallace, Mark I. *Finding God in the Singing River: Christianity, Spirit, Nature.* Minneapolis: Fortress, 2005.

———. *Green Christianity: Five Ways to a Sustainable Future.* Minneapolis: Fortress, 2010.

Weaver, Jace, ed. *Defending Mother Earth: Native American Perspectives on Environmental Justice.* Maryknoll, N.Y.: Orbis Books, 1996.

Wensveen, Louke van. *Dirty Virtues: The Emergence of Ecological Virtue Ethics.* Amherst, N.Y.: Humanity Books, 2000.

Westley, Frances, Michael Quinn Patton, and Brenda Zimmerman. *Getting to Maybe: How the World Is Changed.* Toronto: Vintage Canada, 2007.

Westra, Laura, and Peter S. Wenz, eds. *Faces of Environmental Racism: Confronting Issues of Global Justice.* London: Rowman & Littlefield, 1995.

Wigg-Stevenson, Tyler. *The World Is Not Ours to Save: Finding the Freedom to Do Good.* Downers Grove, Ill.: InterVarsity, 2013.

Wilkens, Steve. *Beyond Bumper Sticker Ethics.* Downers Grove, Ill.: InterVarsity, 1995.

Wilson, Edward O. *Biophilia.* Cambridge, Mass.: Harvard University Press, 1984.

———. *The Creation: An Appeal to Save Life on Earth.* New York: W. W. Norton, 2006.

———. *The Future of Life.* New York: Vintage Books, 2002.

Winright, Tobias, ed. *Green Discipleship: Catholic Theological Ethics and the Environment.* Winona, Minn.: Anselm Academic, 2011.

INDEX

Printed in the USA
CPSIA information can be obtained
at www.ICGtesting.com
LVHW050733030224
770777LV00002B/113